Case Grammar Theory

Walter A. Cook, S.J.

GEORGETOWN UNIVERSITY PRESS, WASHINGTON, D.C.

Library of Congress Cataloging-in-Publication Data

Cook, Walter Anthony, 1922-
  Case grammar theory.

    Bibliography: p.
    1. Case grammar.   I. Title.
P163.C64   1989   415   88-33553
ISBN 0-87840-276-4

Contents

Preface

Case grammar theory is a semantic valence theory that describes the logical form of a sentence in terms of a predicate and a series of case-labelled arguments such as Agent, Object, Location, Source, Goal. The theory provides a language universal approach to sentence semantics as well as a semantic description of the verbs of a language.

The theory is presented in seven concrete models: Fillmore (1968), Fillmore (1971), Chafe (1970), Anderson (1971), the thematic relations of Gruber (1965) and Jackendoff (1972), case theory in tagmemic analysis (Pike and Pike 1977), and the matrix model (Cook 1979). Each model is examined with regard to its logical structure, list of cases, case tactics, derivational system, and use of covert case roles.

In generative grammar, case grammar theory was introduced as a transformational grammar with a case base, incorporated into the general framework (Stockwell, Schacter and Partee 1975), and then dismissed as 'a convenient, if somewhat arbitrary, way of classifying the roles that nouns play in sentences' (Newmeyer 1980). Cases then reappeared as theta-roles in a system of thematic relations, an essential part of the description of logical form in Government and Binding theory. 'Logical form (LF) must be so designed that arguments are assigned theta-roles, that is, are assigned the status of terms in a thematic relation' (Chomsky, 1981). These thematic relations have recently been used to investigate the problem of control, the problem of determining the antecedents of abstract pronouns (PRO) that occur in complement structures.

In computational linguistics, case grammar theory has assumed a central role in augmented transition networks used for both sentence analysis and sentence generation. Case theory describes the essential properties of verbs, and cases are used as labels for the required arguments that enter into the network. This research is evident in Roger Schank's *Computer Models of Thought and Language* (1973) and in later works on natural language processing such as Terry Winograd's *Language as a Cognitive Process* (1983:311-326) and Mary Dee Harris's *Natural Language Processing* (1985:183-217). Cases are used in parsers developed for LISP and PROLOG type programming languages by linguists as well as professional programmers.

In theoretical linguistics, case theory is used as an approach to sentence semantics, as opposed to word semantics, in a predicate calculus framework. The analysis of sentences into predicate and arguments has long been advocated in the study of semantics by linguists such as Allwood, Anderson and Dahl (1977), Leech (1974), Lyons (1977) and works such as James McCawley's 'A program for logic' (1976) and George Lakoff's 'Linguistics and natural logic' (1972). A revitalized case grammar theory uses the predicate-argument approach, and adds the identification of arguments as cases to produce a case-labelled predicate calculus.

In tagmemic analysis, case roles have been introduced as a further semantic classification of the syntactic slot:class unit in the work of Alton Becker (1967), John Platt (1971), Austin Hale (1974), Robert Longacre (1976), and Kenneth Pike (1977). The introduction of case is a new approach which incorporates Kenneth Pike's original (1960, 1967) concept of variants of the subject tagmeme such as subject-as-actor, subject-as-undergoer. Case theory is now widely used by linguists in the Summer Institute of Linguistics.

In foreign language learning, case theory has been used in the description of foreign language. Case grammar descriptions have been developed for many languages in Ph.D dissertations. These include European languages such as Spanish (Aid 1973), French (Anderson 1975), German (Hall 1976), Dutch (Moskey 1978), Portuguese (Nicolacopulos 1981), and Norwegian (Sorenson 1983). They also include many non-European languages such as Japanese (Sasaki 1975), Chinese (Washburn 1975, Astor 1977), Persian (Aghbar 1981), Vietnamese (Tri 1981), Korean (Lee 1984), Thai (S. Chanawangsa 1986) and Arabic (Qahtani 1988).

The theory has been applied in Ph.D dissertations to English (Baer 1976), to teaching English as a foreign language (Reer 1982, Abdullah 1981, Carney 1986) and to child language acquisition (Kasajima 1982, Cha 1983). In teaching English as a foreign language, case theory has been used within a functional-notional approach to teach the language from a semantic viewpoint and appears in *A Comprehensive Grammar of the English Language* (Quirk, Greenbaum, Leech, and Svartvik 1985).

Case grammar theory under one label or another is currently in widespread use. Traces of cases are found in the thematic relations of Government and Binding theory, in the verb feature specification of augmented transition networks, in the study of logical form, and as a logical structure for tagmemic analysis. Case grammar theory is used for foreign language description, for teaching English as a foreign language, and in the study of child language acquisition. The detailed comparison of existing case grammar models should be of interest to all those engaged in the many concrete applications of case grammar theory.

1 The Fillmore 1968 Model

1.0 Overview. The classical presentation of the case grammar model is given by Charles Fillmore in 'The case for case' in *Universals in Linguistic Theory* (1968:1-88). A similar model was presented earlier in 'A proposal concerning English prepositions' in the *Georgetown University Round Table on Languages and Linguistics 1966* (1966:19-36). This model was later revised in 'Toward a modern theory of case' in *Modern Studies in English* (1969:357-371). These are the principal sources for the Fillmore 1968 case grammar model.

'The case for case' was first presented at a conference on language universals. In the introduction to that conference, Fillmore's paper is described as presenting 'a universal underlying set of case-like relations that play an essential role in determining syntactic and semantic relations in all languages' (1968:vii).

Fillmore describes his own approach as one based upon two principles: (1) the centrality of syntax, and (2) covert categories. By 'centrality of syntax' Fillmore means an approach which works downward from the sentence syntax rather than upward from the morphological form; by 'covert categories' Fillmore is referring to the meaning underlying the use of traditional case categories. A clear distinction is made between syntactic categories, such as subject and direct object, and deep structure categories. In Fillmore's words, 'what is needed is a conception of base structure in which case relationships are primitive terms of the theory, and in which such concepts as subject and object are missing' (1968:2). The subject and object categories belong to surface structure not to deep structure.

Fillmore's principal objective then is to explain what is meant by deep case structure, how these are universals belonging to the base of a transformational grammar, and how they can be used to derive surface structures. His hope is that 'by distinguishing between surface and deep structure case relationships, by interpreting subject and object as aspects of the surface structure, and by viewing the phonetic shape of nouns as determinable by many factors' (1968:19) case systems can be shown to be compatible across languages.

1.0.1 Traditional case. In traditional grammars language is described in terms of words and their uses. Word classes are first described in a section devoted to word formation, and then the use of these words is described in a section devoted to syntax. The approach is from morphological form to sentence construction.

A typical grammar describes the noun class and inflections which may occur with the noun. This set of inflections applied to any noun is called a DECLENSION. A noun is generally classified as belonging to a grammatical gender but inflected for number and case. Charles E. Bennett, in his *New Latin Grammar* (1918), describes the inflection of Latin nouns in terms of six cases: Nominative, Genitive, Dative, Accusative, Ablative, Vocative. The inflectional endings indicating these cases are given for both the singular and the plural. Once the case forms have been explained, a large section of the work is devoted to illustrating the various uses of the cases. These uses are explained sometimes in terms of syntactic function, such as the nominative is the case of the subject, and sometimes they are explained in semantic terms, such as the ablative expresses the meaning of Agent in the sentence context.

(1) **Nominative.** In Latin grammar the nominative case is used for the syntactic positions of subject, predicate noun, and appositive. Nothing is said in this definition of the semantic role played by the subject. Similarly, in Sanskrit, the nominative is described as CASUS SUBJECTIVUS, the case of the subject (Edward Perry 1936:28). One of Fillmore's objections to these traditional descriptions is the failure to specify the semantic role of the nominative (1968:6). There is no reason why the nominative could not be specified as nominative-of-agency, nominative-of-affected-object, and so on, since the subject nominative is used with many different meanings.

(2) **Genitive.** In Latin the genitive case is described as the case which defines the meaning of a noun more closely. In other words the genitive performs a modifying function. Likewise in Sanskrit the genitive is described as CASUS ADJECTIVUS (Perry 1936:31), a modifier denoting all kinds of belonging. The semantic role played by the noun inflected for the genitive case is described in various terms, such as genitive of origin, possession, material, as well as subjective and objective genitive.

(3) **Dative.** The dative case in Latin expresses in general the relations expressed in English by the prepositions *to* and *for* (Bennett 1918:129). Its principal syntactic function is that of indirect object. The semantic roles of the dative are described as dative of agency, possession, purpose, and direction. In Sanskrit grammar dative is described as a 'more remote' object used for such roles as purpose, direction, and reference (Perry 1936:31).

(4) **Accusative.** The Latin accusative is the case of the direct object, its principal syntactic function. It is used to denote the person or thing affected or the result produced; it is also used for duration of time and space, or for place-to-which. In Sanskrit the accusative is CASUS OBJECTIVUS, denoting direct and sometimes remote objects according to Perry (1936:28).

(5) Ablative. The Latin ablative case, compared to the grammar of Sanskrit, is really a combination of three cases; the ablative or *from* case, the instrumental or *with* case, and the locative or *where* case (Bennett 1918:142). Sanskrit keeps these three cases distinct.

(a) The ablative, or *from* case, may denote separation, source, or agent, and answers the questions *whence?*, *from what place?*

(b) The instrumental use of the ablative includes ablatives of means, cause, manner, instrument, accompaniment, specification, quality, and price. It answers the questions *with what? by what means?*

(c) The locative use of the Latin ablative includes ablatives of place-where and place-from-which, as well as ablatives of time-when and time-within-which.

Within the case system three concepts must be kept distinct. First, there is the case form, a morphological surface signal represented by an affix which is added to a noun. Next, there is the syntactic use of that case form, how the case affix fits the noun for use in syntax as subject, object, or modifier. Finally, there is the meaning which is carried by the case affix in context. It is the meaning underlying the case form, not the case form and not its syntactic use, that is of interest to the case grammarian.

1.0.2 Case grammar. According to Fillmore 'the concepts underlying the study of case uses may have a greater linguistic significance than those involved in the description of surface case systems' (1968:19). The surface case system of the language consists of the set of inflectional case endings that are possible with nouns. These inflections, expressed in the declension of nouns, fit the nouns for use in surface syntax, including their use as subject, direct object, indirect object, modifier, and various adverbial adjuncts. Surface case systems are not comparable across languages.

The deep case system consists of the semantic roles which these nouns play in the meaning of the sentence. The list of deep cases is a list of these roles and, if it turns out that this is a limited set with cross-linguistic validity, then case systems may be compared across languages. The list of case roles will include those case 'uses' familiar from traditional grammar, notions such as Agent, Object, Source, Goal, Location, Instrument, and Accompaniment.

Fillmore presents his 1968 model of case grammar as 'a substantial modification to the theory of transformational grammar' based upon 'a reintroduction of the conceptual framework interpretation of case systems, but this time with a clear understanding of the difference between deep and surface structure' (1968:21).

Fillmore's model is based upon a clear distinction between CASE FORM and CASE USE, suggested by the distinction between deep and surface structure (Chomsky 1965). In case grammar case use belongs to the deep structure and case form belongs to the surface structure. Nouns are inflected for case and the case markings are the visible sign of the kind of syntactic relations that the system provides. Case uses are the meanings that the case forms are used to convey and are universal across languages. It is the 'concepts underlying the study of case uses' (1968:19) that are linguistically significant in the study of the content underlying language expression; concepts are comparable across languages.

There should be no problem in using the term CASE for the underlying semantic relationships provided that this term is properly understood as applying to the deep structure semantic relationships. NUMBER, as a semantic category referring to the one and the many, is universally understood but is expressed in different ways in languages that contrast singular and plural and those that contrast singular, dual and plural. GENDER, as a semantic category dealing with male /female differences, is universally understood but is expressed differently in those languages which contrast masculine and feminine and those languages which contrast masculine, feminine, and neuter genders. Semantically number and gender are comparable across languages; grammatically number and gender work differently in different languages. Similarly the term CASE, in its deep structure sense, must be distinguished from those surface case forms which are proper to individual languages. Fillmore's case notions are 'a set of universal, presumably innate concepts, which identify certain types of judgments human beings are capable of making about the events going on around them such as *who did it, who it happened to, what got changed*, and so forth' (1968:24). It is these meanings which are universal across languages and constitute the deep structure cases of the case grammar model.

According to Fillmore (1968:20) the value of this view of case can be demonstrated 'if there are recognizable intrasentence relationships, if they can be shown to be comparable across languages, and if there is some predictive or explanatory use to which they can be put'.

1.1 Deep structure

1.1.1 Semantic formation rules. Fillmore (1968:21) presents his model as a substantial modification to the standard theory as proposed by Chomsky in *Aspects of the Theory of Syntax* (1965). According to Chomsky's theory, base structures are generated by phrase structure rules from an initial string #S#. Fillmore's case grammar has base structures generated by phrase structure rules from an initial string #S#. Fillmore's case grammar is intended to be a transformational grammar with a case base.

The deep structures generated by the 1968 case grammar model are characterized by the following features: (1) the sentence is initially separated into a proposition and a modality, (2) the proposition consists of a verb and a series of cases ordered from right-to-left, and (3) prepositions or case markers occur in the deep structure.

The sentence (S) consists of a proposition (P) and a modality (M). The PROPOSITION is 'a tenseless set of relationships involving verbs and nouns' (1968:23); the MODALITY 'includes such modalities on the sentence-as-a-whole as negation, tense, mood, and aspect' (1968:23).

The first rule of the base is formulated:

Rule 1: S --> M + P   (1968:24)

The proposition (P) consists of a central verb (V) and a series of case-marked noun phrases (C). The verb is placed in the leftmost position and the associated cases are listed in a right-to-left order with the most probable subject choice to the far right in the deep structure. According to Fillmore 'at least one case category must be chosen, and no case category appears more than once' (1968:24). The second rule of the base is formulated:

Rule 2: P --> V + C_1 + ...C_n (1968:24)

Each case-marked noun phrase (C) consists of a case marker (K) and a noun phrase (NP) with the case marker preceding the noun phrase in deep structure. The case marker is a universal element of language which may be realized as preposition, postposition, or case affix (1968:33). The third rule of the base is formulated:

Rule 3: C --> K + NP   (1968:33)

In the generation of the base structure for a sentence these three rules are applied in order. One or more concrete cases, such as Agent, Object, Instrument, are substituted for the case categories in rule 2. Concrete case markers proper to these cases are entered under the case marker (K) in rule 3.

Lexical insertion takes place after the base rules apply. Verbs are chosen from the lexicon to fit the case environment provided by the structure generated. Noun phrases are supplied according to the sentence which is being generated. Modalities such as tense, aspect, and certain optional adverbials are inserted into the modality. Each verb is classified in the lexicon with its case frame features. These include the set of case frames that will accept that particular verb. For example, one of the case frames for the verb *break* is + [___O,I,A]. This means that the verb *break* may occur with an Object (O), the thing that gets broken, an Instrument (I), which aids in the breaking process, and an Agent (A), who does the breaking. The blank in the case frame shows that this case frame is an environment for the verb (V). The plus sign and square brackets indicate that this case frame is a feature of the verb. The cases are listed within the frame according to Fillmore's subject choice hierarchy with the most probable subject choice listed to the far right in the case frame. Within the O-I-A case frame the process of subject choice occurs according to the following subject choice rule:

'If there is an A, it becomes the subject; otherwise,
if there is an I, it becomes the subject; otherwise
the subject is O.' (Fillmore 1968:33)

Each case occurs in the deep structure with its case marker and a noun phrase. In English the case markers are prepositions. The case marker for Agent is *by*, for Instrument is *with*, and for Object is ∅ (1968:32). When the phrase structure rules are applied the lexical verb is listed under the V node and tense is entered under the modality constituent. The cases are listed right-to-left with their case markers. The structure of sentence (1) is given in Figure 1.1.

(1) John /broke /the window /with a hammer.
    A   V   O   I

Figure 1.1 Deep structure (1968:35).

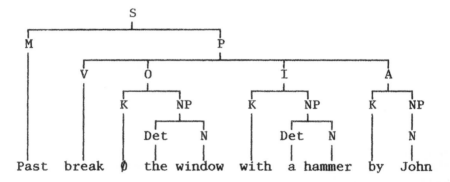

1.1.2 Surface structure derivation. From this deep structure the surface structure is derived by subject formation, object formation and tense incorporation. The case chosen as subject is moved to the far left and the case label and preposition are deleted. The case chosen as direct object moves next to the verb with the same deletions. The Instrument case retains its preposition. Finally tense is incorporated into the verb. The surface structure of the active sentence is given in Figure 1.2.

Figure 1.2 Active surface structure (1968:35).

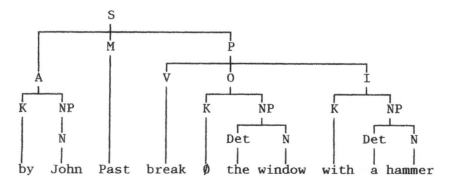

After application of the subject formation rule the NP chosen as subject is an NP dominated by S. After object formation the NP chosen as direct object is an NP dominated by P, which, after the removal of the subject NP, is similar to a derived VP. The subject and object now conform to standard configurational definitions of subject and object given by Chomsky in *Aspects* (1965:69).

Passive sentences are derived from the same deep structure as their active counterparts. If the Object case noun is chosen as subject this non-normal choice of subject requires that the feature [+ Passive] be registered in the verb (1968:37). This feature triggers a BE incorporation rule in the modality to carry the tense and changes the main verb to a past participle. The surface structure of sentence (2) is given in Figure 1.3.

(2) The window /was broken /with a hammer /by John.
    O   V   I   A

Figure 1.3 Passive surface structure (1968:39).

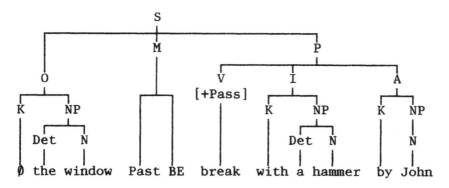

In the application of the subject formation rule the case label, the K label, and the preposition are deleted when the O-case is fronted; the NP formerly under the O case is now directly dominated by S and is the subject. The other noun phrases, Agent and Instrument, retain their prepositions.

1.1.3 Other applications. After describing the derivation of simple active and passive sentences from case-based structures, Fillmore adds other examples of syntactic problems in which case analysis is useful. Among these are parallel sentences with *have* and *be*, as in sentences (3-4).

(3) Many toys /are /in the box.   O,L /O-subject
    O   V   L
(4) The box /has /many toys /in it.   O,L /L-subject
    L   V   O   L-copy

These two parallel sentences have the same case frame but a different choice of subject. In sentence (3) the O case is subject. Fillmore considers this to be a verbless sentence which requires the insertion of the verb *be* from the modality. In sentence (4) the L case is subject. According to Fillmore the verb *have* is obligatorily inserted if the subject is not the O case. (1968:47). The L-subject is copied in a prepositional phrase and the NP is pronominalized. Thus *have* and *be* sentences are equivalents which differ only in subject choice.

Other syntactic applications include the use of the rules of THERE-INSERTION and EXTRAPOSITION. Sentences in which these rules have applied have the same case frame as those in which the rules have not applied. Thus sentence (3), after the rule of *there*-insertion, is written as sentence (5).

(5) There /are /many toys /in the box.
    L-copy V   O   L

In a similar way, sentences in which extraposition has applied have the same case frame as sentences in which the rule has not applied (1968:41). For example, sentence (6) has the same case frame as sentence (7).

(6) That John loves Mary /is true.
    O=S   V
(7) It /is true /that John loves Mary.
    O-copy V O

In both *there*-insertion and extraposition Fillmore considers *there* and *it* to be copies of cases expressed elsewhere in the sentence. These particles could also be considered as dummy particles inserted by syntactic rule. In either interpretation the case frame remains unchanged.

All of these practical examples are given by Fillmore to show the usefulness of a deep structure case base within the context of a transformational grammar. They are not part of case theory as such. In the following chapters, other authors take the same case base but use it within the context of generative semantics, interpretive semantics, dependency grammar, or tagmemics. What remains constant in all case models is the semantic classification of verbs by deep case roles.

1.2 Case system. Case grammars have a case system which consists of (1) a small number of cases, (2) which are sufficient for the classification of the verbs in a language, and (3) which have cross-language validity (Fillmore 1975:7). These cases are arranged according to a subject choice hierarchy.

The initial list of cases proposed by Fillmore includes: Agentive (A), Instrumental (I), Dative (D), Factitive (F), Locative (L), and Objective (O) (1968:24). But he immediately qualifies this statement by suggesting that other cases will certainly be needed. In listing the prepositions that are required for the individual cases he includes these six cases but adds Benefactive (B) and Time (T) (1968:32). In dealing with coordination he mentions the possibility of a Comitative (C) case. This same list of cases, with the exception of Factitive, is found in Fillmore's revision (1969:366).

Fillmore states that 'certain cases will be directly related to the modality constituent, as others are related to the proposition itself' (1968:23). In the discussion that follows cases related to the modality will be called MODAL cases and cases related to the proposition will be called PROPOSITIONAL cases. Only the propositional cases are relevant to the subclassification of verbs. The cases occurring in subject and object position, and 'adverbial elements capable of becoming subjects or objects' (1969:366) are propositional. All other adverbials, such as (outer) Time, (outer) Benefactive, and Frequentative (1969:366) are modal cases. The seven cases listed below constitute the essential case system of the 1968 model.

1.2.1 Agentive (A). The Agentive case is 'the case of the (typically animate) perceived instigator of the action identified by the verb' (1968:24). As the highest ranking case the Agentive must always be chosen as subject in simple active sentences. The Agentive is listed as typically animate in order to include the possibility of considering nouns like *robot* and *nation* as Agents (1968:24 fn.31). The Agentive case is marked with the preposition *by*, as in sentences (8-9).

(8) John /broke /the window.   A = S
    A   V   O
(9) The window /was broken /by John.   A = PP
    O   V   A

1.2.2 Instrumental (I). The Instrumental case is 'the case of the inanimate force or object causally involved in the state or action identified by the verb' (1968:24). Natural forces such as *wind* (1968:27) are called instruments. The Instrumental case may occur as the subject of the verb, as the direct object of the verb *use*, and also in prepositional phrases (1968:25). The typical case marking for the Instrument case is the preposition *by* if there is no Agent present in the structure and is the preposition *with* if there is an Agent present (1968:32), as in sentences (10-13).

(10) The hammer /broke /the window.   I = S
     I   V   O
(11) John /used /a hammer.   I = DO
     A   V   I
(12) The window /was broken /with a hammer.   I = PP
     O   V   I
(13) The window /was broken /by the storm.   I = PP
     O   V   I

1.2.3 Dative (D). The Dative case is 'the case of the (animate) being affected by the state or action identified by the verb' (1968:24). The Dative case may occur as the subject, direct object, or indirect object of nonaction verbs; it may also occur as the indirect object of state or action verbs but is not simply an indirect object. The Dative is typically marked with the preposition *to*, as in sentences (14-17).

(14) John /believed /the story. D V O	D = S
(15) The book /was boring /to John. O V D	D = IO
(16) The movie /pleased /John. O V D	D = DO
(17) John /gave /the book /to Mary. A V O D	D = IO

1.2.4 Objective (O). The Objective case is 'the semantically most neutral case, the case of anything representable by a noun whose role in the action or state identified by the verb is identified by the semantic interpretation of the verb itself' (1968:25). Since there is also a Factitive case in the list of cases, Fillmore adds that the Objective case should probably be limited to things which are affected by the verbal action. Things which are effected or created by the verbal action more properly belong to the Factitive case. The Objective case may occur as either subject or object with nonaction verbs and as the direct object of action verbs, but the notion of the deep structure Objective case is not to be confused with the surface notion, direct object. The prepositional marker for the O case is $\emptyset$. Fillmore (1968:28 fn.38) adds that sentences may be embedded only under the O case, as in sentences (18-21).

(18) The story /is true. O V	O = S
(19) John /liked /the movie. D V O	O = DO
(20) Mary /opened /the door. A V O	O= DO
(21) We /persuaded /John /he could win. A V D O=S	O = Sent

1.2.5 Factitive (F). The Factitive case is 'the case of the object or being resulting from the state or action identified by the verb, or understood as part of the meaning of the verb' (1968:25). The Factitive case is used to distinguish the EFFECTED OBJECT, which does not exist prior to the verbal action, from the AFFECTED OBJECT, which preexists and is acted upon. The Factitive is also used for cognate object constructions (1968:85). Since this case may never occur as subject it is not listed as part of the subject choice hierarchy. Case marking for the Factitive case is $\emptyset$, as in sentences (22-23).

(22) John /built /a table.   F = effected O
        A   V   F

(23) Mary /dreamed /a dream.   F = cognate O
        D   V   F

1.2.6 Locative (L). The Locative case is 'the case which identifies the location or spatial orientation of the state or action identified by the verb' (1968:25). Locative includes both stative and directional locatives 'since locational and directional elements do not contrast' (1968:25) and are in complementary distribution. Locative prepositions are optional choices occasionally dictated by the character of the verb itself or by the associated noun (1968:32). The stative prepositions *at*, *in*, *on* occur with state verbs; the directional prepositions *to* /*from*, *into* /*out of* occur with motion verbs. The Locative case may occur as subject or direct object but more often occurs in a prepositional phrase, as in sentences (24-27).

(24) The toys /are /in the box.   L = PP
        O   V   L

(25) The box /contains /the toys.   L = S
        L   V   O

(26) John /sprayed /paint /on the wall.   L = PP
        A   V   O   L

(27) John /sprayed /the wall /with paint.   L = DO
        A   V   L   O

Outer Locative (L), a propositional case, must be distinguished from inner Locative (L$_m$), a modal case. This distinction corresponds to locatives inside the VP and locatives outside the VP (Fillmore 1968:26 fn.34). Verbs like *keep*, *put*, *leave* require inner locatives; verbs like *polish*, *wash*, *build* have optional outer locatives; verbs like *believe*, *know*, *want* allow no locative at all, as in sentences (28-29).

(28) John /keeps /his car /in the garage.   inner-L
        A   V   O   L

(29) John /washes /his car /in the garage.   outer-L
        A   V   O   L$_m$

1.2.7 Comitative (C). This case is not defined. It is mentioned under coordinate conjunction (1968:81) and listed as a propositional case in the revised version (1969:366). From the examples given it seems to be a typically animate case used to express accompaniment. The prepositional marker is *with*. This case may become the subject of the verb *have* (1969:372), as in sentences (30-31).

(30) The children /are /with Mary.   C = PP
        O   V   C

(31) Mary /has /the children /with her.   C = S
      C   V   O   C-copy

The seven cases described above form a CASE SYSTEM. These cases are used in various combinations to form case frames which are the environments for particular verbs. Within the case frame the cases are arranged according to a subject choice hierarchy and not according to the order of occurrence of the phrases in surface structure. Since Factitive never occurs as a subject, it is excluded from the hierarchy and may be considered as a variant of the O case. It replaces the O case when the object is an effected or cognate object. Comitative seems to be an alternative for Locative and would occur in the hierarchy in the same position as Locative. The subject choice hierarchy can then be listed reading from left to right as: Agentive, Instrumental, Dative, Objective (Factitive), Locative (Comitative), abbreviated as: A–I–D–O–L.

In this description of the original cases listed for the 1968 case grammar model the definitions posited by Fillmore have been placed side by side with the examples that are used to illustrate the various cases and in particular those examples which illustrate how the same cases occur in different surface structure configurations. The surface notions of subject, direct object, indirect object, and prepositional or adverbial adjuncts form a system of surface syntactic contrasts. This system is totally independent of the underlying deep structure case system. In order for a case system to be viable the cases must be able to move freely in and out of various surface structure positions. The surface structure positions are syntactic; the deep structure cases are semantic and independent of syntax.

According to Fillmore: (1) The case system must consist of a small number of elementary case notions. In practice, Fillmore limits the number here to fewer than ten cases. (2) The case system must be universal in scope. This means that this same list of cases is used to describe the verbs of any language, not just English. (3) The case system must be capable of being extended to the whole vocabulary of predicating words in the language. The list of cases must be necessary and sufficient to classify all the verbs of a given language; necessary in that all the cases listed are needed to classify the verbs, and sufficient, in the sense that no other cases are needed.

1.3 Case frames. The case frame (1968:27) is an array of cases into which the central verb may be inserted to describe the propositional content of a sentence. Cases are the units in the system which occur in definite configurations in the language. There are limitations, expressed or implied, on the ways in which the various cases may combine into case frames. These limitations, taken together, constitute a set of case tactics.

(1) In every frame at least one case must occur (1968:24). Fillmore's 1968 system does not allow zero-place predicates; every sentence must have at least one case-marked noun. Even sentences such as *It is raining* must be considered as one-place predicates with *it* serving as the case-marked noun. In practice, case frames in the

1968 model have one, two or three cases; but, in principle, Fillmore does not exclude case frames with four or more cases.

(2) No case category may appear more than once in a single sentence. The one-instance-per-clause principle is one of the cornerstones of Fillmore's early model, a principle he considers as a necessary claim (1968:21). Apparent counterexamples are to be explained as two different cases or as an example of a complex sentence (1968:21 fn.26)

(3) The Agentive and Objective cases are more fundamental than the other cases. With their surface case markings they help define the transitivity system of a language. But in Fillmore's model there is no obligatory O case nor any rule demanding that either the O case or the A case appear in the frame. In fact Dative, Locative, and even Instrumental occur as the only case in the frame.

(4) In practice, all cases except the A case and the O case seem to be mutually exclusive. Again, this is not a restriction in principle but a generalization from the examples used.

(5) Fillmore always lists the cases in the frame in right-to-left order and the symbol S is used to indicate a sentence embedded under the O case. For comparative purposes, however, the practice here will be to list the cases in left-to-right order. When a sentence is embedded under the O case the case will be listed as O in the case frame followed by the notation that O=S, meaning that the O case dominates a sentence.

If the tactics listed above are followed the case frames of the 1968 model can be grouped into: (1) basic case frames, which use only the A case, the O case, or both; and (2) secondary case frames, which use at least one of the mutually exclusive cases, Instrumental, Dative, Locative, in conjunction with the A case, the O case, or both. The resulting verb types can be classed as Basic, Instrumental, Dative, or Locative verbs. These groupings separate the verbs of a language into semantic subtypes and, taken together, constitute one dimension of what can be described as a case frame matrix.

The other dimension of the matrix is based upon verb type. In the definition of each of the cases Fillmore refers to the 'state or action identified by the verb' (1968:24). This state versus action distinction is based upon the article *On stative adjectives and verbs* by George Lakoff (1966). In this interesting article Lakoff identifies state verbs as being [-progressive, -imperative] and action verbs as being [+progressive, +imperative]. Lakoff's conclusion is that, although most adjectives are states, there are also action adjectives such as *be quiet*, *be noisy*. Although most verbs are actions there are also state verbs such as *know*, *want*, *like*. Lakoff found exceptions to his state versus action distinction which seem to be neither states nor actions, among which he lists the durational verbs *stay*, *keep*, *remain* and the position verbs *sit*, *stand*.

Following Lakoff's two way distinction of verbs into state and action, Fillmore draws the following false conclusions regarding verb types as represented in case frames (1968:31).

(1) No stativity feature need be added to verbs since state verbs are those whose case frames contain no A case. The resulting verb classification, with stativity unmarked, fails to distinguish between state verbs like *be dead* and process verbs like *die*, both of which are not Agentive.

(2) The progressive aspect can only occur in those verbs whose case frames contain an A case. Yet Fillmore (1968:29) cites an example of the O case frame which contains no A case but which uses the progressive aspect, namely, *the potatoes are cooking*.

The verb types which occur in the Fillmore 1968 model may be arranged in a two-dimensional matrix with the verb types -- state, action -- in one dimension and the case domains -- basic, instrument, dative, and locative -- in the other, as given in Figure 1.4.

Figure 1.4 Case frame matrix based on Fillmore 1968.

Verb Type	Basic	Instrument	Dative	Locative
1. State	O break,iv	I ... I,O break,tv	D be sad D,O like	L be hot O,L be in
2. Action	A run A,O break,tv	A,I use A,I,O break,tv	A,D ... A,D,O give	A,L ... A,O,L put

The verb *die* is listed as D and the verb *kill* as A-I-D (1968:30), but this D case is later changed to the O case (1969:372). The verbs *plant*, *smear* are listed as A-I-L (1968:48) but changed to A-O-L (1969:369). This summary adopts the 1969 version of these case frames, excluding A-I-D and A-I-L frames in favor of A-I-O and A-O-L frames.

1.3.1 Basic verb types. Basic verbs use either the A case, the O case, or both, but use no other cases. State verbs make use of only the O case; action verbs use the A case alone or use both the A case and the O case.

State verbs, using only the O case.
+ [___O] /O=S   *be true, turn out*
+ [___O]   *break,iv, cook,iv, die, open,iv,*
                   wake up,iv, bend, move, rotate, turn

Action verbs, using only the A case.
+ [___A]   *run* (1968:27)

Action verbs, using the A case with the O or F cases.

+ [___A,O]   *break,tv, buy, cook,tv, kill, murder,*
                open,tv, terrorize, wake up,tv, learn,
                listen to, look at, remove, say
+ [___A,F]   *build*

It seems that all predicate adjectives, used statively, would fall within the O frame and all action adjectives, such as *be careful, be noisy, be polite* would belong to the A frame. The inclusion of *bend, move, rotate, turn, remove* as O verbs seems over hasty since these are motion verbs requiring a locative. Likewise the inclusion of *learn, listen to, look at* as simple action verbs overlooks the fact that all of these are mental state verbs which should require the Dative case in addition to the A case. The verb *buy* probably requires the other party to the transaction and should include both A and D cases. The verb *say* probably requires the A case as speaker, and the D case as hearer. Both *buy* and *say* should be A-D-O.

1.3.2 Instrumental verbs. These verbs include the Instrumental case but may also include the O case, the A case, or both. State instrumental uses the I case, or I and O cases with the I case chosen as subject. Action instrumental verbs use A and I, or A, I, and O cases with the A case as subject.

State Instrumental, using the I case or the I and O cases.

+ [___I]   *be warm* (1971:40)
+ [___I,O]   *break,tv, kill, open,tv (Ins),*
                wake up,tv (Ins)

Action Instrumental, using the A and I or the A,I and O cases.

+ [___A,I]   *use* (1968:25)
+ [___A,I,O]   *break,tv, kill, murder, open,tv,*
                wake up,tv

What makes the Instrumental verbs suspect is that all of the verbs listed as Instrumental verbs have four different deep structures, namely O, I-O, A-O, and A-I-O. There are no verbs that are properly speaking instrumental except perhaps the verb *use*. This makes one wonder whether Instrumental should not be treated as a modal case which is optional to a wide range of action verbs but is not contained in the deep structure of any verb. As far as Fillmore is concerned, Instrument represents another of the cornerstones of his 1968 and later models.

1.3.3 Dative verbs. These verbs are characterized by the presence of the D case. State dative verbs use the D case only or the D and O cases. With D-O verbs either the D or O case may be chosen as subject. Action dative verbs use the A, D, and O cases with the A case chosen as subject.

State Dative, using the D case, or the D and O cases.

+ [___D]	*be sad*
+ [___D,O] /D-subj	*believe, expect, hear, know, like, see, think, want, have*
+ [___D,O] /O-subj	*be apparent, be interesting, please, belong to*

Action Dative, using the A, D, and O cases.

+ [___ A,D,O]	*blame, force, persuade, show, talk, give*

The dative verbs represent a semantic domain which includes sensation, such as *see, hear*; motion, such as *want, like*; and cognition, such as *know, think*. In this model the dative case also includes verbs of possession, later called Benefactive, such as *have, belong to*. Dative verbs also include those three-place predicates in which the Dative is indirect object, such as *blame, persuade, give*. The verb *be interesting* is listed with only the O case (1968:28), but later with both O and D cases (1968:40). The latter analysis seems correct and contrasts with the verb *be true* listed as an O-verb. A story can be true without an observer but can hardly be interesting without some interested party.

1.3.4 Locative verbs. The locative verbs are characterized by the Locative case. Locative states use the L case, or both O and L cases. With O-L verbs either the O case or the L case may be subject. Verbs which are locative actions use the A case, the O case, and the L case with the A case as subject.

State Locative, using only the L case.

+ [___L]	*be hot, be windy* (meteorological)

State Locative, using the O case with the L or C cases.

+ [___O,L] /O-subj	*be in, be on, swarm*
+ [___O,L] /L-subj	*have in, have on, swarm*
+ [___O,C] /O-subj	*be with*
+ [___O,C] /C-subj	*have with*

Action Locative, using the A, O, and L cases.

+ [___A,O,L]	*keep, leave, put; plant, smear, spray, stuff, stack*

The locative verbs represent a semantic domain which deals with both stative location and directional location. State locative verbs use stative locative prepositions; action locatives generally use directional prepositions. There are, however, verbs which are neither state nor action and which take directional prepositions as in *the water flows downhill*. In the development of case grammar models provision must be made for locatives which are neither state nor action but indicate a moving process from source to goal.

1.4 Related lexical entries. Within a case grammar the cases combine to form case frames which serve as environments into which verbs may be inserted. Once the case frames of verbs have been identified the next problem is to find out how lexical entries are related to each other. There are two problems: (1) How are the different uses of the same lexical verb related to each other?, and (2) how are verbs from different roots related to each other?

1.4.1 Different uses of the same verb. Given a single lexical verb that has different meanings represented by different case frames, how can these uses be related to each other? The 1968 model offers at least two methods; the conflated case frame, and moveable cases.

(a) The conflated case frame is a case frame which makes use of optional notation to combine many different case frames in a single notation. Fillmore refers to these conflated frames as 'frame features' (1968:27). Some verbs have different case frames constructed out of the same basic set of cases corresponding to their intransitive and transitive use, or their use with agent or instrument subjects. By listing the cases that occur in all the frames as obligatory and the cases that occur only in some frames as optional, it is possible to write a single conflated case frame that represents the whole set of case frames. For example, the verb *break* has four compatible case frames, formed with A, I and O cases. The case frames are O, I-O, A-O, and A-I-O. These four frames can be represented by a single conflated frame: + [___(A),(I),O]. The conflated entry represents four totally different deep structures, only one of which may occur in a given sentence. The four structures represented by this frame are given in sentences (32-35).

(32) The window /broke.
     O   iV
(33) The hammer /broke /the window.
     I   tV(ins)   O
(34) John /broke /the window.
     A   tV(agt)   O
(35) John /broke /the window /with a rock.
     A   tV(agt/ins)   O   I

With the conflated case frame notation it is possible to have a single lexical entry for the verb *break* rather than four separate entries. Transitive and intransitive uses, as well as use with agentive and instrumental subjects, are all subsumed under this one notation. But it should be understood that this lexical entry is simply an abbreviation for many different deep structures and is not in itself a deep structure. The conflated case frame as a lexical entry is subject to the misinterpretation that all cases listed in the conflated frame are present in all uses of the verb, whereas in fact the entry contains multiple deep structures.

(b) Another method for combining different meanings of the same verb is to provide for moveable cases. The verb may have two different meanings represented by the same set of cases but the cases occur in surface structure in a different order, often with a change of meaning or emphasis. If the subject choice hierarchy is accepted as the basic order then a rule of RANK SHIFT, operating on this basic frame, produces a second frame with a different order of cases.

The particular examples Fillmore has in mind are those three-place predicates which, after the subject has been chosen, offer alternative direct object choices from the remaining two cases. After the subject has been chosen from the cases arranged in a subject choice hierarchy, the direct object must be chosen from the remaining cases. The presumed object choice hierarchy is the subject choice hierarchy with the chosen subject removed. For example, the verb *spray* has the case frame A-O-L. After the Agent has been chosen as subject, the preferred direct object choice is the O case. But with this and other verbs the L case may also occur as direct object, as in sentences (36-37).

(36) John /sprayed /paint /on the wall.   O = DO
    A   V   O   L
(37) John /sprayed /the wall /with paint.   L = DO
    A   V   L   O

Fillmore (1968:48) attributes the original rules relating these sentences to Partee (1965) with additional examples from Fraser and Heringer cited in Fillmore (1969:370 fn.10). These include the A-O-L verbs: *plant, smear, spray, stack, stuff* and the A-D-O verbs: *talk, blame.* The principle of rank shift is extended to subject choice with certain O-L verbs like *swarm* (1968:48 fn.49) as illustrated in sentences (38-39).

(38) Bees /are swarming /in the garden.   O = S
    O   V   L
(39) The garden /is swarming /with bees.   L = S
    L   V   O

Mellema (1974) considers these uses of the verb as different in meaning. In sentence (36), where O is object, the meaning is partitive; only part of the wall need be sprayed with paint. In sentence (37), where L is object, the meaning is holistic with the implication that the whole wall was painted. Sentence (38), with O as subject, refers to some bees somewhere in the garden whereas sentence (39), with L as subject, implies that the whole garden is swarming with bees. But Fillmore is aware of these differences and even suggests that this rank shift be called a meaning changing transformation (1968:48, fn.49). No one makes the claim that verbs with the same case frame have the same meaning; on the contrary, different orderings of the same cases are being used here to explain the different meanings.

1.4.2 Different lexical verbs. In relating any two verbs from different lexical roots an attempt is made to relate those verbs which one intuitively feels are semantically related. The principle is similar to the assumption of phonetic similarity in the study of phonology. Not any two sounds, but only sounds that are phonetically similar, may be grouped as allophones of the same phoneme.

In his residual problems chapter in *Aspects* (1965:162) Chomsky states the need for a 'still more abstract notion of semantic function' to explain the similarity between such pairs of verbs as *like /please*, *strike /regard*, *buy /sell*, a similarity which cannot be explained in terms of deep or surface structure relations within the standard theory. Fillmore (1968:30) suggests that these perceived similarities might possibly be explained by similarity at the level of deep case structure with the differences between the verbs in each pair to be expressed in terms of either (1) different subject choices, or (2) the addition of a case, or (3) the substitution of one case for another in the case frame.

(1) Subject choice. (1968:30) Two different lexical verbs may be related if they are semantically similar, have the same case frame, and differ only in the case which is chosen as subject. One verb will have the cases in subject hierarchy order, while the other verb will have the same cases but with a non-normal choice of subject. A rank shift rule specific to this verb type will give the order of the cases, as is illustrated in sentences (40-41).

(40) John /liked /the movie.   D = S
     D   V   O
(41) The movie /pleased /John.   O = S
     O   V   D

(2) Add-a-case. (1968:30) Two different lexical verbs may be related if, under the condition of semantic similarity, their case frames are identical except for the addition of one case. For example, the verbs *see* and *show* differ in that *see* has the case frame D-O and *show* has the case frame A-D-O. The verb in sentence (43) differs from the verb in sentence (42) by the addition of a new case, the A case. Likewise the case frame for the verb *die* is O and the case frame for the verb *kill* is A-O. The verb in sentence (45) differs from the verb in sentence (44) by the addition of the A case.

(42) John /saw /the snake.   D,O
     D   V   O
(43) Harry /showed /John /the snake.   A,D,O
     A   V   D   O
(44) Max /died.   O
     O   V
(45) Harry /killed /Max.   A,O
     A   V   O

It is interesting to note that, in the examples which Fillmore uses to illustrate the add-a-case principle, the case which is added is always the A case. The verb with the A case seems to be the causative of the verb without the A case. Thus *show* with the A-D-O frame is the causative of *see* with the D-O frame, if *show* means 'cause to see'. Similarly, the verb *kill* with the A-O frame is the causative of *die* with the O-frame, if *kill* means 'cause to die'.

(3) Substitute-a-case. (1968:31) Two different lexical verbs may be related if, under the condition of initial semantic similarity, their case frames differ by a single case. In these examples, the difference is not in the addition of a new case but in the substitution of one case for another. For example, consider the pairs: *hear* / *listen to, see* / *look at, know* / *learn*. The initial verb of each of these pairs has the D-O frame and the second verb of each pair has the A-O frame according to Fillmore's analysis. The first verb of each pair is a nonagentive verb; *hear, see, know* are dative state verbs. The second member of each pair is an agentive verb; *listen to, look at, learn* are action verbs, as in sentences (46-47).

```
(46) John /saw /the snake.                          D,O
     D    V    O
(47) John /looked at /the snake.                    A,O
     A    V          O
```

In dealing with these examples of case substitution one suspects that these examples may also be examples of the addition of an Agentive case to form the causative counterpart of the state verb. It is at this point that one feels the need for coreferential case roles. The verb *listen to* does not deny that the person can hear but only adds the notion that he is now hearing with deliberate attention. The subject of *listen to* is Agentive but does not for that reason cease to be also Dative, since the person experiences the sense of hearing. This relation could be shown if, in adding the A case to the frame, the subject of the verb is both Agentive and Dative.

The pair *buy* / *sell* should probably be treated as two verbs that have the same case frame; they differ from each other in that one has the buyer as Agent while the other has the seller as Agent. In 1968 Fillmore does not treat this pair of verbs directly, and they would not fit neatly into any of the above three categories. These verbs are not related by subject choice, or by substituting or adding cases. But if both verbs are assigned the case frame A-D-O they would then differ only in that the buyer is Agent with *buy* and the seller is Agent with *sell*, as in sentences (48-49).

```
(48) David /bought /a book /from John.              A,D,O
     A     V        O       D
(49) John /sold /a book /to David.                  A,D,O
     A    V     O        D
```

1.5 Covert case roles. The term 'covert category' is adapted from Fillmore. In the 1968 model all case relationships are described as categories that are 'in large part covert but nevertheless empirically discoverable' (1968:5). All case roles are covert in Fillmore's description and these covert case roles, or concepts underlying case forms, are opposed to the overt forms used to express these case relationships in various languages.

In the present work the term COVERT CASE ROLE is used only for those cases which appear only sometimes, or never appear, in the surface structure. Cases which are always manifested in the surface structure are called OVERT CASE ROLES. Given a deep structure with a well defined set of cases, these cases are described as overt or covert depending upon whether or not they regularly appear in the surface structure. Cases which occur sometimes but not always in the surface structure are called PARTIALLY COVERT CASE ROLES, or deletable roles. Those cases which can never appear in the surface structure but nevertheless are present in the deep structure are called TOTALLY COVERT CASE ROLES. These include coreferential case roles and lexicalized case roles. The different ways in which deep case roles are manifested are represented schematically in Figure 1.5.

Figure 1.5 Covert case roles.

```
          ┌ Overt . . . . . . . . . always present
          │
Cases ┤
          │              ┌ Partially . . sometimes present
          └ Covert ┤
                          └ Totally . . . . . never present
```

Overt case roles are those cases which are present in the deep structure and always occur in the surface structure whenever that verb occurs. For example, the Agent always appears in action verbs when used in the active voice. The sentence must have a subject in English and Agent is the first choice for subject. For certain verbs the direct object is obligatory in the surface structure and therefore considered to be an overt case, as, for example, the verb *build*. Certain locative verbs, such as the verb *put*, require a locative phrase in the surface structure and are not considered grammatical without that locative, as in sentences (50-52). With most verbs the majority of the cases within the case frame will be obligatory in surface structure; however, covert case roles are the exception.

(50) John /broke /the window.
     A   V   O
(51) Harry /built /a house.
     A   V   O
(52) He /put /the book /on the table.
    A V   O   L

1.5.1 Deletable case roles. Those cases which are always present in the deep structure but sometimes appear and sometimes do not appear in the surface structure are partially covert roles. They are optional to the surface structure despite the fact that they are required by the verb. They are easily recognized by the fact that they occur in some sentences with the verb but are missing in other sentences.

Fillmore illustrates deletable case roles in the context of verbs with deletable objects (1968:29). The verb *cook* may be used intransitively with the case frame O or transitively with the case frame A-O. When the verb is used intransitively the one O case may not be deleted. But when the same verb is used transitively the A case always appears as subject and the O case, the direct object, sometimes appears and sometimes does not appear. This does not mean that there are two different transitive verbs, one with the A case alone and one with the A and O cases. It simply indicates that the verb in transitive use, with the A-O frame, has a direct object which is deletable in surface structure. The meaning of the verb *cook* requires that whoever does the cooking must cook something but this something can be either expressed or implied. In other words, the object of the verb in this case is a partially covert role which sometimes appears in surface structure and sometimes does not appear, as in sentences (53-55).

(53) The potatoes /are cooking.   O
     O   V
(54) Susan /is cooking /the potatoes.   A,O
     A   V   O
(55) Susan /is cooking /(something).   A,O /O-del
     A   V   (O-del)

The use of deletable case roles allows the analyst to unify the uses of the verb when it occurs either with or without a surface object by listing both uses under a single case frame. These two uses will not be listed as transitive and intransitive forms but as a single transitive verb with deletable object. The transitive verb with an A-O frame can then be clearly distinguished from the intransitive with the O-frame.

The principle of partially covert case roles, which are present obligatorily in the deep structure but optionally present in the surface structure, has widespread application within the context of the deletable object verbs described by Fillmore. But the principle is easily extended to a wide range of cases and their surface manifestations. For example, verbs of communication require a speaker, a hearer, and the information that passes between them. They may be listed universally as requiring the A-D-O case frame. But the hearer (the D case), or what is said (the O case), or both may be deleted from the surface structure depending upon which particular verb of communication is chosen, as in sentences (56-59).

(56) He /spoke.   A,D,O /D,O-del
     A   V

(57) He /spoke /to me.   A,D,O /O-del
    A   V   D

(58) He /spoke /about that.   A,D,O /D-del
    A   V   O

(59) He /spoke /to me /about that.   A,D,O
    A   V   D   O

Despite the fact that the verb *speak* is able to occur in four different surface structures, A, A-D, A-O, A-D-O, the verb is listed once in the lexicon as an A-D-O verb and all occurrences are explained by the principle of deletable roles. Obviously, for any model using deletable case roles the cases manifested in the surface structure are not in a one-to-one correspondence with the cases present in the deep structure.

1.5.2 Coreferential case roles. Totally covert case roles are those case roles which are present obligatorily in the deep structure but which never occur in the surface structure. These totally covert roles are of two types: coreferential case roles, where two case labels are applied to the same surface noun phrase, and lexicalized case roles, where an essential case is incorporated into the verb. Coreferential roles do not occur in Fillmore's 1968 model but appear later in his 1971 model. Coreferential case roles are two or more cases that are applied to the same surface NP. This deep structure coreferentiality is not to be confused with surface reflexivization. In fact, they are mutually exclusive. Surface reflexivization occurs when there are two surface NPs with the same external referent. But if two deep cases are coreferential the lower ranking case may not appear at all in surface structure; it is totally covert. Consequently, surface reflexivization is prima facie evidence that there is no deep structure coreferentiality.

The principle of deep structure coreferential cases begins with Gruber (1965). Starting with an obligatory theme case which must be present in every deep structure, roughly equivalent to Fillmore's O case, Gruber was easily led to coreference. For example, the theme with motion verbs is the moving object and the Agent is the intender of the action. It is not difficult to find examples where a surface NP is both an agent and the moving object. The subject of sentence (60) is only a moving object but the subject of sentence (61) is both an agent and a moving object.

(60) The rock /rolled /down the hill.   O,L
    O   V   L

(61) Max /rolled /down the hill.   A,*O,L /A=O
    A=O V   L

One of Jackendoff's principal reasons for adopting Gruber's thematic relations rather than Fillmore's 1968 case grammar was the idea of coreference in which the Agent subject 'can simultaneously bear other thematic relations' (Jackendoff 1972:32).

1.5.3 Lexicalized case roles. Lexicalized roles are totally covert roles that never appear in the surface structure because they are lexicalized into the verb form. The principle of lexicalization is based upon Gruber's (1965) theory of prelexical structure. According to Gruber the lexical verb often has a complex underlying structure that may consist of Verb-Preposition, Verb-Noun, Verb-Preposition-Noun, Verb-Noun-Preposition. This underlying structure is then incorporated into a single lexical verb form.

When one of the NPs that expresses an underlying propositional case is incorporated into the verb it will not normally appear in the surface structure and is called a lexicalized case role. For example, the verb *dine* is a surface intransitive verb with the meaning 'eat dinner'. The noun *dinner* is incorporated into the lexical verb *dine*, as in sentences (62-63).

(62) They /ate /dinner /at 5 o'clock.   A,O
     A   V   O T_m
(63) They /dined /at 5 o'clock.   A,*O /O-lex
     A   V+O T_m

The process of lexicalization is very widespread in English. Both modal cases and propositional cases may be lexicalized into the verb. The fact that a role is lexicalized is not evidence that the role is propositional, but when propositional roles are lexicalized they should be entered as part of the case frame.

Instrumental roles are frequently lexicalized but are not necessarily propositional. The verb *slap* means 'hit-with-the-palm-of-the-hand,' and the verb *kick* means 'hit-with-the-foot'. These lexicalized roles do not normally appear on the surface. But if the role is modified in some way then the lexicalized role is forced to the surface as a copy of the lexicalized role which can then be modified, as in sentences (64-65).

(64) She /slapped /him /(*with her hand).   A,*I,O
     A   V+I   O
(65) She /slapped /him /with her left hand.   A,*I,O
     A   V+I   O   I-copy

A case grammar that does not have a theory of covert roles is just another labelling system for surface structure. But with a theory of covert case roles some attempt is made to understand the prelexical structure of the verb. This type of analysis is a more complete semantic analysis in that all the essential roles are listed whether they appear in the surface structure or not. This system is oriented towards deep structure semantic analysis and not towards surface analysis. Such a system is not subject to the objection that surface NPs and deep structure cases are in one-to-one correspondence (Jackendoff 1972:34). Deletable roles, coreferential roles, and lexicalized roles all occur in the Fillmore 1971 model.

1.6 Evaluation of the Fillmore 1968 model. The Fillmore 1968 model as presented in 'The case for case' is the first case grammar model. While many features of the model were to change over the years the essentials of a case grammar model were presented for the first time and had widespread acceptance. The essential idea of classifying the verbs of a language according to the combinations of cases with which they occur, the distinction between traditional case forms and their uses, and the possibility of a verb classification which has cross-language validity, all helped to get case grammars off to a strong start. But the details of the model change as they are adapted by various authors, including Fillmore himself.

1.6.1 Deep structure. The deep structure of the 1968 model is characterized by the separation of proposition and modality, the right-to-left ordering of the cases, and the presence of case marking prepositions in the deep structure. Prepositions in deep structure are abandoned in 1971 in favor of preposition selection rules which add case markers to NPs as the surface structure is formed. Also in 1971 the right-to-left ordering of the cases is abandoned in favor of the left-to-right ordering, a VSO order which is easier to read and more in accordance with the order of arguments in most systems of logic. Proposition and modality remain separate in Fillmore's later model but there is more concentration on propositional structure. The modality component was never fully developed.

Modal elements must be incorporated into the surface structure. Fillmore's original plan to sort out and then abandon all the modal elements allows him to concentrate fully upon the propositional content of the sentence. At one point, Fillmore (1968:23 fn.29) suggests that certain sentence adverbials may be introduced as higher sentences. It is possible that all modality elements that modify the sentence as a whole could be introduced as higher sentences following the practice of generative semantics. Fillmore, however, does not explore these possibilities. He is more concerned with developing the propositional elements of the case grammar model.

1.6.2 Case system. Fillmore, speaking of the case system, admits that he does not know: (1) What is the correct list of deep structure cases? (2) How can we know when the list is complete? (3) How are cases to be defined? (1975:3) He simply insists that the list of cases be small, sufficient for the classification of the verbs in a language, and with cross-language validity. Within these parameters the case systems proposed by later authors vary a great deal.

Fillmore's 1968 system contains five useful cases: A-I-D-O-L. In addition, there is a Factitive case which serves as an alternate for the O case with creative verbs and a Comitative case which serves as an alternate to the Locative case for accompaniment. The primary cases, Agentive and Objective, appear in all future case models and are essential to any case grammar. The list of secondary cases changes from model to model.

The Instrumental case is emphasized in Fillmore's 1968 model and in all future Fillmore models but is not universally accepted by other authors as a propositional case. The Dative case covers too wide a semantic domain and is later subdivided into Experiencer and other cases. Fillmore advances strong arguments for the unity of a Locative case which includes both stative and directional locatives in complementary distribution. Those case grammarians who prefer a unified Locative will appeal to these arguments despite the fact that Fillmore later abandons the unified Locative in favor of Location, Source, and Goal cases.

1.6.3 Case frames. Fillmore lays down certain basic principles for combining cases into case frames: (1) Every case frame must have at least one case, (2) the same case may not appear twice in the same case frame, and (3) sentences are embedded only under the O case. In practice, the two primary cases, Agent and Object, have assumed more importance but they are not obligatory to the case frame since Fillmore has frames without either an A case or an O case. The secondary cases, in practice but not in principle, are mutually exclusive. In effect, they divide the verbs of a language into separate semantic domains. Fillmore proposes case frames with one, two or three cases. Meteorological verbs are treated by Fillmore as having the L case only but this practice is not followed by subsequent case grammarians.

The greatest defect in case tactics is the acceptance of the Lakoff binary State /Action distinction for verb types. This leads Fillmore into the erroneous assertions that stativity need not be marked in the case frame or that progressive occurs only with verbs which contain an A case in the frame.

Once the case system is expanded to a three-way system including: (1) state verbs, classified as [-progressive,-imperative], (2) process verbs, classed as [+progressive,-imperative], and (3) action verbs, classed as [+progressive,+imperative], then a proper classification can be made. Within a three-way classification stativity must be marked in the case frame to distinguish state from process verbs which have the same case inventory. The progressive inflection may occur with both process and action verbs.

It is unfortunate that Fillmore's O case, as the semantically most neutral case, never attained the status of an obligatory theme as in Gruber (1965). The case frames in which the O case does not appear are relatively few in Fillmore's 1968 model. These examples include meteorological verbs with the L case, experiential adjectives such as *be sad* with the D case, and the action verb *run* with the A case. If these few examples were explained away an obligatory O case could be established. Meteorological verbs could be analyzed as simply the O case, experiential adjectives as an O coreferential with D, action verbs as A coreferential with O. But Fillmore's later work takes him further away from, rather than closer to, a case system with an obligatory theme.

1.6.4 Related lexical entries. In the 1968 model Fillmore suggests various ways in which lexical entries can be related by case frames. These methods are different: (a) for those verbs which have the same lexical root in which the spelling of the verb imposes a presupposition of semantic similarity, and (b) for those verbs which come from different lexical roots in which semantic similarity is not so evident.

(a) For those verbs which have the same lexical root Fillmore suggests the conflated case frame which combines many deep structures into one notation by making use of parentheses for optional elements. The disadvantages of this conflated frame are: (1) the state form is not included in the entry, (2) the optional cases could be interpreted as deletable roles, and (3) the frame is subject to the misinterpretation that all cases in the conflated frame occur in all uses of the verb. The problem with combining many uses of the verb under a single entry is that their differences are deemphasized. Little attention is given to which use is basic and which use is derived. What is required here is not an abbreviation system to make things notationally simple but a derivational system to explain the derivation of one verb form from another. Such a system was suggested by Lakoff's (1965) work with inchoative and causative proforms and is later developed by Chafe (1970).

Fillmore also uses the principle of movable cases to unite two uses of the verb into a single notation for verbs such as *spray* which occur with the cases sometimes in A-O-L and sometimes in A-L-O order. Fillmore lists these two uses of the verb under a single A-O-L entry and lets the flip rule account for the change in order of the cases and the subsequent change in meaning from partitive to holistic.

(b) For those verbs which are based upon different lexical roots there must be a strong presupposition of semantic similarity. Fillmore relates these entries by different subject choice, by adding a case to the frame, or by substituting a case in the frame. Different subject choice is an effective tool for relating some pairs: *like /please, have /belong to, be in /contain*. Even if there is not perfect identity of feature specification, the meaning of the case roles with these pairs is similar enough. However, the add-a-case and substitute-a-case analyses seem far more superficial. The relationships between the pairs *see /show* and *die /kill* are not just add-a-case relations in which the A case is added to the frame but a relationship of causality in which one verb is the causative of the other. Likewise the substitute-a-case relationship seems to be based too much on surface structure. The relationship between *hear /listen to* is not simply that the A case has replaced the D case. The A case does not replace the D case but is added to the case frame and is coreferential with D. In this analysis *hear* has the case frame D-O and *listen to* has the case frame A-D-O /A=D. But this kind of analysis, using coreferential roles, was not possible for Fillmore in 1968 in a model that di not deal with coreference.

1.6.5 Covert case roles. Fillmore considers all case roles to be covert in the deep structure sense and does not develop a system of covert case roles which sometimes or never appear on the surface. He does lay the foundation for partially covert roles in his examples of verbs with deletable objects. But the principle of deletable roles has a much wider application in unifying the description of various surface expressions involving the same lexical verb. There are no totally covert roles in the Fillmore 1968 model but both coreferential roles and lexicalized roles appear in his 1971 model. The principle that two case labels can be applied to the same NP, already used by Gruber (1965), and the principle that case roles can be lexicalized into the verb, suggested by Gruber's(1965) prelexical structures, are adopted by Fillmore in his later work and to some degree by most other case grammarians.

1.7 Conclusion. The Fillmore 1968 model was a solid case grammar model, the first of its kind in modern linguistics, and prompted many to attempt a similar approach. Fillmore's object was to create 'new conceptual tools' (1975:2) for the analysis of language. What he arrived at was a semantic analysis at a certain level of clause structure which manifests the semantic relationships between the essential elements of a clause, the central verb and one, two or three noun phrases, in much the same way as logic analyzes the relationships between a predicate and its arguments. Although Fillmore's goal was to provide a case base for a transformational grammar, the model which evolved was more of a kind of semantic valence theory which analyzed the clause in predicate-argument terms, independently of such surface grammatical relationships as subject and object. Chomsky had noted the need for a new level of semantic analysis not provided by the standard theory. Part of Fillmore's success was that his model seemed to provide that level of semantics.

The wider appeal of case grammar is probably due to the fact that, after a long period in which meaning was first ignored then relegated to an interpretive role, semantics could be approached directly. The linguist could now deal with meaning in much the same way as logicians do but with more attention to the differences to be found in natural language. Case grammar provided a system for analyzing the content behind the clause rather than its surface structure. If syntactic studies were based on visible language structures, then the meaning behind the structure was 'empirically discoverable' (1968:5), given that any language is a system of communication. The data is not in language expression but in the content behind the expression. This content could now be expressed in case grammar terms. The attempt to analyze meaning, no matter how defective the model, directly turned the minds of analysts towards meaning rather than form and this attempt to analyze meaning is the principal challenge offered by the introduction of the theory of case grammar.

Exercise 1. Write the case frame for the main verb in each of the following sentences. The cases available are A-I-D-O-L. One, two, or three cases may appear in the frame. If the flip rule has applied write the two cases in the order in which they occur in surface structure. If a sentence is embedded in the O case add O=S after the case frame. If a case is deleted list the deleted case after the case frame. For passive verbs write the case frame for the active verb.

1. It was apparent to Max that he would win. _____

2. The studio is hot. _____

3. There are many toys in the box. _____

4. Mary was very sad. _____

5. It is true that John likes Mary. _____

6. He blamed the accident on Fred. _____

7. A hammer broke the window. _____

8. Mary is cooking. _____

9. The old man died. _____

10. My brother was given the books. _____

11. The box has many toys in it. _____

12. Harry didn't hear the bell. _____

13. The door opened. _____

14. The janitor opened the door with a key. _____

15. They persuaded John that he would lose. _____

16. The music will please him. _____

17. He put the car in the garage. _____

18. Harry was running. _____

19. He sprayed the wall with paint. _____

20. He sprayed paint on the wall. _____

21. John wanted to leave early. _____

Fillmore 1968 Lexicon. The Fillmore 1968 lexicon is a collection of eighty verbs with the case frames as far as they can be determined from 'The case for case'. Where the flip rule has applied to two place or three place verbs the cases are written in the order in which they occur in surface structure after the flip rule has applied.

be apparent	O,D	look at	A,O
be hot	L	murder (agt)	A,O
be in	O,L	murder (ins)	A,I,O
be interesting	O,D	open,iv	O
be on	O,L	open (ins)	I,O
be sad	D	open (agt)	A,O
be true	O	open (agt/ins)	A,I,O
be with	O,C	persuade	A,D,O
be windy	L	plant in	A,O,L
believe	D,O	plant with	A,L,O
belong to	O,D	please	O,D
blame for	A,D,O	predict	A,O
blame on	A,O,D	put	A,O,L
break,iv	O	remove	A,O
break (ins)	I,O	run	A
break (agt)	A,O	say	A,O
break (ins/agt)	A,I,O	see	D,O
build	A,F	show	A,D,O
buy	A,O	smear on	A,O,L
cause	A,O	smear with	A,L,O
cook,iv	O	spray on	A,O,L
cook,tv	A,O	spray with	A,L,O
die	O	stack on	A,O,L
expect	D,O	stack with	A,L,O
force	A,D,O	stuff into	A,O,L
give	A,D,O	stuff with	A,L,O
have	D,O	swarm in	O,L
have in	L,O	swarm with	L,O
have on	L,O	take	A,O,L
have with	C,O	talk to	A,D,O
hear	D,O	talk about	A,O,D
keep	A,O,L	terrorize	A,O
kill (ins)	I,O	think	D,O
kill (agt)	A,O	turn out	O
kill (ins/agt)	A,I,O	use	A,I
know	D,O	wake up,iv	O
learn	A,O	wake up (ins)	I,O
leave	A,O,L	wake up (agt)	A,O
like	D,O	wake up (agt/ins)	A,I,O
listen to	A,O	want	D,O

2 The Fillmore 1971 Model

2.0 Overview. The Fillmore 1971 model has a revised deep structure and a new list of cases. This model was first presented in the Linguistic Institute of 1970 and is summarized in Cook (1979:16-27). The revised model is also reflected in an article entitled 'Some problems for case grammar' in the *Georgetown University Round Table on Languages and Linguistics 1971* (1971:35-56). Later reminiscences by Fillmore concerning his work are found in the author's preface to *Principles of Case Grammar* (1975) and in 'The case for case reopened' in *Syntax and Semantics*, volume 8 (1977:59-81).

Writing in 1975 Fillmore declares that his intention in presenting the case grammar model was to provide 'new conceptual tools' (1975:2) for general grammatical theory. The detailed analyses of particular verbs were meant to be 'suggestive rather than definitive' (1975:3). Case grammar was not meant to be a description of any particular language, such as English, but a method for analyzing any language.

Fillmore's motives for taking the case grammar position fall into two general categories: (1) the level of analysis at which grammatical relations are defined, and (2) the organization of the lexicon (1975:3).

(1) The first problem of how to distinguish grammatical relations from grammatical categories is twofold. How are we to represent nuclear relations like subject and object as distinct from the noun phrase category that manifests these functions, and also how are we to represent, for peripheral functions like time, place, and manner, the relational information contained in these labels and at the same time represent the categorial information that these ideas may be represented by prepositional phrases, by adverbs, or by adverbial phrases?

(2) The second problem, the organization of the lexicon, is also twofold. How are we to subcategorize the verbs or governing words in a clause, and, secondly, will this classification be adequate in relating morphologically different verbs like the pairs of verbs given in Chomsky's (1965:162) residual problems chapter such as *buy /sell*, *like /please*, *strike /regard*? These problems are treated more explicitly in the 1971 model than they were in the 1968 model.

Case grammar subcategorizes the verbs in a language according to case frames which provide a 'semantic valence description' for the verb (1975:6). Valence is a term taken from atomic chemistry in which the valence of an atomic nucleus represents the positive power of the nucleus to hold a specified number of electrons in its configuration.

Syntactic valence theories, popularized in Europe, were those in which syntactic constructions were described in terms of a governing word and the constituents that could or must occur in construction with them. Case grammar describes the governing word of a clause in terms of the noun phrases that are required by the meaning of that predicate. This valence is semantic not syntactic, but there are syntactic correlates that follow from the semantic description of predicates as expressed in the case frame.

Standard transformational theory subcategorized verbs in terms of the surrounding noun phrases and their features. Verbs were subcategorized as transitive or intransitive depending upon whether they did or did not take an NP direct object. They were then further subcategorized by selectional rules which indicated the features of NPs in both subject and object position. In this system the nouns are central and are clearly defined in terms of intrinsic semantic features such as [± common], [± count], [± animate], [± human]. The verbs of the system have no intrinsic features but are totally characterized in terms of the nouns that surround them.

Case grammar accepts the verb as the governing word and lists the surrounding nouns in terms of the deep structure roles which they represent in the state or action described by the verb. The system is verb-centered and case relations are read onto the nouns from the verb. The resulting case frame subcategorization represents a deeper semantic level of analysis than the syntactic subcategorization of the standard theory. The two systems are compared in Figure 2.1.

Figure 2.1 Subcategorization in Chomsky and Fillmore.

(1) The window /broke.
  break, iv $\qquad$ +[NP$_{in}$ ___] $\qquad$ +[___ O]
(2) A hammer /broke /the window.
  break, tv (ins) $\qquad$ +[NP$_{in}$ ___ NP$_{in}$] $\qquad$ +[___ I,O]
(3) John /broke /the window.
  break, tv (agt) $\qquad$ +[NP$_{an}$ ___ NP$_{in}$] $\qquad$ +[___ A,O]
(4) John /broke /the window /with a hammer.
  break, tv (agt/ins) $\qquad$ +[NP$_{an}$ ___ NP$_{in}$ PP$_{in}$] $\qquad$ +[___ A,I,O]

In the standard theory the verb *break* must be entered four times in the lexicon to represent the four different syntactic configurations in which the verb occurs. In the case grammar notation the four case frames can be conflated into a single case frame which represents the four structures. The verb *break*, for example, is +[___(A),(I),O]. If A is present it is chosen as subject; if there is no A, the I is chosen as subject; if neither A nor I is present, the O is chosen as subject (Fillmore 1968:33).

The case frame subcategorization is not more informative simply because the frames can be combined into a single notation. The case elements in the frame give a different kind of information which is proper to the semantic interpretation of the verb rather than its syntactic use. In sentences (1–4) the O case is consistently the Object which is broken, the I case is consistently the Instrument used in the breaking process, and the A case is consistently the Agent performing the action. The case subcategorization represents a deeper level of the grammar because it deals with semantic relations ultimately based on the meaning of the verb and is not dependent upon particular syntactic constructions. Some modern interpretivists, such as Jackendoff (1972), use a similar system which is called THEMATIC RELATIONS. His method is to enter into the lexicon both the syntactic configurations of the standard theory and a semantic subcategorization in terms of thematic relations with subscripts to indicate which NP of the syntax is identified with which case role in the thematic relations (Jackendoff 1972:38).

Case frame subcategorization helps to relate different uses of the same lexical verb. It also serves to relate morphologically different verbs of the type mentioned in *Aspects* (1965:162). Chomsky admits that beyond the notions of deep structure and surface structure 'there is some still more abstract notion of semantic function still unexplained' (1965:163). Some new kind of semantic level is required to explain the meaning relationships that exist between *like /please*, *buy /sell*, *strike /regard*. The standard theory has no way of expressing these relationships. Fillmore (1971:35) believes that case grammar provides a way of dealing with these meaning relationships. Basically these pairs of verbs have the same case frame but differ from each other in choice of subject and object or other case-related features, as in sentences (5–10). The 1968 Dative case (D) is replaced by the Experiencer case (E), and Source (S) and Goal (G) are introduced as new cases. For the complete list of cases see section 2.2.

(5) John /strikes /me /as pompous.   O,E /E object
 = It /strikes /me /that John is pompous.
  O-copy V E   O
(6) I /regard /John as pompous.   E,O /E subject
  E V   O
(7) I /liked /the play.   E,O /E subject
  E V   O
(8) The play /pleased /me.   O,E /O subject
  O   V   E
(9) John /bought /the book /from Bill.   A,O,S,*G /A=G
  A=G V   O   S
(10) Bill /sold /the book / to John.   A,O,*S,G /A=S
  A=S V   O   G

The organization of a lexicon based upon case grammar includes the case frame of the verb with the lexical entry. These case frames help to organize the different uses of the same morphological verb into a single combined lexical entry. Also, certain systematic relationships between verbs from different roots but belonging to the same semantic domain are revealed by these same frames.

Case grammar classifies verbs according to case frames. The frames are made up of those cases which are required by the meaning of the verb. In the case grammar model certain features are considered essential; other features, over a period of time, were rejected as not essential to the model. The essential features of a case grammar model are the cases, the subject choice hierarchy, and verb classification by case frames. The nonessential features are the existence of prepositions in the deep structure, the assignment of features such as [±animate] to cases, and the ordering of the cases at the deepest level.

(1) The first requirement of a case grammar is 'a small number of elementary case notions, universal in scope, capable of being extended to the whole vocabulary of predicating words in a language' (1975:7). Although the small number is not defined, in Fillmore's work it is always less than ten. The cases must be universal in scope, that is, the cases must be applicable to predicating words across languages. And finally, the cases must be necessary and sufficient to describe all the predicating words in a given language. There must be one set of cases for the whole language not different sets of cases for different vocabulary fields.

(2) The second essential requirement is the subject choice hierarchy. Although deep structures may be considered to be unordered at the deepest level, 'more like a mobile than a tree' (Fillmore 1975:6), some order has to be established early in the generation of sentences to provide a hierarchy for listing the cases and determining for each instance the proper choice for subject of the sentence. The model can then provide case frames for each verb in the language and for each meaning of every verb, with the cases arranged in a subject choice hierarchy order. Although the Fillmore 1968 model had the cases in right-to-left order, Fillmore uses the more logical left-to-right order in his 1971 model.

(3) Prepositions are not essential to deep structure. In the 1971 model prepositions may no longer occur in deep structure; cases directly dominate noun phrases. Prepositions or other case markings, according to Fillmore, are added to noun phrases as the surface structure is derived (1975:6; 1977:65).

(4) Cases are no longer described as necessarily animate or inanimate. Cases are relational notions that describe the semantic roles that nouns play in sentences; they are not to be confused with categorial notions like animacy. Fillmore states 'I no longer confuse selection restrictions to animates with true case-like notions' (Fillmore 1971:42), and 'I am now more careful about keeping relational notions (cases) and categorial notions (animate) distinct' (Fillmore 1977:65). He adds the statement: 'This part of the initial formulation of the (case grammar) proposal was wrong' (Fillmore 1975:6).

2.1 Deep structure. The deep structure of Fillmore's 1971 model is characterized by the absence of any modality constituent, the abandonment of the right-to-left ordering of the cases, and the absence of case markers in deep structure. The deep structure now consists of a verb and a series of cases ordered left-to-right in subject choice hierarchy order. The resulting structure resembles the logical structures of generative semantics with two main differences. First, the generative semantics structure uses only the labels S, V, and NP, whereas the case grammar structure replaces the NP labels with case role labels. Second, the NPs in the logical structures of generative semantics are ordered according to the syntactic function they perform as subject, indirect object, and direct object, whereas the case-labelled nouns are ordered according to the subject choice hierarchy. The basic case structure of sentence (11) is illustrated in Figure 2.2.

(11) John /broke /the window /with a hammer.
     A   V   O   I

Figure 2.2 Basic case structure

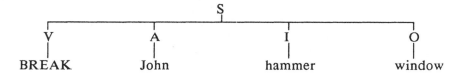

The advantage of this particular deep structure is that it mirrors the case frame exactly. Given that the verb *break* has the case frame + [___ A,I,O], simply add V in the blank space in the case frame and add S as a higher node dominating the V and all the cases within the frame. This structure is then in accord with Fillmore's statement that 'the propositional core of a simple sentence consists of a predicator (V) in construction with one or more entities, each of these related to the predicator in one of the semantic functions known as (deep structure) cases' (1971:37).

If the deep structure represents only the 'propositional core' of the sentence, then the modality is not represented in this deep structure. In the 1971 model Fillmore concentrates upon the proposition and makes little mention of the modality. But given that modality elements exist, how would those modality elements mentioned by Fillmore in earlier models, such as tense, aspect, negation, and modal adverbials, be represented in the deep structure? Fillmore gives several suggestions about the structure of sentences containing modal cases.

In dealing with the modal cases, time and location, which are 'optional complements of essentially any predicator' (1971:49), Fillmore suggests that clauses designating actions and events that can occur in time and space 'are themselves embedded in higher sentences containing as their main verb something like *occur* or *happen*' (1971:49). These verbs are two place predicates relating an event (O) with a time phrase (T). The structure of sentence (12), illustrating the modal time case, is given in Figure 2.3.

(12) John /broke /the window /yesterday.
    A   V   O T_m

Figure 2.3 Modal Time.

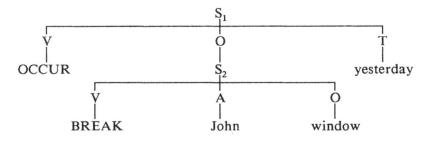

A similar higher sentence analysis (1971:52) is suggested for the Goal case in which the modal Goal (or Benefactive) case, manifested by *for* meaning 'for the sake of', is represented in the deep structure as a case required by a higher verb such as *give* or *offer*. Sentences such as *John did the work for me* would be represented as *John gave it for me* where *it* represents the embedded sentence *John did the work*. The structure of sentence (13) is given in Figure 2.4.

(13) John /did /the work /for me.
    A   V   O B_m

Figure 2.4 Modal Benefactive.

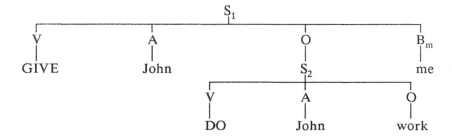

These two examples indicate that Fillmore is considering the general possibility that all adverbial modal cases not contained within the propositional content of the main verb, such as outer Locative, outer Time, and outer Benefactive, are to be represented as complex structures in which the adverbial modal element is contained in a superordinate clause. Fillmore's solution for these modal elements suggests the further possibility that all modal elements should appear as higher predicates. Given the simple logical structure of the verb plus its required cases, the modal elements such as tense, aspect and negation could easily be represented as higher predicates in the deep structure since they represent 'modalities on the sentence-as-a-whole' (1968:23). This is the method used in generative semantics as recommended by Ross (1969) in 'Auxiliaries as main verbs', by McCawley (1971) in 'Tense and time reference in English', and by McCawley (1970) in 'On the deep structure of negative clauses'.

In the 1971 model Fillmore's concerns are evident. He is interested in proposing 'a substantive modification to the theory of transformational grammar' (1968:21) and with answering the basic question 'how can a transformational grammar with a case base be formalized?' (1975:3). His course in case grammar at the Linguistic Institute of 1970 proposed a set of fifteen realization rules to convert deep structures into surface structures. The essentials of such a grammar are (1) that deep structure is to be represented in terms of cases, and (2) that in the derivation of surface structures the subject choice hierarchy will play an important role. The plan of how such a grammar would work is given in Figure 2.5.

Figure 2.5 Sentence Derivation

Deep structure --> Subject choice --> Surface
(case base)   Hierarchy   structures

The concrete realization rules used in the 1970 presentation have been reviewed elsewhere (Cook 1979:21). Four rules deal with subject marking, subject formation, object marking, and object formation. Three rules deal with transformations such as subject-raising, extraposition, and passive, and three rules deal with changes in the subject choice hierarchy. The remaining five rules deal with the selection and placement of prepositions and particles. Without going into details about how each rule works there is something to be learned from the choice of these particular topics.

The realization rules that deal with standard transformations teach us how to set up structures with a case base. In a word, the surface structure must be unravelled and the effect of the transformational rules undone before an accurate assignment of cases can be made in the deep structure.

SUBJECT-RAISING in its most common form raises the subject of the lower sentence to be the subject of the next higher sentence. If subject-raising has taken place the deep structure must show the two sentence structure before raising has taken place and cases can then be assigned to the original two sentence structure. There is no case frame for complex sentences but only case frames for the simplex sentences of which complex sentences are composed. For example, the verb *seem* is a subject-raising predicate, which always takes an embedded sentence as its subject. The deep structure will show the two sentence structure before raising with *seem* as the higher verb and the embedded verb as the lower verb. Sentence (14) has the deep structure given in Figure 2.6.

(14) John seems to me to be sick.
    = It /seems /to me /that John is sick
    = *That John is sick /seems /to me.
        O=S   V   E

Figure 2.6 Subject-Raising

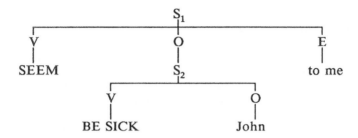

EXTRAPOSITION moves an embedded clause from subject position to the end of the sentence and replaces this subject with the dummy word *it*. Extraposed sentences have no simple case analysis. It is only when the effect of the extraposition rule is undone that one can clearly see that the verb is a predicate with a sentence embedded under the O case as subject. The *it* introduced by rule is described by Fillmore (1968:41) as a 'copy' of the O case already present. This copying rule does not violate the one-instance-per-clause principle but the surface form after the application of the rule of extraposition has two representations of the same case.

PASSIVE sentences are represented in deep structure in their active form. Before assigning cases to them the sentence must be converted into its active form and the downgraded subject, usually the Agent, must be supplied if the *by* phrase has been deleted. Passive is an optional rule which changes the form of the verb and allows a lower ranking case to appear as the subject of the passive verb (1971:42).

The realization rules that deal with changes in the subject choice hierarchy also teach us something about how to formulate case frames. First, the rule of obligatory COREFERENCE DELETION establishes the fact that two cases may be coreferential in deep structure; but if they are coreferential the lower ranking case of the two is obligatorily deleted and cannot appear in any position in surface structure. This principle makes a clear distinction between deep structure coreference and surface structure reflexivization. A coreferential role cannot possibly occur as a reflexive pronoun since it is deleted before the reflexivization rule could apply.

The other two rules deal with RANK SHIFT in the subject choice hierarchy and with the second ranking Experiencer case. The EXPERIENCER-SHUNTING rule moves the Experiencer case out of order so that it will not be chosen as subject. This shunted Experiencer case then becomes the indirect object with verbs like *seem*. The PSYCH

MOVEMENT rule moves the Experiencer case to the next position in the hierarchy where it will be chosen as direct object, as with the verb *amuse* in *The story amused me.*

2.2 Case system 1971. The case system of the 1971 model is developed from the case system of the 1968 model. In the 1968 model the cases were: Agentive, Instrumental, Dative, Objective (Factitive), Locative (Comitative). In the 1971 model Dative, Factitive, and Comitative are dropped. Most of the functions of the Dative case are taken over by a new Experiencer case. The 1968 Locative case, which included both stative and directional locatives, is now split into three cases, Location, Source, and Goal. Factitive is subsumed under the Goal case and Comitative is no longer mentioned, probably to be subsumed under the new locative cases. The case system of the 1971 model is then a nine case system consisting of: Agent, Experiencer, Instrument, Object, Source, Goal, Location, Time, as the cases that Fillmore says he has 'become comfortable with' (1971:42). To these Fillmore later adds 'and possibly Benefactive' (1971:52). The subject choice hierarchy is A-E-I-O-S-G-L-T-B. The 1968 case system is compared with the 1971 system in Figure 2.7.

Figure 2.7 Case systems compared

Fillmore 1968   Fillmore 1971

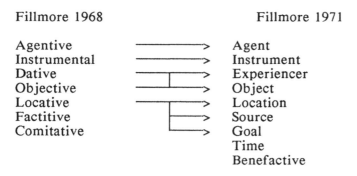

Agentive	⟶	Agent
Instrumental	⟶	Instrument
Dative		Experiencer
Objective		Object
Locative		Location
Factitive		Source
Comitative		Goal
		Time
		Benefactive

2.2.1 Agent (A). Agent is 'the instigator of an action' (1971:37); 'the principal cause of an event' as opposed to the immediate cause (1971:43) but excluding natural forces (1971:44). Immediate causes and natural forces are subsumed under Instrument. The Agent role is not restricted to animate nouns. Inanimate Agents are permitted. In Fillmore's words: 'I no longer confuse selection restrictions to animates with true case-like notions' (1971:42).

2.2.2 Experiencer (E). Experiencer is 'the experiencer of a psychological event' (1971:37); the case required by 'a genuine psychological event or mental state verb' (1971:42). The new Experiencer case takes over most of the functions of the 1968 Dative case but excludes those nonpsychological change-of-state verbs such as *die* and *grow*, which are represented in the newer model by the O case (1971:42). Experiencer also excludes the receiver in transfer of property verbs such as *give*. Transfer of property verbs now use Source and Goal cases with the receiver as Goal (1971:42).

According to this description of the new Experiencer case verbs that were formerly classified as D-O verbs in the 1968 model are now reclassified as E-O verbs, including verbs of sensation: *see, hear*; verbs of emotion: *like, want*; and verbs of cognition: *believe, expect, know, think*. Verbs of emotion such as *fear, love*, and verbs of cognition such as *imagine* are listed as E-O verbs (1971:53) in which the E case is the experiential subject and the O case represents the content of that experience. The indirect object of cognitive adjectives such as *be apparent* and *be interesting*, which were formerly classed as O-D verbs, are now presumably to be reclassified as O-E verbs. Emotional adjectives such as *be sad* (= feel sad) and *be warm* (= feel warm), formerly classed as D verbs, are now reclassed as E verbs in which the E subject expresses the 'emotion-experiencer role' and the 'sensation-experiencer role' respectively (1971:40).

2.2.3 Instrument (I).

Instrument is the 'immediate cause of an event' (1971:42) as opposed to the Agent as principal cause. If Agent and Instrument cooccur the Agent is the instigator of the event and the Instrument is that cause more immediately in contact with the event. When *John breaks the window with a hammer, John* is the principal cause but the *hammer* is the immediate cause. In non-agentive causality the subject of the verb *cause* can be classed as an immediate cause and is therefore assigned the Instrument case as in *the glare of the sunlight caused the accident* (1971:45). Embedded sentences which are subject of the verb *cause* are also immediate causes and are classed as sentences embedded under the Instrument case as in *Susan's screaming caused me to drop the tray* (1971:49).

Natural forces are also subsumed under the Instrument case (1971:44). According to Fillmore there is no reason for a separate Force case since it never occurs in contrast with either the Agent or the Instrument case (1971:44). Natural forces are better classed as Instruments since natural forces are immediate causes rather than instigators of events. This arrangement allows Agent and natural forces to cooccur in human control of natural phenomena but excludes the possibility of the cooccurrence of Instruments and natural forces in the same sentence.

The notion of Instrument as 'immediate cause' is carried over into the domain of psychological predicates where Instrument is identified as 'the stimulus or thing reacted to' (1971:42) or 'the reacted-to situation in the description of a mental event' (1971:53). In 1968 pairs such as *like /please* or *fear /frighten* were both given D-O case frames and differed from each other only in subject choice. But in 1971 *like* and *fear* are analyzed as E-O verbs and *please* and *frighten* are analyzed as I-E verbs. The semantic relationship between these pairs has been destroyed by this new analysis.

Fillmore's assignment of the I case or the O case with two-place psychological predicates is consistent. If the E case is the object and the other case is subject this other case is the 'stimulus' of the psychological experience and is assigned the I case as in the verb *please*, classed as an I-E verb. If the E case is the subject and the other case is object this other case is the 'content' of the experience and is assigned the O case as in the verb *like*, classed as an E-O verb. The question then arises: should these two cases be given the same label, since they seem to be in perfect complementary distribution? Both cases were classed as O in 1968 with the difference between stimulus and content predictable on distributional grounds. Fillmore's principal argument for assigning two case labels rather than one is that the two cases seem to cooccur with verbs like *remind* as in *the noise (I) reminded me (E) of the accident (O)*. But if *remind* = 'cause to remember' then the verb is complex and the resulting case frame may be analyzed as two frames collapsed into one as in *the noise (I) caused (G)*, where G = the sentence *(E) remembered the accident (O)*. If so, the argument for separate I and O cases does not hold.

2.2.4 Object (O). Object is the most neutral case, the 'wastebasket' case, 'the entity which moves or undergoes change' (1971:42), the 'content' of the experience with psychological predicates (1971:53) when it occurs in direct object position. Sentences are still regularly embedded under the O case but sentences may also be embedded under other cases as long as they are embedded as 'occupants of some case role' (1971:38). For example, sentences are embedded under the I case as subject of the verb *cause* or under the Goal case as object of the verb *cause* (1971:46). With the reassignment of Instrument to psychological verbs and the extension of embedded sentences to Instrument and Goal cases, the 1971 model has drifted further away from any notion of an obligatory O case.

2.2.5 Source (S). Source is the origin or starting point of motion; it refers primarily to the place-from-which the motion begins. It is applied to 'earlier location' with motion verbs, to 'earlier states' with change of state verbs, and to 'earlier time' with time verbs (1971:41). This case is regularly marked in English with the motion prepositions *from, away from, out of, off of*.

2.2.6 Goal (G). Goal is the end point of motion; it refers to the place-towards-which the motion tends. It represents 'final location' with motion verbs, 'final state' with change of state verbs, and 'final time' with time verbs. This case is regularly marked in English with the directional prepositions *to, towards, into, onto*. With change-of-state verbs the Goal case replaces the 1968 Factitive case (1971:42), as in *he wrote a poem*. In causative constructions, those embedded sentences which function as direct object and identify the resulting state or event are represented as embedded under the Goal case (1971:423).

2.2.7 Location (L). Location is the place where an object or event is located. When Location is used in a case system with Source and Goal cases the L case is restricted to stative locatives and the directional locatives are listed as Source or Goal. Fillmore notes that multiple locative phrases referring to a single location do not violate the one-instance-per-clause principle as in *he was sitting under a tree in the park on a bench.* 'It is clear that we have in this sentence one place specification' (1971:51). This stative Location is frequently a modal case, an 'optional complement of essentially any predicator' (1971:49). When Location is a modal case it may be represented in a higher predicate with a verb like *happen* or *occur* (1971:49).

2.2.8 Time (T). Time is the time at which an object or event is located. Multiple time expressions may refer to a single time specification (1971:51) as in *Tuesday afternoon about three o'clock.* Time is also often used as a modal case, an optional complement of essentially any predicator. However, 'some verbs take Location and Time complements directly' (1971:51) so that Location and Time are used as propositional cases, as in *Jeffrey spent Tuesday afternoon (T) at the beach* or *the meeting lasted an hour (T).*

2.2.9 Benefactive (B). Benefactive is the one who benefits from an event or activity. It is listed as a possible case by Fillmore (1971:52). He seems to have in mind those Benefactive phrases introduced by *for* meaning 'for the sake of'. This case seems to be a modal Benefactive case, optional in agentive sentences in which the Agent's role is 'deliberate or voluntary' (1971:52). Here again Fillmore suggests a higher sentence analysis with the Benefactive case occurring with a higher verb, such as *give* or *offer.* Fillmore does not seem to have here a clear notion of a Benefactive case which is a propositonal case required by the verb.

The nine case system of the 1971 model is a mixed case system. This system is partially localistic in that it introduces the notion of Source and Goal. Within a localistic case system Location, Source, and Goal are used as prime analogates to describe not only physical location and motion in space but abstract location and motion. It is this extension of locational terms to describe nonlocal events that constitutes the essence of a localistic system. Thus the cases Location, Source, and Goal are used in the domain of possession and transfer of property to express possession and the beginning and end points of transfer of property as in *I (S) gave it (O) to you (G).* They are used with time expressions to express beginning and end points in time as in *from five (S) until six (G) o'clock.* With change of state verbs Source and Goal represent the beginning and end points of the change of state as in *he (O) changed from a frog (S) into a prince (G).* The consistent use of the same prepositions in Source and Goal expressions across different semantic domains is one of the more more attractive aspects of localistic systems. But a fully localistic system would use only Location, Source, and Goal.

2.3 Case frames 1971. In the 1971 model Fillmore attempts to outline tactics for determining the emic status of cases with the purpose of limiting the number and kind of case frames. The first principle is the one-instance-per-clause principle; the second principle is the principle of contrast and complementation.

2.3.1 The one-instance-per-clause principle. According to this principle cases occur in a case frame only once. The principle that 'no case category appears more than once in a given case frame' is enunciated in the early model (1968:24) and is also confirmed in the 1971 model. Apparent counterexamples must be resolved either by establishing two distinct cases, or by analyzing the situation as an instance of clause embedding (1971:38).

For example, predicate nominals seem to be the same case as their respective subjects. In those nonreversible similarity predicates like the verb *resemble* the fact that *John resembles his uncle* cannot be reversed to equal *John's uncle resembles him* suggests that 'observable' properties in the subject are related to 'attributable' properties in the predicate noun (1971:39). Fillmore's conclusion is that these two nominals must receive different case labels but he does not suggest what those labels might be. In 1968 Fillmore had suggested the term 'essive' (1968:84) but in 1969 he lists predicate-noun constructions as one of case grammar's unsolved problems (1969:375). Predicate nominals remain a problem in case analysis as long as no exception is made to the one-instance-per-clause principle. Fillmore would retain this principle but other case grammarians, such as Anderson (1977:38), openly advocate the repetition of the O case with predicate nominals as a justifiable exception to the general rule. This exception, it seems to me, would then be extended not only to states like *John (O) is president (O)* but also to process predicates like *John (O) became president (O)* and even to those action verbs which contain a direct object and an object complement, as in *they (A) elected John (O) president (O)*. The passive of this structure would become a stative proposition with two O cases as in *John (O) was elected president (O)*.

An example of clause embedding might be the transitive use of the verb *walk* in *John walked the dog*. Here *John* is the Agent but *the dog* which does the walking is also an Agent, so that there seem to be two Agents in the structure, violating the one-instance-per-clause principle. But if *walk* is considered to be a complex predicate meaning 'cause to walk' then the sentence is composed of two clauses; *John caused something* with John as Agent and *the dog walked* with the dog as Agent. The verb *cause* has the case frame A-O with O as an embedded sentence. The verb *walk* has the case frame A-*O-S-G with A=O. It is the conflation of these two clauses with the single transitive verb *walk* that creates a case frame that seems to have two Agents in the same structure. Other examples include the verb *work* in *He worked the staff hard* and the verb *march* in *He marched the men home*.

2.3.2 The principles of contrast and complementation. The principles of contrast and complementation are adapted from phonological and morphological studies. According to these principles, elements in contrast are considered emic units within the system but units in complementary distribution, either in mutually exclusive distribution or with partial overlap, may be grouped as subunits of the same emic unit. Fillmore mentions in passing the terminological horror of 'allocases of the same caseme' (Fillmore 1971:41).

According to the principle of contrast, two cases that occur in parallel distribution in the same position and which contrast with each other semantically in that position are separate emic case units. For example, if the same verb has subjects with different meanings then these subjects should be assigned different case labels. This case assignment would then have to be confirmed by the use of these cases elsewhere in the system or by appealing to coordination principles, where only like cases can be conjoined (1971:40). The principle of contrast is illustrated with the verb *be warm* in sentences (15-18).

(15) John /is (=feels) warm.   E = experiences warmth
     E   V

(16) This jacket /is warm.   I = induces warmth
     I   V

(17) Summer /is warm.   T = warmth when
     T   V

(18) Texas /is warm.   L = warmth where
     L   V

However, Anderson (1977:126) suggests that these are not necessarily distinct cases, since the difference in interpretation may be a function of the different type of nouns used not an indication of predicates with different meanings.

According to the principle of complementation, two cases may be grouped as allocases of the same case if they are in some kind of complementary distribution. The essential fact to remember about complementation is that contrast is not immediately evident. Further principles of pattern congruity, semantic similarity, and economy would be required to make the decision that two noncontrastive cases are to be grouped into a single case. Fillmore grouped stative and directional locatives under one Locative case in the 1968 model (1968:25). In the 1971 model Fillmore illustrates this principle with the Source and Goal cases placed in complementary distribution, as in sentences (19-21).

(19) He /went /from the chapel /to the cemetery.
   A=O V   S   G

(20) He /changed /from a weakling /to a strong man.
   O   V   S   G

(21) The play /lasted /from noon /until sundown.
   O   V   S   G

2.3.3 Verb types. Case frames in the 1971 model use the system of nine cases arranged in a subject choice hierarchy as A-E-I-O-S-G-L-T-B. The resulting case frames may be roughly divided into (1) basic verb types including instrumental verb using the A, I, and O cases, (2) experiential verbs using the Experiencer case, and (3) locative verbs using the Location, Source, or Goal cases.

(1) Basic verb types, using the A, I, and O cases.

State verbs, using the O and I cases (G as effected object).
+ [___O]   *die, grow, float, slip, be true*
+ [___I]   *be warm* (Ins); *be sad* (Ins)
+ [___I,G]   *cause* (inanimate)

Action verbs, using the A, I, and O cases (also G object).
+ [___A]   *drive, run, swim, walk, ride, scream*
+ [___A,O]   *do, hit*
+ [___A,G]   *construct, write*
+ [___A,I,O]   *break, hit, strike, kick, kiss, slap*

(2) Experiential verbs, using A, I, O with the E case.

State verbs, using the E case with I and O cases.
+ [___E]   *be warm* (=feel); *be sad* (=feel)
+ [___E,O]   *fear, love, imagine, regard, suspect, expect*
+ [___I,E]   *amuse* (-agt), *frighten*; *strike* (=impress)
+ [___I,E,O]   *remind* (= cause to remember)

Action verbs, using the E case with the A, I, O cases.
+ [___A,E,I]   *amuse* (+agt)

(3) Locative verbs, using A and O cases with L, S, G.

State verbs, using the O case with L, S, G.
+ [___O,L]   *be in, live in, sit, occur, happen*
+ [___O,S,G]   *change, last, float* (=go), *slip, fall*
                      come, go, move (-agt)

Action verbs, using A and O cases with L, S, G (or T).
+ [___A,O,G]   *lean,*tv, *push, hit, strike* (= hit)
+ [___A,T]   *spend* (time)
+ [___A,*O,S,G] /A=O *come, go, move, drive, run, swim, walk*
+ [___A,O,*S,G] /A=S *give, offer, sell, send, throw*
+ [___A,O,S,*G] /A=G *buy, get, receive, rob, steal, take*
+ [___A,O,S,G]   *drop, push, shove*

Note that the notion of 'time' may be represented by the T case, as in the verb *spend* (time); this concept may also be represented by S and G cases, as beginning and end time points.

2.3.4 Localism. The localistic case system using Location, Source, and Goal cases has some disadvantages. The first and most obvious disadvantage is the levelling of distinctions between semantic domains. A large number of verbs from different semantic domains are all analyzed as A-O-S-G. The distinction between possession, physical location, and other domains is lost. The second disadvantage is that Location, Source, and Goal are not the only possible locative expressions with motion verbs.

In applying the localistic system Location, Source, and Goal are the case names and the various semantic domains must be understood. To distinguish between these domains the localist case label would have to be subscripted with domain labels. In the non-localist system, the names of the semantic domains are highlighted and the concepts of Source and Goal, if used at all, would have to be subscripted. The contrast between the two systems is seen in the case analyses in sentences (22-25).

(22) He /went /from the chapel /to the cemetery.　　　(localist)
　　　A=O V　　S_L　　　　　　　　G_L
(23) He /went /from the chapel /to the cemetery.　(nonlocalist)
　　　A=O V　　L_S　　　　　　　　L_G
(24) The play /lasted /from noon /until sundown.　　　(localist)
　　　O　　　　V　　　S_T　　　　G_T
(25) The play /lasted /from noon /until sundown.　(nonlocalist)
　　　O　　　　V　　　T_S　　　　T_G

If Source and Goal are used as cases then the concepts of 'time' and 'place' must be subordinated to them; if Location and Time are the cases then the concepts of 'source' and 'goal' must be subordinated to Location and Time. Obviously a choice must be made. One must either accept the localist theory and use it consistently or adopt a nonlocalist theory.

The second problem with localistic systems deals with the kinds of complements that motion verbs can take. Source and Goal do not exhaust the possibilities. One can also express the whole Path of the motion (1971:50), or a series of partial paths, or even transit points. Languages can express not only starting and end points but the whole path of the motion in one expression, as in sentence (26).

(26) John /went /across the river.
　　　A=O　V　　　Path

Should Path constitute a case separate from the Source and Goal cases? Fillmore argues that multiple expressions of Path do not violate the one-instance-per-clause principle as long as these are subparts of the same path (1971:51). Other case grammarians (Gruber 1965:77) consider Source and Goal to be a cooccurring pair. In this view the so-called Path case is an instance of Source and Goal combined, eliminating the need for a separate Path case.

2.4. Related lexical entries. There is no derivational system to relate lexical entries in either the 1968 or the 1971 Fillmore models. In the 1971 model case frames such as *break*, + [___(A),(I),O], are still conflated. Case frames still differ from each other by subject choice as with *have /belong to*, or by object choice as with the *spray* type verbs. But there is no mention of the type of inchoative and causative proforms used by Lakoff (1965) to relate verbs which are derived from the same morphological root. However, Fillmore does deal with different meanings of the same lexical predicate by a process called conflation, adapted from Leonard Talmy's 1970 work, with passing reference to McCawley's 1968 predicate-raising rules. The basic process is to paraphrase the meanings of a verb and list these various paraphrases as the underlying structure, which is then conflated into an expression with a single lexical verb. This process can be applied to both motion verbs and impact verbs.

2.4.1 Motion verbs. In the semantic domain of motion verbs Fillmore postulates that the most basic motion verbs are *come*, *go*, and *move* since these verbs have no manner, means or medium incorporated into them (1971:41). These verbs are then used as basic elements to describe other verbs of motion, reminiscent of Ikegami's 1965 study of the semological structure of English verbs of motion.

Motion verbs like *drive, run, swim*, and *walk* receive two case analyses depending upon whether they are meant to describe types of activities, or types of movements (1971:41). When used as activity verbs they tend to occur with durational phrases; used as movement verbs they tend to occur with directional phrases of the Source /Goal type. In movement contexts the verbs are interpreted as conflations of *go-by-driving* or *go-by-running* in which the underlying verb is *go* and the surface verb adds the manner, means, or medium of the motion. The contrast between these verbs used as an activity and as a movement is given in (27) and (28).

(27) John /walked /for an hour.   A
     A   V T_m
(28) John /walked /to the store.   A,*O,S,G /A=O,S-del
     A=O   V   G

Similarly, verbs like *float* may express either the process of being suspended in a medium or movement through that medium (1971:48). When the verb expresses movement it is interpreted as a conflation of *go-by-floating*. The difference between the two case analyses is illustrated in sentences (29) and (30). Suspension in a medium has an O case frame, movement has an O,S,G case frame.

(29) The bottle /is floating /on the water.   O
     O   V L_m
(30) The bottle /is floating /into the cove.   O,S,G /S-del
     O   V   G

2.4.2 Impact verbs. The process of conflation may also be applied to verbs of impact, such as *hit, push, shove, strike*, in which the event of hitting causes an object to move. Normally verbs of impact will receive a simple A–O analysis but when the impact causes movement then the same verbs are interpreted as two clauses conflated into one. Sentences like *John hit the ball over the fence* are interpreted as *John hit the ball* and *it went over the fence*. The verb *hit* has the meaning *cause-to-move-by-hitting* (1971:47). The conflation theory seems to suggest that there is some remote structure in which the original two clauses are related to each other by the verb CAUSE. The event of John-hit-the-ball causes the event ball-go-over-the-fence. This complex verbal structure is then reduced to a single lexical verb. Sentence (31) is represented by Figure 2.8.

(31) John hit the ball over the fence
= CAUSE (John-hit-ball, ball-go-over-the-fence)

Figure 2.8 Impact verbs.

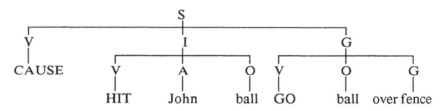

The conflation process would then have to combine the three verbs into a single predicate in which *hit = cause-go-by-hitting* but the details of this derivation are less than clear. An alternate solution is to postulate two different meanings for the verb. In the first meaning *hit = X hits Y* and the verb is a simple A–O verb. In the second meaning *hit = X causes-Y-to-move-by-hitting it* and the verb is an A–O–S–G motion verb with the lexical verb indicating the cause of the motion. The contrast is illustrated in sentences (32–33).

(32) John /hit /the ball.   A,O
     A   V   O
(33) John /hit /the ball /over the fence.   A,O,S,G /S-del
     A   V   O   G

In this solution impact verbs receive two different case analyses. Just as motion verbs may have two different meanings associated with verbs of activity and verbs of movement, so impact verbs may have two different meanings associated with verbs of simple impact and verbs of movement caused by impact. The different meanings of these verbs would then be entered into the lexicon with the choice of meaning determined by context.

2.4.3 Instrumental verbs. Another problem which makes it difficult to construct a set of lexical redundancy rules to relate morphologically similar verbs is Fillmore's fascination with the Instrument case. There is no simple way to link similar verbs which seem to be sometimes accompanied by the Instrument case and other times without it. Yet Instrument remains one of the hallmarks of the Fillmore models and it is hard to imagine a Fillmore-type case grammar without it. There are three positions an analyst can adopt with regard to the Instrument case. (1) The Instrument case is always present in the meaning of the verb, (2) the Instrument case is sometimes present in the meaning of the verb, or (3) the Instrument case is never present in the meaning of the verb.

(1) Instrument always present. In this position, the analyst holds that certain verbs always require the Instrument case as a propositional case and as part of the case frame, whether or not that case appears in the surface structure. According to this first position verbs like *break*, which sometimes occur with instrumental phrases and sometimes occur without them, always have the Instrument case in their deep structure. This amounts to a psychological claim that Instrument is in the mind of any speaker who uses such a verb, whether he expresses it or not. It is as though the speaker, on uttering a sentences like *John broke the window*, already expects the hearer to ask: *with what?* It is not certain that anyone holds this extreme position. Even those linguists like Fillmore, that require some kind of Instrument case to be part of the system, would not go so far as to say it is present in any single verb all the time. The only real candidate might be a verb such as *use*, where the meaning of the verb itself indicates instrumentality.

(2) Instrument sometimes present. According to this position, the same lexical verb may occur with Instrument in the deep structure in some contexts but occur without Instrument in the deep structure in other contexts. This seems to be Fillmore's position when he describes the verb *break* as having four different case frames. In nonagentive use the verb *break* has the case frames O, or I-O; in agentive use the verb *break* has the case frames A-O or A-I-O. Even though these four case frames are conflated into a single lexical entry, there is no reason to believe that Instrument is present when the O frame or the A-O frame is used since there are parallel I-O and A-I-O case frames for those instances in which the Instrument occurs.

The problem with this position is economy. For every O verb there must be a parallel I-O verb and for every A-O verb there must be a parallel A-I-O verb to insure that the Instrument, when it does occur, is a deep structure or propositional case. The result is that the lexicon contains two verbs where it should contain one. Every instrumental case frame described in such a system has its parallel non-instrumental case frame. The Instrument case seems to have no domain of its own.

(3) Instrument never present. According to this position, the Instrument case is always a modal case, never a propositional case. Therefore it is never included in the list of cases and is never a part of any case frame. The modal Instrument may occur with virtually any action verb, wherever the meaning of that verb allows the expression of secondary causes. Most case grammarians except Fillmore adopt some similar position.

The principal objection against this position is the use of the Instrument case as subject. If Instrument is not part of the case system, how is one to distinguish between the sentences *John broke the window*, where *John* is an Agent, and *the hammer broke the window*, where the *hammer* is an Instrument? The answer is you can not and need not distinguish them.

The point at issue is whether the nouns in the structure determine the case frame of the verb or whether the verb in the structure determines the roles the nouns play in the structure. In the noun-centered system initially adopted by Fillmore, the nouns were first given case labels and then grouped together as an environment in which the verb might occur. In a verb-centered system, such as advocated by Fillmore in 1977, nouns are not cases, they are CASE CANDIDATES. The verb determines the roles that the nouns will play. The case roles are read onto the nouns from the verb, not vice versa.

Therefore, if a verb like *break* is essentially an A–O verb, the case role of Agent will be read onto the subject and the case role of Object will be read onto the direct object, no matter what nouns happen to be there. If the noun happens to be an inanimate noun like *hammer* the notion of Agency is read onto that noun. Since Agency is no longer necessarily limited to animate nouns and cases are relational and not categorial notions, there is no problem is ascribing agency to inanimate nouns. When a noun is assigned a role by the verb, the fit may not be perfect and we may have the beginning of metaphor. But when *the dish runs away with the spoon* it is the dish that takes on the features of an Agent due to the verb but the verb does not change its meaning at all.

The result of listing the Instrument case as always a modal case and never a propositional one is that the concept of Agency is broadened. The original Agent and Instrument of the Fillmore models coalesce into a supercase which includes what elsewhere might be considered either Agents or Instruments. Under this supercase are also included those nouns which are listed as natural forces. Agent, Force, and Instrument are all one.

This is not necessarily a disadvantage. In the noun-centered system it was often difficult to choose between Agent and Instrument, once Agent was listed as only 'typically' animate. Debates raged over particular nouns, with the determining factor often listed as mere size. Thus, hammers, chisels, knives were classed as Instruments, but tractors, piledrivers, computers were classed as Agents. Assuming Agent and Instrument as well as natural forces under a single case relieves the analyst of these tiresome measurements.

2.5 Covert case roles. The theory of covert case roles is more fully developed in the 1971 than in the 1968 model. Covert case roles are those cases which are present in the deep structure but often not present in the surface structure. The importance of covert roles is that they allow the case grammarian to perform a deeper analysis of the case structure, thus avoiding the criticism of Jackendoff (1972) that deep cases are in a one-to-one relationship with surface noun phrases. If this were true, case grammar would be no more than an arbitrary labelling system for NPs already existing on the surface. The 1971 model has a complete theory of covert roles, including deletable roles, coreferential roles, and lexicalized roles.

2.5.1 Deletable case roles. The deletable roles, once called 'vacant' roles in the 1971 Fillmore model, are those cases which sometimes appear in the surface structure and sometimes do not. They are discovered by comparing two sentences, one which contains the role in question in the surface structure and one of which does not contain this role in the surface structure. Fillmore already had deletable case roles in his 1968 model with reference to 'deletable object' verbs (1968:29). In the 1971 model Fillmore uses the notion of deletable roles to distinguish between verb types on the basis of what case is deletable. For example, the verbs *rob* and *steal* are similar but differ in that *rob* has a deletable Object case whereas *steal* has a deletable Source case, as in sentences (34-35).

(34) John /robbed /a bank /(of money).   A,O,S,G /A=G,O-del
　　 A=G　 V　　 S　　 O-del
(35) John /stole /money /(from a bank). A,O,S,*G /A=G, S-del
　　 A=G　 V　　 O　　 S-del

Deletable roles are empirically discoverable but require the use of the analyst's judgment. Verbs are found in different contexts with a wide array of possible surface structures. It is up to the analyst to observe the different cases that occur. But for each case role he must make the judgment either (1) that this case is a modal case not required by the meaning of the verb and therefore should be excluded from the case frame, or (2) that this case, although not always present, is required by the meaning of the verb and should be included within the case frame. The frequency of occurrence of the case role in surface structure is often an indication that the case role is associated with the meaning of the verb and required in the case frame. Compare sentences (36-37) in which the G and O cases are essential to the meaning of the verb but deletable, whereas the unmarked T and L cases are optional modal cases.

(36) John /spoke /to me /about that /yesterday /in the hall.
　　 A=S　 V　　 G　　 O
(37) John /spoke /(to someone) /(about something).
　　 A=S　 V　　 (G)　　　　 (O)

2.5.2 Coreferential case roles. In the 1968 model there were no totally covert case roles. The concept of cases that are required in the deep structure but which do not and can not appear on the surface was absent from that model. But in the 1971 model both coreferential and lexicalized roles appear.

Coreferential roles are two deep case roles which are applied to the same NP in the surface structure. The doubly labelled NP has two case functions within the sentence. Fillmore reenforces the notion of coreferential roles by adding a specific rule of required coreference deletion. According to this rule the lower ranking of the two case roles according to the subject choice hierarchy is obligatorily deleted and may not appear as a separate NP in the surface structure. In all of the examples given the Agent role is coreferential with some lower ranking role and, according to the rule, the lower case role is deleted. But this does not exclude the possibility of coreference existing between two case roles, neither of which is an Agent. The notational convention followed here is to include the two coreferential case roles within the case frame and mark the lower ranking role with an asterisk (*) to indicate that it may not occur in the surface structure. The reason why the totally covert case role, marked with an asterisk (*), cannot appear in the surface structure is indicated after the case frame. When two roles are coreferential they are joined by an equals sign. Thus, for an A-O-S-G verb with coreferential A and O cases, the case frame of the verb is written as + [___A,*O,S,G] /A=O. Some examples of coreferential roles are given in sentences (38-40).

(38) John /went /to Chicago.   A,*O,S,G /A=O,S-del
    A=O V   G
(39) John /gave /the flowers /to Mary.   A,O,*S,G /A=S
    A=S V   O   G
(40) John /got /a book /from the library.   A,O,S,*G /A=G
    A=G V O   S

In sentence (38) *John* is the instigator of the action and therefore an Agent, but he is also the moving object and therefore has the semantic role of Object. With motion verbs, agentive or nonagentive, the O case is always the moving object. The subject NP then is both Agent and Object and the A case and the O case are marked as coreferential. Although the deep structure case frame is A-O-S-G, the O case, since it is coreferential with A, may not appear in the surface structure. The surface structure expression always appears as A-S-G, with S or G or both deletable.

In sentence (39) *John* is simultaneously the instigator of the action of giving and the source of the gift. The Agent role is coreferential with Source, therefore Source will not appear in the surface structure. Similarly, in sentence (40), *John* is simultaneously the instigator of the action of getting the book and the receiver of the property. The Agent is coreferential with the Goal of the activity and Goal may not appear on the surface.

The principle of coreferential roles is not to be confused with the grammatical process of REFLEXIVIZATION. In fact, one excludes the other. Coreferential roles are two roles that are applied to the same surface NP. The lower ranking of the two receives no independent realization on the surface. Since this rule involves a single NP, reflexivization is impossible. The rule of reflexivization applies to two coreferential NPs in the same clause and operates independently of case relationships. The appearance of a reflexive pronoun is an indication of two NPs coreferential in the surface structure and is prime facie evidence that the two roles are not coreferential in the deep structure sense. When a surface reflexive pronoun appears it must be given a different case role from the NP with which it is coreferential. In sentence (41), for example, the object is reflexivized but the subject has the case role of Agent (A) while the direct object has the case role of Object (O).

(41) John /washed /himself.   A,O
     A   V   O

2.5.3 Lexicalized case roles. Lexicalized roles appear in the 1971 model, sometimes called 'built-in' or 'incorporated' roles. Lexicalized roles are case roles that are incorporated into the predicate and therefore do not normally appear in the surface structure. Lexicalized case roles are a special application of a more general process of incorporation. Many elements are incorporated into the meaning of specialized verbs. For example, manner, means, or medium are often incorporated into motion verbs (1971:48). Lexicalized roles occur when one of the roles essential to the case frame is incorporated into the verb and therefore is not represented in the surface structure. The notational convention followed here is to list the lexicalized propositional role as part of the case frame and mark it with an asterisk(*) to indicate that it does not appear on the surface. The reason why it does not appear in the surface structure is indicated by adding the notation after the frame that the role is lexicalized. Thus the case frame of the verb *slap* is A-I-O with the I lexicalized and is written as + [___A,*I,O] /I-lex.

It is possible to repeat the lexicalized role in the surface structure if the role is modified in some way. In this instance there is no change in the case frame of the verb. The case is still lexicalized but a copy of the lexicalized role appears on the surface with its modification. In sentence (42) with the verb *slap* the unmodified instrumental phrase may not occur in the surface structure, but if the instrumental phrase is modified as in sentence (43) then the modified phrase may occur in the surface structure of the sentence.

(42) Mary /slapped /John /(*with her hand).   A,*I,O /I-lex
     A   V   O
(43) Mary /slapped /John /with her left hand.   A,*I,O /I-lex
     A   V   O   I-copy

Both propositional roles and modal roles may be lexicalized into the verb. The lexicalization process is a general process which allows a wide range of surface parts of speech in various combinations to be lexicalized into the verb. These combinations include V + NP: *dine* = 'eat dinner'; V + Prep: enter = 'go in'; V + Prep + NP: *jail* = 'put in jail'; and V + NP + Prep: *skin* = 'remove skin from'. The case grammarian is interested primarily in those lexicalized NPs which are propositional cases and required by the meaning of the verb in order to arrive at the correct case frame for each verb no matter what the surface form. Lexicalized modal cases may be ignored. The fact that a role is lexicalized is no guarantee that it is a propositional case since both propositional and modal cases may be lexicalized.

Lexicalized case roles have a much wider application that the few examples of lexicalized Instruments cited by Fillmore. Lexicalized roles are often discovered in conjunction with those lexical items in which the same morphological form is used as both noun and verb. Given a noun *comb*, there is often a corresponding verb *comb* which incorporates the meaning of the noun into the verb as *comb* = 'to arrange the hair with a comb'. When matching noun-verb entries are found in the lexicon there is a strong possibility that the noun has been incorporated into the verb and may be an essential part of its case frame.

Verbs of imposition (put-on verbs) and verbs of removal (take-off verbs) frequently incorporate their object noun into the verb. Put-on verbs include: *bait, color, clothe, dress, grease, hook, oil, powder, paint, plaster, polish, roof, salt, saddle, water, wax*, with the meaning 'put X on'. Take-off verbs include: *core, gut, husk, peel, pit, scale, shell, skin*, with the meaning 'take X off'. In case analysis the verb must be paraphrased in terms of its corresponding noun in order to reveal the complete case frame prior to the lexicalization of one of the essential nouns into the verb form, as in sentences (44-45).

(44) Lucy /powdered /her nose.　　　　　A,*O,S,G /O-lex
　　　A　　put-powder-on G
(45) Dan /watered /the lawn.　　　　　　A,*O,S,G /O-lex
　　　A　　put-water-on G

Although lexicalized roles are not limited in principle, the main examples of lexicalized roles seem to be the Object case when in direct object position. But the Goal case may also be lexicalized into the verb. This occurs with inanimate nouns in verbs such as *box, bag, pocket, can, bottle, bank* with the meaning 'put into X', and with animate nouns in verbs such as *cage, jail, imprison*, as illustrated in sentences (46-47).

(46) He /had boxed /all the oranges.　　　A,O,S,*G /G-lex
　　　A　put-into-boxes　O
(47) They /had jailed /Robin Hood.　　　　A,O,S,*G /G-lex
　　　A　　put-into-jail　O

2.6 Evaluation of the 1971 model. Compared to the 1968 model the new 1971 model has certain advantages. The deep structure of the 1971 model is greatly simplified and directly reflects the content of the case frame. Since this structure is identical except for the case labels with the structures used in generative semantics, it has the potential for expansion with all the modal elements and modal cases representable as higher predicates. The omission of prepositions in the deep structure and the absence of rules that add features to nouns is also an advantage as it stresses the relational character of the cases as opposed to categorial notions. Cases are semantic relations originating in the verb and case roles are imposed upon the nouns by the verb.

The list of cases in 1971 is different but not necessarily better that the list of cases in 1968. In the 1971 list the localist and nonlocalist systems are mixed. The local cases Location, Source, and Goal are extended to the domains of change of state and transfer of property but are not extended to the domain of mental state verbs which here use, instead, the Experiencer case. The resulting framework is inconsistent. There is doubt, for example, whether in verbs of communication one should apply the localist theory and use the Source and Goal cases for speaker and hearer, or whether one should use the nonlocalist theory and use Agent and Experiencer cases for speaker and hearer. There is, however, one solid improvement over the 1968 model. The place of covert case roles (deletable roles, coreferential roles, and lexicalized roles) is made explicit, with the result that the semantic analysis is now deeper than the mere surface labelling of cases. Case frames are improved by the addition of those roles which do not always appear in the surface structure.

2.6.1 Problems with the 1971 model. There are, however, some serious defects that apply to both the Fillmore models. The principal problems are: (1) the way in which the modality is expressed, (2) the state /action dichotomy for verb types, and (3) the lack of any derivational apparatus to relate different verb forms derived from the same lexical root.

(1) In the 1968 model the semantic content of the sentence is represented as composed of a proposition and a modality, with the modality including tense, aspect, mood, and negation. To these are added the modal cases. The distinction between proposition and modality is an important one but not much more is said about it in 1968. The modality constituent is hardly mentioned in 1971 but it is suggested that some, if not all, of the modal elements may be represented as higher sentences. Once it is agreed that case grammar deals with the proposition only and that modal elements are recognized only to be swept aside in the analysis, then the division into proposition and modality makes some sense. Still there should be some long-range plan by which the modal elements can be treated in a consistent way so that all the semantic elements have a place in the system of representation.

(2) The acceptance of the state /action dichotomy for verb types based upon Lakoff's 1966 study is a lasting defect which is common not only to Fillmore's case grammar but to many works on generative semantics as well. It raises the crucial issue of whether the stativity feature should be marked within the case frame. If verbs consist of only two classes, states and actions, then stativity should not be marked in the case frame. But then there is no way to distinguish between such common pairs as *die /dead*. The adjective predicate *dead* is a state verb which cannot take the progressive and *die* is a process verb which can take the progressive. Fillmore's statement that 'the progressive occurs only with verbs that take Agents' (1968:31) is falsified by the example *the potatoes are cooking*, a sentence which has no Agent in the case structure and yet includes a verb used in the progressive form.

George Lakoff (1966) proposes that state verbs are [-progressive, -imperative], and action verbs are [+progressive, +imperative]. The possibility that was not considered by Lakoff, although mentioned as an exception, is that some verbs pass the progressive test but fail the imperative test. This class of verbs, later classified as process verbs, are [+progressive, -imperative]. They are not exceptions but a large class of verbs constituting roughly 10% of the verbs in running text. The extent of this class may be deduced if one considers Lakoff's (1965) work on inchoative and causative proforms. The addition of the inchoative, without the causative, to any state verb will produce a verb of the *become* type which has the characteristics [+progressive, -imperative]. If the adjective *thick* is a state verb, there is a corresponding process verb *thicken,iv* meaning 'become thick' which is no longer a state and may take the progressive. Verbs can no longer be classified as states and actions but must now be classified as states, processes, or actions. Therefore the stativity feature must be marked in the case frame to distinguish states from processes.

(3) Another defect in the Fillmore models is the lack of any derivational system. Since state and process were not distinguished, it is not surprising that the systematic relations between states, processes, and actions were not discovered. Yet there is a regular system deriving processes from states by the addition of inchoative elements and deriving actions from processes by the addition of causative elements. Fillmore's method of conflating case frames into a single notation tended to obscure rather than solve the derivational problem. His intent was to simplify the lexicon notationally by grouping similar uses of the same verb root. But this notation of many case frames under one label tends to obscure the problem of how these frames are related to one another. Add to this the fact that the state form was not recognized as separate from the process form, and the state form is not included at all in the conflated frame. It is no wonder then that the systematic relation between states, process, and action verbs through the addition of inchoative and causative elements was not recognized in Fillmore's models.

2.6.2 Case grammar revisited, 1978. Almost ten years after the publication of 'The case for case' Fillmore reviews the case grammar position in 'The case for case reopened' (1977). In this article he discusses the basic assumptions of the theory, some apparent and real challenges to the theory, and then adds a new interpretation of case grammar within a more general semantic framework.

The basic assumptions of the model are clarified. Case grammar is not a grammar; it deals with a level of organization of the clause, describes certain aspects of lexical structure, and offers a convenient way for describing clause types (1977:62). It is not 'a general model of linguistic structure' and certainly does not deal with intonation. Case grammar describes 'the inner structure of a clause' (1977:60) and deals with internal semantics, the relation of verb to nouns, and not with external semantics, such as truth value, entailments, or illocutionary force. It deals with that semantic level which considers such relations as Agent /Recipient, but not with the grammatical level of subject /object, or the rhetorical level of topic /comment.

Case grammar theory offers 'a semantic valence description of verbs and adjectives' (1977:60), comparable to the syntactic valence theories prevalent in Europe. Such a description is semantically oriented with semantics as central. As a semantic valence, the system is also verb-centered, not noun-centered, since the valence of the verb determines the nouns that go with that verb and not vice versa. The semantic valence of the verb is now expressed in terms of a case frame which 'indicates the case notions conceptually present in a sentence' (1977:64). The use of deletion transformations (1977:64) makes certain case roles deletable from the surface structure and enables the case analyst to distinguish between case roles that are not conceptually present in the deep structure and case roles which are conceptually present in the deep structure but sometimes not expressed in the surface structure.

Fillmore again rejects the position that all nouns in English are marked by prepositions in the deep structure, a position he held in 1968 but had rejected in his later model (1971:65). He also rejects the position, which he held in 1968 but rejected in 1971, that some cases are necessarily animate. Since cases are relational, not categorial notions (1977:65), and [± animate] is a feature of the noun category, these features should not be applied to the description of cases.

The basic assumptions of case theory include a list of cases, their use in case frames, and a subject selection hierarchy. The list of cases represents case uses, not case forms (1977:66); cases are relational, not categorial, and represent roles played by objects in the ontological universe, not a list of categories in the universe. Fillmore admits that he still does not know what the cases are or how many of them there are (1977:59). He still lists as unanswered questions: what is the correct list of cases, how do we know when the list is complete, and how are cases defined? However, he does strongly stress that cases are to be defined as relational entities relative to the meaning of the verb and not categorically.

Cases are arranged into case frames as an 'essential feature of the theory of deep cases' (1977:61). For a particular sentence the case frame expresses the cases required by the verb in that particular context and constitutes one meaning of that verb. The semantic analysis provided by the case frame is related to the surface syntactic structure containing subjects and objects by means of a subject choice hierarchy. Some subject choices will be language specific, as, for example, those languages which do not allow inanimate causes as subjects. Other subject choices will be verb-specific, as in the pairs *like /please*, *strike /regard*. These verb-specific choices must be registered in the lexicon.

In his 1977 review of the case grammar model Fillmore places case grammar within the context of general semantic theory. His position is described in the slogan: 'Meanings are relativized to scenes' (1977:59). This new semantic context uses the terms: scene, perspective, and salience. By putting case grammar into this framework Fillmore gives us a better understanding of the case frame, the ways in which sentences should be understood, and how semantic material is separated into figure and ground.

The SCENE is the event in the real world that is activated by any of the verbs relating to that scene. Within a scene there are many elements which are activated within the scene but not directly expressed in the utterance. For example, in the scene Fillmore (1977:72) calls the commercial scene there is an event which may be described, in part, by many different sentences including such verbs as: *buy*, *sell*, *cost*, *pay*. In this scene there are at least two Agents, the buyer and the seller, and at least two objects changing hands, the goods and the money.

The PERSPECTIVE is a point of view relative to this scene which is determined by the particular verb chosen. If, for example, we choose the verb *buy* then the buyer becomes the Agent and is foregrounded, the Agency of the seller is overlooked, and the seller is treated as the Source in the transaction. The object in focus is the goods bought, and the fact that money changes hands is left in the background. The verb determines the perspective and the case frame expresses the case roles that are required, not by the scene in general, but by this particular perspective on the scene. The feature of SALIENCE is much less developed and deals with the various possibilities of what is more likely to be foregrounded and what is more likely to be left in the background. Using scene and perspective, case frames are now intelligible as expressing one of many possible perspectives on a given scene, a perspective that is determined once the verb and its accompanying case frame are chosen.

Exercise 2. Write the case frame for the main verb in each of the following sentences. Cases available are A-E-I-O-S-G and L-T-B. For deletable roles, include the deletable role in the case frame and add C-del after the frame. For coreferential roles, mark the lower ranking of the two coreferential roles with an asterisk and add $C_1 = C_2$ after the case frame. For lexicalized roles, mark the lexicalized role with an asterisk and add C-lex after the case frame.

1. The clown amused me with his tricks. _____

2. John was sad. _____

3. The movie was sad. _____

4. The room is too warm. _____

5. Summer is warm. _____

6. Mary bought a car last weekend. _____

7. Susan's screaming caused me to drop the tray. _____

8. John dropped the dishes onto the floor. _____

9. I sometimes fear the devil. _____

10. The soap floated on the water. _____

11. The bottle floated into the cove. _____

12. Thunder frightened the baby. _____

13. John gave the flowers to Mary. _____

14. He hit the ball over the fence. _____

15. The play lasted over an hour. _____

16. The noise reminded me of the accident. _____

17. He sat under a tree on a bench in the park. _____

18. Harry spent Wednesday at the seashore. _____

19. Susan stole the money. _____

20. He swam from the dock to the shore. _____

21. Donald wrote several long poems. _____

Fillmore 1971 Lexicon. The Fillmore 1971 lexicon is a collection of 80 verbs with the case frames as far as they can be determined from Fillmore's 1971 article 'Some problems for case grammar'. Deletable roles are unmarked but coreferential roles and lexicalized roles are marked with an asterisk.

amuse (-agt)	I,E	lean,tv	A,O,G
amuse (+agt)	A,E,I	live,iv	O,L
be in	O,L	love	E,O
be true	O	move,iv	O,S,G
be sad (ins)	I	move,iv (agt)	A,*O,S,G
be sad (=feel)	E	occur	O,L
be warm (ins)	I	offer	A,O,*S,G
be warm (=feel)	E	push against	A,O,G
break,tv (agt/ins)	A,I,O	push (=move)	A,O,S,G
buy	A,O,S,*G	regard	E,O
cause (-agt)	I,G	receive (agt)	A,O,S,*G
cause (+agt)	A,G	remind	I,E,O
change,iv	O,S,G	resemble	O_1,O_2
come,iv (-agt)	O,S,G	ride (=action)	A
come,iv (+agt)	A,*O,S,G	ride (=go)	A,*O,S,G
construct	A,G	rob	A,O,S,*G
die	O	run (action)	A
do	A,O	run (=go)	A,*O,S,G
drive (agt)	A	scream	A
drive (=go)	A,*O,S,G	sell	A,O,*S,G
drop (agt)	A,O,S,G	send	A,O,*S,G
expect	E,O	shove against	A,O,G
fall	O,S,G	shove (=move)	A,O,S,G
fear	E,O	sit	O,L
float,iv	O	slap	A,*I,O
float,iv (=go)	O,S,G	slip,iv	O
frighten (-agt)	I,E	slip (=move)	O,S,G
get	A,O,S,*G	spend (time)	A,T
give	A,O,*S,G	stab	A,*I,O
go (-agt)	O,S,G	steal	A,O,S,*G
go (+agt)	A,*O,S,G	strike (=hit)	A,O,G
grow,iv	O	strike (=impress)	I,E
happen	O,L	suspect	E,O
hit against	A,O,G	swim (action)	A
hit (=move)	A,O,S,G	swim (=go)	A,*O,S,G
imagine	E,O	take (away)	A,O,S,*G
kick	A,*I,O	throw	A,O,*S,G
kill (-agt)	I,O	walk (action)	A
kiss	A,*I,O	walk (=go)	A,*O,S,G
last (time)	O,S,G	write	A,G

3 The Chafe 1970 Model

3.0 Overview. A new type of language model was developed by Wallace Chafe in *Meaning and the Structure of Language* (1970). After reviewing the structuralist models prevalent up to the late 1950s and the generative transformational models prevalent in the 1960s, Chafe concludes that linguistics needs some 'new alternatives'. The model he proposes is a generative semantics model in which semantics is central.

The history of linguistic science is traced in terms of prevalent linguistic paradigms. In the structuralist period, from Bloomfield (1933) to Chomsky (1957), the emphasis was on surface structure with immediate constituent analysis as the dominant methodology. During this period there was a bias towards phonology which stressed the importance of hard physical data, accompanied by a deep distrust of meaning. In the syntacticist period syntax became central but the phonological bias and the distrust of meaning remained. During this period language was viewed as a generative process and a distinction was drawn between deep and surface structures. Chafe views his own model as belonging to a semanticist paradigm in which semantics, not syntax, is the central system.

According to Chafe, 'LANGUAGE is a system which mediates in a highly complex way between the universe of meaning and the universe of sound' (1970:15). The universe of meaning consists of the infinite number of concepts which the speaker wants to express; the universe of sound consists of the limited number of articulatory sounds which the speaker uses to communicate these concepts. Although the number of sounds is limited, these sounds may be used in a great variety of combinations and permutations to represent concepts through the process which Chafe calls symbolization.

Deep structure is semantic structure (1970:9). The speaker creates a semantic structure and converts it into sound (1970:59). The directionality of the generative process is always from meaning to sound (1970:57). The creative aspect of language resides in the deep structure (1970:64) and the well–formedness of linguistic utterances is determined in the semantic structure (1970:65).

The STRUCTURALIST VIEW that Chafe describes is typically represented in *A Course in Modern Linguistics* (Charles Hockett 1958). This work, published twenty-five years after *Language* (Leonard Bloomfield 1933), is a modern version of structural linguistics which remains faithful to the basic principles outlined by Bloomfield and followed throughout the period.

Figure 3.1 Contrasting Views of Language Structure

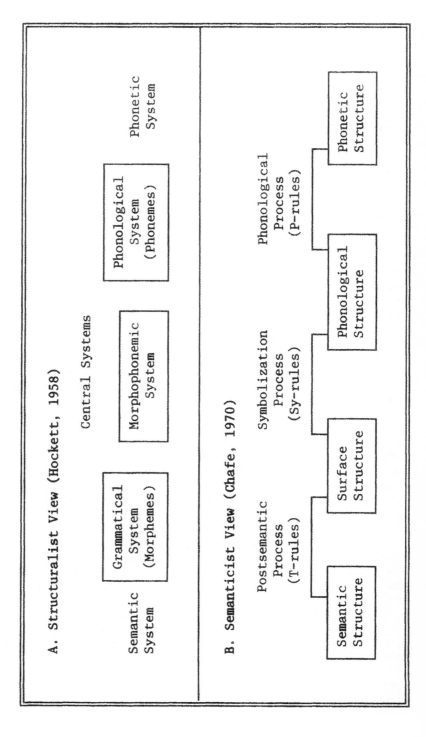

In Hockett's presentation language structure consists of three central systems and two peripheral systems (1958:137). The three central systems are the grammatical system, the phonological system, and the morphophonemic system. The grammatical system is 'a stock of morphemes and the arrangements in which they occur', the phonological system is 'a stock of phonemes and the arrangements in which they occur', and the morphophonemic system is 'the code which ties together the grammatical and the phonological systems'. The peripheral systems are the semantic system and the phonetic system. The semantic system relates morphemes to meanings, and the phonetic system relates phonemes to physical sounds. The model is illustrated in Figure 3.1.A.

The SYNTACTICIST VIEW is represented in Chomsky's *Syntactic Structures* (1957) and later in his *Aspects of the Theory of Syntax* (1965) which is now known as the standard theory. In this standard theory sentences are generated from a central syntactic component. The syntactic base with its phrase structure rules, subcategorization rules, and lexicon generates deep structures, which, by means of transformational rules, are converted into surface structures. The semantic component and the phonological component are interpretive. The semantic component gives a semantic interpretation to deep structures and the phonological component gives a phonological reading to surface structures. The standard theory is dynamic, not static, but semantics remains peripheral and interpretive.

The SEMANTICIST VIEW as presented by Chafe views language as consisting of grammar and phonology joined by a symbolization process (Sy rules). On the grammatical side, semantic structure is converted into surface structure by postsemantic processes (T rules). On the phonological side, the underlying phonological structure is converted into a phonetic structure by generative phonological rules (P rules) of the Chomsky /Halle (1968) type. The principal difference between the semanticist and the syntacticist position is the fact that in the semanticist position semantics is central and the only deep structure is semantic structure. Using the semantic structure as a starting point, the surface structure is generated and then converted into a sequence of sound.

The semanticist view as presented by Chafe can be represented in terms of four states and three processes. Semantic structure becomes surface structure by postsemantic processes (T rules); surface structure becomes underlying phonological structure by symbolization processes (Sy rules); underlying phonological structure becomes phonetic structure by phonological processes (P rules). The model is illustrated in Figure 3.1.B.

Chafe's model can probably be best understood by recognizing the clear break between grammatical processes on the one hand and phonological processes on the other. Chafe first separates language into grammar and phonology and then bridges this gap with the symbolization process. Human language can then be compared with artificial communication systems and animal communication systems.

On the phonological side the underlying phonological structure is separated from the phonetic structure. In the production of language utterances man acts like an 'internal reconstruction device' (1970:37) generating new phonetic strings that in many cases he has never heard before. Both from the point of view of descriptive convenience and psychological reality (1970:34) the process view, that phonetic strings are freshly generated, is to be preferred to the allomorph view, in which all the phonetic variants are remembered. The process view of language tends to move the phonetic structure away from underlying phonological structure so that generative phonological rules are required.

On the grammatical side the distinction between deep and surface structure in Chomsky's syntactic model suggested the possibility that surface structure should be separated from deep semantic structure. This separation turned out to be useful for the description of IDIOMS which often have a surface structure which may carry a literal meaning but may also carry meanings that cannot be deduced from the sum of its parts. The adoption of the view that surface structures are generated from semantic structures requires the use of postsemantic processes including transformations.

The model was now substantially complete. Symbolization linked concepts with sound. On the grammatical side, deep semantic structure and surface structure were accounted for; on the phonological side, underlying phonological structure and phonetic output were accounted for. The universe of meaning, represented by grammar, was linked to the universe of sound, represented by phonology.

Chafe's *Meaning and the Structure of Language* (1970) is divided into two sections. Part I, chapters 1-8, deals with language in general and develops his generative semantic model of language, summed up in 'the resulting picture' (1970:56). Part II, chapters 9-20, deals with language in particular and illustrates how the model works, especially with regard to English.

Although Chafe does not call himself a case grammarian he uses a set of cases, inspired by Fillmore's 1968 model (1970:10), to describe what Chafe calls 'verb-noun relations'. His semantic structures are built around a central verb, which then requires nouns bearing case relations to that verb. The resulting verb-noun structure is a case labelled generative semantics model which can be compared to other models with regard to (1) the deep structure, (2) its case system, (3) the verb types, (4) the derivation which relates verb roots, and (5) its use of covert roles.

3.1 Semantic structure. Semantic structure is 'built around a central verb' (1970:10). This central verb is accompanied by nouns related to the verb by a series of case roles, adopted from Fillmore 1968, called noun-verb relations. But it is the central verb which determines what these relations will be. Chafe presents a picture of a semantic valence theory in which all noun-verb relations depend upon the meaning of the verb.

The elements of semantic structure are called verb and noun but they could as well have been called PREDICATE and ARGUMENT. Chafe justifies his terminology by stating that predicates are generally verbs with the function of describing states and events; arguments are generally nouns with the function of referring to things, including physical objects and reified abstractions (1970:96). The verb is central and the nouns are peripheral.

Chafe lists three reasons for the centrality of the verb: (1) the verb is present semantically in all sentences; (2) the verb determines what nouns will accompany it, for example, in the sentence *the chair laughed* the verb retains its meaning but the noun *chair* is interpreted as capable of laughter; and (3) inflectional units, like Past, which are added to the verb, are added simultaneously to the entire sentence (1970:96). Since the verb is dominant Chafe sees no reason for using an S symbol to generate a sentence. The semantic structure is generated from an initial empty V symbol.

On the grammatical side of language Chafe distinguishes between processes of FORMATION, by which semantic structures are formed, and processes of TRANSFORMATION, which convert semantic structures into surface structures (1979:55). Although Chafe develops a full set of semantic formation rules he admits that rules are not absolutely necessary. They could be replaced by a set of well-formedness conditions (1970:vii) which would convey essentially the same information.

3.1.1 Semantic formation processes. Semantic structure is generated from an initial empty V symbol which is then converted into the semantic structure by means of a set of semantic formation rules (S rules). The principal kinds of formation rules, in order of application, are: (1) rules that develop V by adding semantic features to the verb, (2) rules that add nouns to the central verb according to the verb's features, and (3) rules that develop the nouns in the structure by adding semantic features.

(1) Rules that develop V. This set of rules adds selectional units, the lexical unit, and inflectional units. Selectional units are inherent features of the verb that are part of its semantic description out of context. They include such features as State, Process, Action, Benefactive, Experiential, and Locative. They are added directly below the V and above the lexical unit.

The lexical unit, selected from the lexicon in accordance with the selectional features generated, is a concrete lexical verb. This lexical unit is entered below the selectional features and underlined. The inflectional units are contextual features that are added to the verb in a particular sentence context such as Progressive, Perfective, Present, and Past. They are not part of the lexical meaning of the verb and are added below the lexical item. For a V that is fully developed with selectional, lexical, and inflectional units according to the Chafe model, see Figure 3.2.A.

Figure 3.2 Semantic surface structure (Chafe 1970).

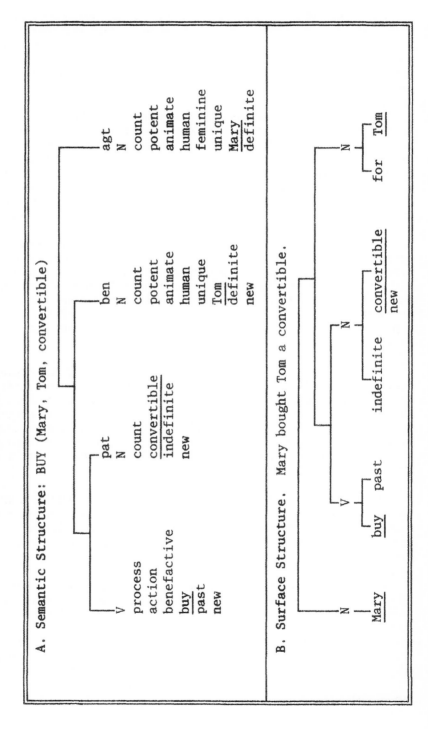

(2) Rules that add nouns to the verb. These rules are applied after the verb is fully developed. Nouns are added to the verb in accordance with the selectional features of the verb. The features State and Process require a Patient noun, the feature Action requires an Agent noun. Selectional verb features are then selectional in two senses: taken together, they select the lexical verb unit, but taken singly, they select the case roles to be filled by nouns.

(3) Rules that develop N. These rules add selectional units, the lexical unit, and inflectional units. For nouns, the selectional units are inherent features from the lexicon such as Count, Potent, Animate, Human, Unique. The lexical unit is chosen in accordance with these features. Inflectional units are contextual features which the noun has in particular contexts. For nouns fully developed with selectional, lexical, and inflectional units, see Figure 3.2.A.

The semantic structure resulting from the application of these semantic formation processes has no higher S node and no modality. The elements include fully developed nouns and verbs. The nouns are added to the verb in immediate constituent fashion and are ordered right-to-left with the probable subject choice to the far right in VOS order. There are no prepositions in the semantic structure and articles are represented by the Definite feature. The resulting structure is 'more like a mobile than a tree' (1970:5) so that the subject noun can be swung around to the left to take up the subject position. The complete semantic structure is given in Figure 3.2.A.

3.1.2 Postsemantic processes. Surface structures are generated from semantic structures by postsemantic processes called T rules. These T rules include (1) subject, object and agreement rules, (2) literalization rules, and (3) linearization rules.

(1) Subject, object, and agreement rules. These rules are basic rules for establishing the surface structure. There are rules for choosing and marking the subject and direct object of a sentence and there are rules for the marking of subject-verb agreement. When subject and object are chosen these terms are used as labels to replace the case labels on the nouns. Subject-verb agreement is indicated by adding the inflectional feature Present, meaning third person singular present tense marking, to the verb when the context requires it (1970:240-246).

(2) Literalization rules. These literalization rules replace semantic units with surface syntactic units, including idiomatic expressions. For example, the semantic unit PROGRESSIVE becomes *be + ing* and the semantic unit PERFECTIVE becomes *have + en* (1970:246). At this stage literal forms may be replaced by idioms. For example, the semantic unit *disclose* might be replaced, according to literalization rules, by the idiomatic expression *spill the beans*.

(3) Linearization rules. These are rules that place semantic units in their proper linear order in surface structure. They are of two kinds: (a) PRIMARY LINEARIZATION rules that put the words, the nouns and verbs, in their proper surface structure order, and (b) SECONDARY LINEARIZATION rules that put the parts of a lexical item in order. Suffixes are placed after the noun or verb and articles are placed before the noun. After primary and before secondary linearization there is a general deletion rule that deletes all selectional units which will not receive any surface realization (1970:250-256).

The surface structure resulting from the application of all these postsemantic processes has no selectional units or case labels due to the general deletion rule that deletes all unnecessary selectional units. The subject N is in subject position due to primary linearization. The suffixes and articles are in their proper position due to secondary linearization. In this example there was no literalization process. The surface structure is now ready for the symbolization process which will change surface structure into an underlying phonological structure, which, in turn, will be converted by phonological rules into phonetic structure. The complete semantic structure is given in Figure 3.2.A, with the corresponding surface structure in Figure 3.2.B.

3.1.3 New and old information. Essential to Chafe's model of grammar is the distinction between new and old information (1970:10). In semantic structure the V is always marked as new information and every N, except the N to be chosen as subject, is marked as new information. In the semantic structure represented in Figure 3.2.A, every element is marked 'new' except the N to the far right which will be chosen as subject. A sentence 'will always contain one and only one noun root which is not new' (1970:217).

In semantic structure the verb root is always 'new', but in surface structure the verb remains 'new' only when there is no 'new' noun present. Therefore the verb remains 'new' in zero and one-place predicates, where it occurs in final position and receives sentence stress as in *It is raining, David laughed.* But when a 'new' noun is present, that is, when there is some noun in the sentence other than the subject, the verb loses the 'new' feature (1970:253).

For nouns in subject position there is no 'new' feature. All other nouns retain the feature 'new' in normal noncontrastive sentences. But in contrastive sentences only one noun, the one that is being stressed, can retain the 'new' feature. Thus for sentences like *David gave Lisa a picture* both *Lisa* and *picture* retain the 'new' feature. However, contrastive sentences must be analyzed on an ad hoc basis with the feature 'new' assigned only to stressed elements, and deleted from other elements.

The distribution of new and old information will have an effect on other syntactic processes such as pronominalization. The non-new elements in a sentence are those which are usually pronominalized (1970:223) because they are old information.

3.2 Chafe's case system. The semantic structure of a simple sentence consists of a central verb and a series of nouns, each noun related to the verb by one of a set of noun-verb relations parallel to Fillmore's cases. According to Chafe, these were relations of 'truly semantic significance not necessarily tied to particular surface constructions' (1970:10). Chafe's system consists of seven cases: Agent, Experiencer, Beneficiary, Instrument, Patient, Complement, and Location (1970:163). Of these cases Agent and Patient are more fundamental since either Agent or Patient appears in every semantic structure except those structures later to be described as Ambient. Fillmore's Dative case is divided into Experiencer and Beneficiary (1970:148) and Fillmore's Factitive case is subsumed under the Complement case (1970:156). The Instrument case is of lesser importance in the system and has no matching selectional feature in the verb.

Chafe's system is a verb-centered system in which the verb determines the number of nouns in the structure as well as the case relations that the nouns bear to the verb. 'It is the verb which dictates the presence and character of the nouns, rather than vice versa' (1970:97). Fillmore's 1968 model is a noun-centered system in which the nouns provide an environmental feature into which verbs may be inserted, called the case frame. In a truly verb-centered system the case roles are read onto the noun from the verb. In such a system also the cases are defined in terms of the verbs with which they occur and not in absolute terms. If one recalls the process of semantic formation it should be evident that semantic features are first added to the verb, then the verb is chosen, and then the number of nouns and their cases is determined, all before the first lexical noun is inserted. In the formation of a sentence with the verb *break*, for example, the V is labelled as action-process, the lexical item *break* is chosen from among the action-process verbs, and then two Ns are added with the case labels Agent and Patient. The structure before the lexical nouns are added is as follows:

Figure 3.3 Initial structure.

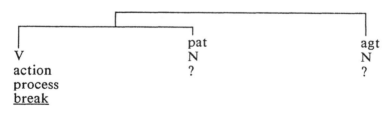

It should be evident at this stage of formation in Chafe's model that no matter what noun is chosen as subject it will be classed as an Agent, and that no matter what noun is chosen as object it will be classed as Patient. In a sentence like *the dish ran away with the spoon* the noun *dish* will be interpreted as an Agent.

3.2.1 Agent (agt). Agent is the case required by an action verb (1970:103). One of the rules for adding nouns to verbs provides for the addition of an Agent noun to every verb with the action feature as long as the verb is nonambient. The Agent specifies 'something (or some one?) which performs the action' (1970:100). An action sentence will answer the question: *What did N do?* in which N is the Agent noun. The Agent occurs in both action and action-process sentences and is always chosen as subject when the verb is used in the active voice, as in sentences (1-2).

(1) Harriet /sang.   (Action)
     agt   (Ac)
(2) Harriet /broke /the dish.   (Action-Process)
     agt   (Ac-Pr) pat

Agent nouns will always have the semantic feature 'potent', which means it 'has the power to do something, has a force of its own' (1970:109). Although the potent feature is regularly associated with animate, 'there seem to be some nouns which are not animate but which may nevertheless occur as Agents' (1970:109). These 'potent' nouns are always Agents, not Instruments. Even inanimate nouns which are not intrinsically potent can be given a 'derived potency' (1970:155) in some contexts. The assignment of the Agent case is perfectly consistent with Chafe's verb-centered approach. If the verb is an action or an action-process verb its subject will be an Agent, whatever features the noun might have, as in sentences (3-4).

(3) The wind /opened /the door.   [+Potent, -Animate]
     agt   (Ac-Pr) pat
(4) The rock /broke /the window.   [-Potent, -Animate]
     agt   (Ac-Pr) pat

3.2.2 Patient (pat). Patient is the case required by a state or process verb (1970:102). One of the rules for adding nouns to verbs provides for the addition of a Patient noun to every verb with either the state feature or the process feature, provided the verb is non-ambient. For state verbs, Patient specifies 'what it is that is in that state' (1970:98). For process verbs, Patient specifies a noun which is said to have 'changed its state or condition' (1970:100). State verbs do not take the progressive; nonstate verbs do take the progressive. A nonstate is an event and answers the question: *What happened?* (1970:99). Among nonstate verbs, process is distinguished from action by answering the question *What happened to N?*, where N is the Patient noun, as in sentences (5-6).

(5) The dish /is broken.   (State)
     pat   (St)
(6) The dish /broke.   (Process)
     pat   (Pr)

The use of the Patient case label for two different semantic concepts can be confusing. State is not adequately distinguished from Process by the case frame alone unless one remains aware that the Patient noun in sometimes derived from the State feature and sometimes derived from the Process feature.

3.2.3 Experiencer (exp). Experiencer is the case required by an experiential verb (1970:146). One of the rules for adding nouns to verbs adds an Experiencer noun to every verb which has the experiential feature. The Experiencer specifies 'one who is mentally disposed in some way' (1970:145). This vague definition can be made more explicit by noting that the examples chosen by Chafe deal with sensation: *see, hear, feel,* with emotion: *want, like,* and with cognition: *know, learn, remember.* The Experiencer case takes over part of Fillmore's Dative case (1970:148). The Experiencer may occur with state, process, or state-ambient verbs. It also occurs with action-process verbs but these seem to be derived causatively from underlying process verbs (Chafe 1970:146), as in sentences (7-10).

   (7) Tom /is (=feels) hot.   (State-Ambient)
       exp (St-amb)
   (8) Tom /knew /the answer.   (State)
       exp (St)   pat
   (9) Tom /saw /the snake.   (Process)
       exp (Pr)   pat
 (10) Harry /showed /Tom /the snake.   (Action-Process)
       agt   (Ac-Pr)   exp   pat

3.2.4 Beneficiary (ben). Beneficiary is the case required by a benefactive verb (1970:150). One of the rules for adding nouns to verbs adds a Beneficiary noun to every verb which has the benefactive feature. The Beneficiary specifies 'the one who benefits from whatever is communicated by the rest of the sentence' (1970:147). This vague definition is made more explicit by noting the examples used by Chafe which indicate a state of possession: *have, own,* the transfer of property with nonagentive verbs: *acquire, find, lose, win,* and with agentive verbs: *buy, sell, send, give.* According to these examples, the Beneficiary is interpreted as the possessor in state verbs and as the nonagentive party in transfer of property verbs. The Beneficiary noun occurs with state, process, and action-process verbs, but not with action verbs (1970:150). There is also an optional Beneficiary, similar to the modal Benefactive of Fillmore, which may occur with any simple action or action-process verb. Beneficiary occurs as subject in sentences (11-12) and as indirect object in sentences (13-14).

 (11) Tom /owns /a convertible.   (State)
       ben (St)   pat
 (12) Tom /acquired /a convertible.   (Process)
       ben (Pr)   pat

(13) Mary /bought /Tom /a convertible.   (Action-Process)
    agt   (Ac-Pr) ben pat
(14) Mary /knitted /Tom /a sweater.   (Action-Process)
    agt   (Ac-Pr) B_m pat

3.2.5 Instrument (ins). Instrument has no selectional feature in the verb but may be added to action-process verbs (1970: 152). The Instrument is 'some object which plays a role in bringing a process about, but which is not the motivating force, cause, or instigator; something which the Agent uses' (1970:155), as in sentence (15).

(15) Tom /cut /the rope /with a knife.   (Action-Process)
    agt (Ac-Pr) pat   ins

3.2.6 Complement (comp). Complement is the case required by a completable verb (1970:157). A completable verb optionally takes a complement noun which 'completes or specifies more narrowly the meaning of the verb' (1970:156). In creative verbs it specifies 'what it is that is created' (1970:156). Complement nouns occur with state verbs and action verbs as direct object, as in sentences (16-17).

(16) The book /weighs /two pounds.   (State)
    pat   (St)   comp
(17) Tom /sang /a song.   (Action)
    agt   (Ac) comp

3.2.7 Location (loc). Location is the case required by a locative verb (1970:159). Location specifies the place in which an object is located. Consequently 'a Location noun does not occur without a Patient noun' (1970:217) since the patient noun will represent the object to be located. Only state verbs can be intrinsically locative (1970:159) but there are derived locative process, action, and action-process verbs, as in sentences (18-21).

(18) The knife /is in /the box.   (State)
    pat   (St)   loc
(19) Tom /fell off /the chair.   (Process)
    pat (Pr)   loc
(20) The baby /crawled under /the table.   (Action)
    agt   (Ac)   loc
(21) Tom /threw /the knife /into the box.   (Action-process)
    agt (Ac-Pr) pat   loc

In every locative predication Chafe considers the locative preposition, *in*, *off*, *under*, *into*, to be the locative predicate (1970:159). Consequently in state locative predications it is not the verb *be* but the preposition which is the locative verb root. In nonstate predications the locative root is added to the verb to form compound verbs like *fall off*, *crawl under*, as in sentences (19-20).

3.3 Chafe's verb types. Semantic structure in the Chafe model consists of a central verb and a series of case marked nouns. The distribution of cases depends upon semantic features in the verb. Features are added to the verb by a series of semantic formation rules and these features determine how many and what kinds of cases will be added to the verb.

3.3.1 Basic verb types. Basic verb types are described in Chapter 9 (1970:95-104) and include state, process, action, and action-process verbs. These four basic verb types are developed by Chafe's first two rules of semantic formation.

S.1   A verb is a state or a nonstate (1970:99).

S.2   A nonstate verb is a Process, an Action, or Action and Process (1970:101).

By rule 1 the [+State] feature may be added to the verb. This feature requires the addition of a Patient noun. But if the verb is non-state then rule 2 applies and adds the features [+Process], [+Action], or both. Verbs with the [+Process] feature require a Patient noun, verbs with the [+Action] feature require an Agent noun, and verbs with both [+Process] and [+Action] features require both Agent and Patient nouns. If State-Patient is Os, Patient is O, and Agent is A, the four basic verb types can be translated into Fillmore type frames, as illustated in Figure 3.4.

Figure 3.4   Verb types.

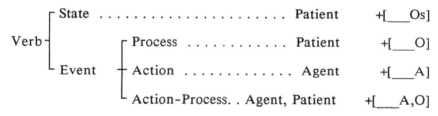

Chafe considers sentences with weather *it* to be semantic structures in which no noun is present (1970:101) and he represents them by adding the feature 'ambient' which removes a noun from the basic structure (1970:102).

S.3   A nonprocess verb may be specified as ambient (1970:102).

Rule 3 permits the formation of state ambient verbs, *It is hot*, and action ambient verbs, *It is raining*. The subject *it* 'covers the total environment' (1970:101) not just some object within it. Action ambient verbs answer the question: *What's it doing?* (1970:102).

Figure 3.5 Case Grammar Matrix (Chafe 1970)

Verb Types	Basic types	Experiential	Benefactive	Locative	Completable
1. State	Os be broken be dead be dry	E,Os know want like	B,Os have have got own	Os,L be in be on be under	Os,C cost measure weigh
2. Process	0 break, iv die dry, iv tighten, iv	E,O feel hear learn see	B,O acquire find lose win	*0,L fall sink	**0,C ...
3. Action	A laugh pounce run	**A,E ...	**A,B ...	*A,L crawl under sit in	A,C fight play run
4. Action–Process	A,0 break, tv dry, tv kill, tv. tighten, tv	*A,E,0 remind show teach	A,B,0 buy give sell send	*A,0,L throw in place next to	**A,0,C ...

** These verb types do not exist.
* These verb types exist but are derived from other verb types.

3.3.2 Other relations of noun to verb. Additional verb types are developed by Chafe in Chapter 12 (1970:144-166) by testing the features experiential, benefactive, instrumental, completable, and locative against each of the four basic verb types. The method suggests that Chafe considers these features to be mutually exclusive since they are tested one at a time with the various combinations of Agent and Patient in the four basic verb types.

S.4   A nonaction verb may be specified as experiential (1970:146).

According to rule 4 there are state experiential verbs, *want, know, like,* and process experiential verbs, *see, hear, feel, learn, remember.* There are no action experiential verbs, and the action-process experiential verbs, *show, teach, remind* seem to be causatively derived from process verbs, *see, learn, remember.*

S.5   A state experiential verb may be specified as ambient (1970:147)

By rule 5, state ambient verbs occur with the Experiencer noun, but with the Patient noun cancelled by the ambient feature. This produces the case frame + [___E], as in *Tom is (=feels) hot.*

S.6   Any verb, except simple actions, may be specified as benefactive (1970:150).

Rule 6 allows state benefactive verbs: *have, own, has got,* process benefactive verbs: *acquire, find, lose, win,* and action-process benefactive verbs: *buy, give, sell, send,* but no simple action verbs.

S.7   A nonprocess verb may be specified as completable (1970:157).

Rule 7 allows state completable verbs: *weigh, cost, measure,* and action completable verbs: *sing, play, win, run, fight.* It does not allow process completable or action-process completable verbs.

S.8   A state verb may be specified as locative (1970:159).

Rule 8 permits state locative verbs, *in, on, under.* All other locative verb types are derived, and include process locatives, *fall off, sink into,* action locatives, *sit in, crawl under,* and action-process locatives, *throw in, place next to.*

All of the verb types generated by Chafe's rules of semantic formation, except the ambient verbs, can be summarized in a sixteen cell case frame matrix with the four basic verb types in one dimension and with basic, experiential, benefactive, locative, and completable verb types in the other, as shown in Figure 3.5.

3.3.3 Subject choice hierarchy. The rules of semantic formation add semantic features to the verb and determine the number and kinds of cases to be added to the verb in the semantic structure. The cases used in the model are ranked hierarchically according to which case is normally chosen as subject. Like Fillmore in 1968, Chafe arranges these cases in a right-to-left order with the probable subject choice to the far right in the structure.

Chafe establishes his subject choice hierarchy on the basis of the distribution of new and old information. Working on the principle that 'a sentence will always contain one and only one noun root which is not new' (1970:217) and knowing that the non-new noun will be in subject position, Chafe establishes his own subject choice hierarchy which he lists in right-to-left order as 'this hierarchy consisting of Location, Patient, Beneficiary, Agent' (1970:217). This subject choice hierarchy is later expanded to include the Experiencer in Chafe's rules of subject formation which are reminiscent of Fillmore's 1968 subject choice rule:

'an Agent or Experiencer noun takes priority in becoming subject,... a Beneficiary noun has the next priority,... otherwise a Patient noun becomes the subject' (1970:244).

Assuming that the Agent is always the subject of active sentences when it cooccurs with the Experiencer case, the complete subject hierarchy is listed in left-to-right order as: Agent, Experiencer, Beneficiary, Patient, and Location. Of the seven cases listed as belonging to the case system (1970:163) the Instrument and Complement cases are not part of the subject choice hierarchy. According to Chafe, the Instrument case is optionally added to action-process verbs (1970:152) and therefore can never be chosen as subject. And since the Complement case completes the meaning of the verb (1970:157) it will always occur in object position and is not a viable subject choice.

According to the rules of object formation (1970:244), the Patient noun not chosen as subject will be chosen as object and 'other nouns will be converted postsemantically into indirect objects or prepositional phrases' (1970:245). Chafe gives no rules for adding prepositions to these other cases.

The subject choice hierarchy governs the choice of subject in active sentences. However, in an immediate constituent semantic structure of the type used by Chafe, the hierarchy must also govern the ordering of the other cases in the structure so that the direct object remains an immediate constituent of the verb. Although Chafe treats passive as an example of the non-normal choice of subjects (1970:219), he has nothing to say about those verbs which demand, idiosyncratically, a different subject choice as in the pairs *own* /*belong to, be in* /*contain, be with* /*have with*, where the second member of the pair is a flip version of the first and requires an exception to the normal rules for subject choice.

3.4 Related lexical entries. In the formation of semantic structure the lexical unit is chosen after the selectional units are added to an unspecified verb root. The number of lexical verb units is equal to the number of verbs in the language. But given that all verbs belong to one of the four basic verb classes, it is highly likely that some verb roots are derived from others. This suspicion is confirmed in English by the existence of derivational affixes evident in such pairs as *break /broken, wide /widen,* which show several verb forms derived from the same lexical root.

Rather than list all the lexical verb roots in his lexicon Chafe proposes a distinction between INTRINSIC and DERIVED verbs. In this lexicon the derived verbs need not be entered since they can now be represented in terms of a basic verb root and one or more derivational units. These derivational units are added to the intrinsic root after lexical insertion of the intrinsic verb root but before the generation of any contextual features. The derivational units are explained and organized into a system in Chapter 11 (1970:119-143). These derivational units are listed as inchoative, resultative, causative, deactivative, deprocessive.

3.4.1 The derivational system.

(1) Inchoative. A derivational unit which converts an intrinsic state verb into a derived process verb (1970:122). For absolute states such as *be open* the process form indicates the change from nonstate to state; for relative states such as *be wide* the form indicates a change from a former state to a different degree of that former state.

Rule 1. State verb + inchoative = process verb
wide,adj + inchoative = *widen,iv*

(2) Resultative. A derivational unit which converts an intrinsic process verb into a derived state verb (1970:124). This unit has the opposite effect of the inchoative unit with the result that derivation is bidirectional. States can then be derived from processes by the inchoative derivation, or processes can be derived from states by the resultative unit.

Rule 2. Process verb + resultative = state verb
break,iv + resultative = *broken,adj*

(3) Causative. A derivational unit which converts an intrinsic or derived process verb into a derived action-process verb (1970:129). The addition of the causative derivational unit will require the addition of an Agent noun to the structure as the process verb becomes an action-process verb.

Rule 3. Process verb + causative = action-process verb
break,iv + causative = *break,tv*

(4) Deactivative. A derivational unit which converts an intrinsic action-process verb into a derived process verb (1970:131). This unit is the opposite of the causative unit and could as well be called the decausative. The rule applies only 'under limited circumstances' and removes the Agent noun in sentences such as *This paper cuts easily.* The resulting process verbs are pseudointransitives.

> **Rule 4.** Action-process + deactivative = process verb
> *cut,tv* + deactivative = *cut,iv*

These four derivational units, grouped in opposing pairs as inchoative versus resultative and causative versus deactivative, form a closed derivational system which links state, process, and action-process verbs, as illustrated in Figure 3.6.A.

Figure 3.6.A Derivational system (1970:132).

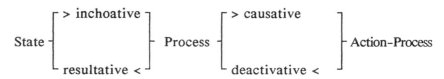

This derivational scheme excludes one of the four basic verb types, namely, the action verbs. Chafe suggests that action-process verbs might be changed into action verbs by a deprocessive derivation to account for those sentences in which the action verbs occur without direct objects.

(5) Deprocessive. A derivational unit which converts an intrinsic action-process verb into a derived action verb (1970:133). This unit is used only for intrinsic action-process verbs.

> **Rule 5.** Action-process + deprocessive = action verb
> *cut,tv* (+obj) + deprocessive = *cut,tv* (-obj)

Chafe asks whether there is a derivational unit which would convert an action into an action-process verb, but says there is none. The obvious candidates for such a rule, such as *laugh, dance, sing,* are action-completable verbs and freely add a Complement not a Patient. Deprocessive is included in the derivation as in Figure 3.6.B.

Figure 3.6.B Derivational system extended (1970:133).

...Action-Process ⎡ > deprocessive ⎤ Action
⎣ no derivation < ⎦

3.4.2 Choosing the intrinsic form. The existence of a bidirectional system which links state, process, and action-process forms presents the analyst with a problem. Given a set of morphologically related forms, how can one discover which is the intrinsic form and which are the derived forms? Chafe provides answers for a limited number of forms which he uses to illustrate various derivational units. The related forms, and the direction of derivation between them, are summarized in Figure 3.7.

Figure 3.7 Intrinsic and derived forms.

State	inch.-->	Process	caus.-->	Action-Process
deaf,adj		.....		*deafen,tv*
dry,adj		*dry,iv*		*dry,tv*
heavy,adj		.....		.....
hot,adj		*heat,iv*		*heat,tv*
long,adj		*lengthen,iv*		*lengthen,tv*
open,adj		*open,iv*		*open,tv*
tight,adj		*tighten,iv*		*tighten,tv*
tired,adj		*tire,iv*		*tire,tv*
wide,adj		*widen,iv*		*widen,tv*

State	<-- res.	Process	caus.-->	Action-Process
broken,adj		*break,iv*		*break,* tv
dead,adj		*die,iv*		*(kill,tv)*
melted,adj		*melt,iv*		*melt,tv*
sunk,adj		*sink,iv*		*sink,tv*

State	<-- res.	Process	<-- deact.	Action-Process
cut,adj		*cut,iv*		*cut,tv*
kicked,adj		*kick,iv*		*kick,tv*
lifted,adj		*lift,iv*		*lift,tv*

The first set represents intrinsic state verbs which become process verbs by the inchoative derivation and then become action-process verbs by the causative derivation. There are intrinsic states with no related forms such as *heavy* and intrinsic states that become action-process by the simultaneous addition of the inchoative and causative derivations without any intervening process form such as *deaf*.

The second set represents intrinsic process verbs which may become state verbs by the resultative derivation or action-process verbs by the causative derivation.

The third set represents intrinsic action-process verbs which become derived process verbs by the deactivative derivation and then become derived state verbs by the resultative derivation. These forms are often identical with the passive form.

Chafe arrives at his conclusions by introspection which he defends throughout his work as 'a valid method of scientific observation' (1970:76). In discussing these derivations he goes one step further in stating 'when introspection and surface evidence are contradictory it is the former which is decisive' (1970:122). The question then arises: Given a set of related forms, can a set of rules be developed that will determine which is the intrinsic form and which forms are derived? Will these rules then give the same results which Chafe has obtained through introspection? The following rules are suggested:

Rule 1: Given related state and nonstate forms, the direction of derivation may be established by the following set of rules:

(a) Choose the morphologically simpler form as the intrinsic form. This is called the 'simplicity of form' criterion. This rule predicts *broken* is derived from *break* and *deafen* is derived from *deaf*.

(b) If two forms are equally simple, choose the state form as the simpler form if a distinct past participle exists. For example, given *hot* and *heated* as state forms, choose *hot* as the intrinsic form. The reason is that, if *heated* is related to the verb *heat* by the resultative derivation, *hot* can only be related to the verb *heat* by the inchoative derivation. This principle also applies to similar pairs such as *dry* /*dried* and *open* /*opened*.

Rule 2: Given related process and action-process forms, the direction of derivation is established by the following rules:

(a) Choose the process form as intrinsic whenever the process form is a true intransitive verb. True intransitives are intransitives that occur in simple subject-predicate sentences such as *The window broke*. The verb *break,iv* is a true intransitive and an intrinsic process and the verb *break,tv* is causatively derived from that process.

(b) Choose the action-process form as intrinsic whenever the process form is a psuedointransitive. These intransitive types are defined by John Lyons in *Introduction to theoretical linguistics* (1968:397). Psuedointransitives are intransitives that normally do not occur in simple subject-predicate sentences such as **The paper cuts*. These intransitives normally require manner adverbials and tend to be generic in meaning. In these cases the process verb *cut iv* is derived by a backwards derivation from the intrinsic transitive form *cut tv*, an action-process verb.

When these rules are applied to the sets of related forms suggested by Chafe, they obtain the same results as Chafe does for all the verbs of the basic state, process, and action-process type. There is only one verb treated by Chafe which is not a basic verb and this is the experiential verb *tire*. Chafe states that for the related forms *tired* /*tire* it is *tired* that is the basic form 'even though surface evidence perversely suggests the opposite' (1970:122). This introspective conclusion is backed by the higher frequency of occurrence and the greater cognitive salience of the state as opposed to the process. But the full set of experiential verbs may need further examination.

3.5 Covert roles: Challenging the matrix. Covert roles are case roles that belong to the semantic structure but do not appear in the surface structure. These include deletable roles, coreferential roles, and lexicalized roles. Deletable roles are roles that belong to the semantic structure but sometimes appear and sometimes do not appear in the surface structure. Coreferential roles and lexicalized roles are roles that belong to the semantic structure but never appear in the surface structure. There is little evidence in Chafe's model of any theory of covert roles and this is perhaps the least developed part of Chafe's analysis.

3.5.1 Deletable case roles. The process of deletion, as proposed by Chafe, is based on the principle 'there are many things present in a semantic structure which do not appear in surface representations' (1970:52). Those semantic units which have no surface realization are deleted consistently. Though the deletion process is general and deals mainly with selectional features deleted postsemantically, deletion may affects nouns and their case roles.

(a) Imperative. The second person subject of the imperative is regularly deleted (1970:53). In this deletion the noun which represents the Agent role is deleted but it is still a part of the semantic structure. Chafe illustrated this deletion by indicating that the subject of the imperative sometimes occurs and sometimes does not occur as in *Eat /You eat*. This is a concrete illustration of the proper use of deletable roles. The Agent case present in deep structure is sometimes present and sometimes absent in the surface structure.

(b) Reflexive. There is an optional deletion rule for some verbs which allows a reflexive direct or indirect object to be deleted from the structure as in *Mary bought (herself) a convertible* (1970:151). Sentences with and without the reflexive pronoun are both generated from a semantic structure which contains Agent, Patient and Beneficiary. Again, the Beneficiary case belongs to the semantic structure but it sometimes appears and sometimes does not appear in the surface structure.

Other structures proposed by Chafe that involve deletable roles show a tendency to change the semantic structure based on surface considerations, despite the fact that these surface deletions seem to follow normal syntactic deletion rules.

(c) Passive. One would expect active and passive sentences to have the same semantic structure as in *Lisa saw David* as opposed to *David was seen by Lisa*. Both of the sentences have the Experiencer and Patient roles. In the short form of the passive *David was seen*, where the regular rule of *by* phrase deletion has applied, the *by* phrase is absent. Since the *by* phrase appears in the long form of the passive, this seems to indicate that the down-graded subject is a deletable case role when the verb is passive.

In any standard theory that makes use of the process of deletion active and passive sentences have the same deep structure and the long and short form of the passive have the same deep structure. The only difference between the long and short passives is that the *by* phrase is present in the long form of the passive and absent in the short form. But Chafe's position is different. He claims that in the passive of Agent-Patient or Experiencer-Patient sentences 'it seems more in line with the meanings of these sentences to say that there is no Agent or Experiencer in their semantic structure to begin with' (1970:219). In this view active and passive sentences have different deep structures and long and short passives have different deep structures. This position seems untenable, especially in view of the fact that there exists a well-known optional *by* phrase deletion rule to account for the difference between the long and short form of the passive. There is no need to change the underlying structure.

There is some justification for Chafe's position in the ambiguity of the short passive. Most short passive sentences are ambiguous between a passive reading which implies the presence of a down-graded subject and an adjectival reading in which the predicate is not a passive but a derived resultative adjective. The sentence *the window was broken* is ambiguous, out of context, between the passive meaning 'the window was broken by somebody' and the resultative stative meaning 'the window is in a broken state'. The former expresses an activity and the form *broken* consists of the root *break* and the inflectional affix *-en* used to indicate a past participle. The latter sentence expresses a resultative state and the form *broken* consists of the root *break* but with the derivational affix *-en* indicating state-as-a-result-of-a-process. The former structure consists of a subject followed by the passive form of the verb; the latter structure consists of a subject, the verb *be*, and a derived adjective.

Although Chafe's position seems indefensible for the short passive, it can be defended for the resultative adjectives. There is no need to change the semantic formation rules to account for these resultative adjectives since there is already in place a derivational system containing deactivative and resultative units which are designed to change action-process verbs to process verbs and then to change process verbs to state forms. Once the derivational units are applied, the process verb becomes a derived state and no Agent noun is generated in the semantic structure.

(d) Deprocessive. In the derivational system state, process and action-process are represented by a regular bidirectional set of derivational units. In an attempt to link the action verbs with this derivational system Chafe suggests a deprocessive unit (1970:132) whose function is to change action-process verbs such as *cut, lift, kick*, which occur with direct objects, to action verbs which occur without direct objects. But the direct object is a role which sometimes appears and sometimes does not appear in the surface structure, a deletable role.

Chafe's position on these deletable object verbs is that the verb is action-process and contains both Agent and Patient roles when the verb occurs with an object, while the verb is an action verb with only the Agent role when no object occurs because the Patient noun has been removed by a deprocessive derivation. Fillmore's position would be that the verb always has both Agent and Patient in its semantic structure but that the verb should be listed as one of the 'deletable object' verbs. If Fillmore is correct there is no need for a deprocessive derivation, since the occurrence of action-process verbs with and without objects is explained on the basis of a syntactic object deletion rule which does not in any way affect the semantic structure.

(e) Complement. One of the cases introduced by Chafe is the Complement case which is introduced by a completable feature proper to such verbs as *sing*, *play*, *run* (1970:156). Complement occurs in object position with certain action verbs, which, with the addition of the Complement case, become action-completable verbs. There is a contrast between simple action verbs which contain only an Agent noun as in *Harriet sang* (1970:98) and action completable verbs which contain an Agent and a Complement as in *Mary sang a song.* (1970:156). But this seems to be just another application of a surface syntactic deletion rule which in this case deletes cognate objects. If Fillmore's deletable object rule is applied when the object is sometimes present and sometimes absent then the verb always would be classified as a transitive verb with the two cases present in the semantic structure.

Chafe's position on deletable roles seems inconsistent. On the one hand he seems to allow syntactic rules to change the surface structure without any corresponding changes in the semantic structure when dealing with imperatives and reflexives. On the other hand he postulates changes in the semantic structure corresponding to changes in surface structure for passives, the deprocessive verbs, and completable verbs. An approach closer to the Fillmore model would suggest that each time there is a noun, which sometimes appears and sometimes does not appear in the surface structure, the semantic structure should remain unchanged. The missing nominals would then be accounted for by optional deletion rules that apply postsemantically and change only the surface structure.

The principle involved is whether a verb should be classified according to the full complement of roles that it can take in a given meaning or whether, on the other hand, the verb is to be given a different semantic structure when one of those roles does not occur in a particular surface structure. The former alternative seems preferable, given the fact that deletion rules such as *by* phrase deletion, reflexive deletion, cognate object deletion, imperative subject deletion are quite regular. The application of this principle to the Chafe model would move many verbs from the action class to the action-process or action-completable class and completely eliminate the need for any deprocessive derivation.

3.5.2 Totally covert roles. Totally covert roles are roles which are present in the semantic structure but never appear in the surface structure. They are of two kinds: coreferential roles and lexicalized roles. There are no totally covert roles in Chafe's 1970 model just as there were none in Fillmore's 1968 model.

(a) Coreferential roles. There are no coreferential roles in Chafe, although coreferential roles do appear in Fillmore's 1971 model. The consideration of coreferential roles such as *John went to Chicago*, with *John* filling the role of both Agent and moving object, could substantially change Chafe's analysis. Many of Chafe's action verbs would then become action-process verbs with the Patient case deleted in semantic structure by Fillmore's coreferential deletion rule, allowing these verbs to surface as apparent action verbs.

Chafe postulates the existence of intrinsic action verbs but states that there are no action-experiential verbs, or action-benefactive verbs. Action-locatives occur but are all derived. If the principle of coreference is applied to Chafe's model then there is the possibility that his simple action verbs are really action-process verbs and that all simple action verbs could be excluded. This would also tighten up the derivational system in which action verbs are an anomaly.

(b) Lexicalized roles. In discussing the derivation of verb roots Chafe uses some examples that could be interpreted as lexicalized roles (1940:141). Sentences such as *Roger watered the lawn* are paraphrased as *Roger applied water to the lawn* and *Roger skinned the lion* is paraphrased as *Roger removed the skin from the lion*. Chafe explains these verbs as examples of verb roots derived from noun roots by postulating a zero marked verbalizer derivation. He suggests that in the lexical rules which introduce action-process verbs these entries might be included as *water (n.) + verbalizer*.

But if the paraphrases given by Chafe are exact paraphrases then the verb and its paraphrase should receive the same semantic analysis. If *water* means 'apply water to' then its case frame should contain an Agent noun, *Roger*, a Patient noun, *water*, and a location noun, *lawn*. The sentence *Roger applied water to the lawn* would be then analyzed as an A-O-L verb with all case roles evident in the surface structure. The parallel sentence *Roger watered the lawn* would also be analyzed as an A-O-L verb, but in this case the Patient noun is lexicalized into the verb and the Locative case becomes the direct object.

Since the meaning of the two sentences is the same, the semantic structure of the two should be the same. The only difference between the two sentences is that the Patient occurs in the surface structure in the first sentence but is lexicalized into the verb in the second. The case frame for the verb *apply* is + [___A,O,L] while the case frame of the verb *water* is +[___A,*O,L] /O-lex.

3.6 Evaluation of the Chafe model. Chafe's fresh and innovative approach to the study of language is a landmark in the history of linguistics. Although not many adopted the use of Chafe's model in all its concrete detail, so many subjects are treated with an intelligent insight that those interested in semantic models find Chafe's presentation to be extremely useful.

In the areas dealing with case grammar Chafe's model is strong precisely where Fillmore's models are weak. Chafe's model proves to be a true countermodel to Fillmore and a careful comparison of the two raises issues that will certainly lead to better case grammar models in the future. Any case grammar that seriously considers Chafe's alternatives will profit from them.

For Chafe as for all generative semanticists, semantics is central, not syntax. It is in the semantic area, where thought is organized, that the well-formedness of sentences is determined. Psychologically, we know what we want to say before we determine how we are going to say it. Within the semantic structure the verb is the central element and the cases are determined by semantic features within the verb. Chafe's case system is better organized than Fillmore's, the verb types are much more clearly defined, and there is a well developed system of derivation that binds together the basic verb types.

3.6.1 Semantic structure. The deep semantic structure of the Chafe model is an immediate constituent structure generated from an initial V. There is no higher S node, no modality, and no prepositions in deep structure. The resulting semantic structure consists of a central verb and a series of case marked nouns, ordered according to a subject choice hierarchy from right to left with the normal subject choice to the far right.

The strength of Chafe's semantic structure is the centrality of the verb. The verb is specified by selectional features, which, in turn, select the cases required by the verb. This is a true semantic valence theory in which the valence of the verb, its propensity to attract definite cases, is clearly defined by features and these features individually demand the presence of specific case marked nouns. In effect, cases are read onto the nouns from the verb.

The weaknesses of Chafe's semantic structure are the lack of a higher S node and the immediate constituent ordering of the cases as they are added one by one to the structure. While Chafe does not go into detail for compound sentences and does not directly treat complementation, he does suggest means for handling relative clauses (1970:288) and various surface structure adverbials (1970:307), with the interesting observation that these higher predicates are state verbs. Complementation could be easily handled by embedding sentences under the Patient case. However, a logical structure closer to Fillmore 1971 would be easier to handle.

3.6.2 Case system. Chafe's case system is an improvement over Fillmore's 1968 list of cases, with the Dative case divided into Experiencer and Benefactive cases, but it could be improved still more by the elimination of Instrument, Complement, and the ambient verbs.

A more careful distinction should be made between the modal and propositional cases. Propositional cases are cases required by the meaning of the verb, in Chafe's terms, the cases demanded by features within the verb. If the Instrument case has no matching selectional feature in the verb, if it is simply an option that may or may not occur with action-process verbs (1970:152), then Instrument is a modal case and should not be listed with the other cases. In a similar way the optional Beneficiary which may be added to any action or action-process verb (1970:151) should be classed as a modal case. Also sentence adverbials of location (1970:300), manner (1970:302), and time (1970:305) should be added to the list of modal cases. All of these cases are options which are not demanded by the verb with which they occur.

Complement in other case systems is just another form of Patient. While admitting that the surface realizations in most languages are the same for Complement and Patient (1970:156), Chafe establishes his Complement as a case because the objects classed as Complements do not fit the definition of Patient as a noun which specifies 'something that is in a state or that changes its state' (1970:156). The traditional meaning difference between affected and effected objects is not at issue here. What is at issue is whether the two meanings constitute two distinct cases or should be considered as in complementary distribution under one case label. The fact that Complement only occurs in object position and has no place in the subject choice hierarchy makes it doubtful whether it has true case status. Without Complement, action-completable verbs become action-process, but state-completable verbs like *cost*, *weigh*, *measure*, still pose a problem, given the one-instance-per-clause principle.

3.6.3 Verb types. The organization of cases into case frames is the strongest point in the Chafe model. The division of all verbs into four types -- state, process, action, and action-process -- is a substantial improvement over the state /action dichotomy used in the Fillmore models. The verb types could be strengthened by adding independent tests such as the imperative test, not mentioned in Chafe, and the progressive test, described by Chafe as 'not available to a state' (1970:99). In these tests any state is [-progressive, -imperative], process is [+progressive, -imperative], and both action and action-process are [+progressive, +imperative]. The distinction between state and process verbs indicated in Chafe by the difference between Patient generated from the state feature, 'that which is in a state', and Patient generated from the process feature, 'that which changes its state or condition', contradicts the Fillmore (1968:31) assertion that stativity need not be marked in the case frame.

3.6.4 Derivation. Chafe is the first to propose a bidirectional derivational system linking together the various verb types. Given a well-defined set of verbs, Chafe shows how these verb types are related to one another by specific derivational units. However, it should be noted that the choice of intrinsic forms, which in Chafe are based upon introspection but reductively are based upon the morphology and syntax of a particular language, will be language specific and not universal. In English, for example, given the pair *break,iv./break,tv.*, the process form is the intrinsic form and the action-process form is causatively derived. But in Spanish, given the pair *romperse /romper*, the action-process form is the simpler form and the process *se* form seems to be derived from the action form by a decausative derivation. The strength of the derivational system is that it echoes individual derivational units described elsewhere in linguistic studies and seems to be parallel to the abstract predicates used in generative semantics.

(a) **Inchoative.** Inchoative is a unit added to a state verb to change it into a process verb. Inchoative is found in Lakoff (1970:32) as a proform added to state adjectives to produce *become*-type sentences which indicate change of state, as in *thick /thicken*. The same notion is represented by the abstract predicate BECOME in McCawley's analysis of the verb *kill* (1976:157) and subsequently in David Dowty as the abstract predicate COME ABOUT (1972:38).

(b) **Causative.** Cuasative is a unit added to a process verb to produce an action-process verb. The causative is found in Lakoff (1970:41) as a causative proform and in McCawley (1976:57) and Dowty (1972:41) as an abstract predicate CAUSE. The recognition of CAUSE as an atomic predicate which can be factored out of certain transitive predicates coincides with the treatment by John Lyons (1968:352) of identical transitive /intransitive pairs where the transitive is causatively derived from the intransitive form.

(c) **Resultative.** Resultative is a unit added to a process verb to produce a state verb. The introduction of the resultative derivation is a fairly innovative move but one justified by the ambiguity of the short passive form which may be either a true passive or a derived resultative adjective.

(d) **Deactivative (decausative?).** Deactivative is a unit which is added to action-process verbs to produce process verbs. This type of derivational unit is a handy tool to describe those pseudointransitives mentioned in Lyons (1968:363) which seem to be a back formation from regular transitive verbs in such sentences as *This sweater washes easily, This book will sell quickly.*

The weakness of the derivational system is the fact that action verbs are not part of the system, if one excludes the deprocessive derivation which can be handled by an object deletion rule. This suggests that action verbs do not constitute a separate verb type. The derivational system also needs to be applied to domains other than the basic verb domain.

3.6.5 Covert roles. One of the weak points of Chafe's model is the limited use of covert case roles such as deletable roles, which sometimes appear in surface structure and sometimes do not, and coreferential and lexicalized roles, which never appear in surface structure. However, Chafe's system is strong enough to accommodate covert roles, given the proper postsemantic processes for deletion, lexicalization and coreference. The adoption of covert roles would make substantial changes in the matrix of verb types.

Concerning the verb types which Chafe asserts do not exist, evidence can be found for action-experiential and action-benefactive verbs. In sentences such as *they questioned the suspect*, the surface structure is action-experiential but if lexicalized roles are admitted then *question* = 'ask questions of' and the noun *question* is lexicalized Patient. In sentences such as *they bribed the guard*, the surface structure is action-benefactive but if lexicalized roles are admitted then *bribe* = 'give a bribe to' and the noun *bribe* is lexicalized.

Concerning the verb types which Chafe asserts do exist but only as derived verb types, examples can be found which seem to be intrinsic. For action-process-experiential verbs Chafe cites *show*, *teach* as causatively derived. But there is a whole set of verbs of communication such as *say*, *tell*, which require a speaker (agt), a hearer (exp), and what is said (pat), which should be classed as intrinsic A-E-O verbs. Furthermore, derived locative types are limited by Chafe's impression that the locative predicate is the preposition. If locative verbs are interpreted as those which demand a complementing locative case, then *fall*, *sink* are obvious process locatives, *walk*, *run* are action locatives, and *put*, *bring* are action-process locatives. The matrix then can be completely filled with intrinsic verb types in the locative domain.

In a deeper analysis, one which postulates an obligatory O case, the whole line of action verbs comes into question. Action verbs become A-O verbs with the O deletable, coreferential, or lexicalized. The A-E verbs, A-B verbs, and A-L verbs would be reinterpreted as A-E-O, A-B-O, and A-O-L verbs with the O-case coreferential or lexicalized. The matrix is reduced from 16 cells to 12 cells and there is no need to incorporate action verbs, now eliminated, into the derivational system.

3.7 Conclusion. Chafe's generative semantics model is the most comprehensive model yet proposed. The verb is central and all case relationships originate with the verb. The list of cases is adequate, the verb types are clearly defined and well tied together by a derivational system. In this model the verb type and number of cases required by the verb can be determined before the case labels are assigned to particular nouns. With the cases determined by the meaning and type of verb that occurs in the sentence, the assignment of cases to the nouns in the structure becomes a relatively easy task which can be performed with consistency.

Exercise 3. Write the case frame for the main verb in each of the following sentences. The cases available are A-E-B-O-C-L. Use Os for state Patient, O for process Patient, C for Complement. Since ambient verbs do not have case frames use St /amb for state ambient, Ac /amb for action ambient, and E-St /amb for experiential state ambient. There are no totally covert roles. If a case role is deleted, mark the deleted role after the case frame.

1. The clown amused Michael. _____

2. The wood is dry. _____

3. It's hot. _____

4. Tom is (=feels) hot. _____

5. The knife is in the box. _____

6. The dish broke. _____

7. The rock broke the window. _____

8. The candy cost ten cents. _____

9. Tom fell off the chair. _____

10. Tom found the tickets. _____

11. Mary gave Tom the tickets. _____

12. Tom has a convertible. _____

13. Tom heard an owl. _____

14. The men laughed. _____

15. Tom liked the asparagus. _____

16. Tom placed the book next to the phone. _____

17. It's raining. _____

18. Harry showed Tom the snake. _____

19. Mary sang a song. _____

20. Tom sat down in the chair. _____

21. This book weighs a ton. _____

Chafe 1970 Lexicon. The Chafe 1970 lexicon is a collection of 80 verbs with the case frames as far as they can be determined from Chafe's 1970 *Meaning and the Structure of Language*. Ambient verbs with no case frame are listed as St /amb, E-St /amb, or Ac /amb. The Complement case, when it is optional, is listed in parentheses.

acquire	B,O	kill	A,O
amuse	A,O	knit	A,O
awaken,tv	A,O	know	E,Os
be broken	Os	laugh	A,(C)
be dead	Os	learn	E,O
be deaf	Os	lift,tv	A,O
be dry	Os	like	E,Os
be hot	Os	lose	B,O
be hot (w)	St /amb	measure	Os,C
be hot (E)	E-St /amb	open,iv	O
be in	Os,L	open,tv	A,O
be late	St /amb	own	B,Os
be on	Os,L	place next	A,O,L
be open	Os	play	A,(C)
be tight	Os	pounce	A
be under	Os,L	rain (w)	Ac /amb
be wide	Os	read	A,(C)
break,iv	O	remember	E,O
break,tv	A,O	remind	A,E,O
buy	A,B,O	run	A,(C)
cost	Os,C	see	E,O
crawl under	A,L	sell	A,B,O
cut,iv	O	send	A,B,O
cut,tv	A,O	show	A,E,O
dance	A,(C)	sing	A,(C)
deafen,tv	A,O	sink,iv	O
die	O	sink into	O,L
dry,iv	O	sit in	A,L
dry,tv	A,O	skin,tv	A,O
fall off of	O,L	snow (w)	Ac /amb
feel	E,O	teach	A,E,O
fight	A,(C)	throw into	A,O,L
find	B,O	tighten,iv	O
frighten	A,O	tighten,tv	A,O
give	A,B,O	want	E,Os
have	B,Os	water	A,O
hear	E,O	weigh	Os,C
heat,iv	O	widen,iv	O
heat,tv	A,O	widen,tv	A,O
kick	A,O	win	B,O

4 The Anderson 1971 Model

4.0 Overview. The first localistic theory of case published was the model proposed by John M. Anderson (1971), *The grammar of case: Towards a localistic theory*. According to the localistic theory, all case roles which relate nouns to verbs except Agent and Object can be reduced to stative Location or to directional Source and Goal. These three locational notions are used in conjunction with an obligatory neutral Object, the entity which is moved or located, and an Agent, the instigator of an activity. The locational cases Location, Source, and Goal are used in their concrete meaning to express spatial location but they are also used in an abstract meaning to cover those domains described in other models as experiential, dealing with sensation, emotion, and cognition; or benefactive, dealing with possession or transfer of property.

A similar model was proposed by Jeffrey S. Gruber in his 1965 thesis *Studies in Lexical Relations*. But this thesis was not popularized until Jackendoff adopted it as the basis for his thematic relations (1972) and was not published until 1976, when it appeared as Part I of Gruber's *Lexical Structures in Syntax and Semantics*. Gruber, like Anderson, proposed a localistic case system with Agent and neutral obligatory theme. Spatial concrete locatives are expressed by stative Location or by directional Source and Goal. Other semantic domains, such as experiential and benefactive, are expressed in terms of abstract Location, Source, and Goal.

The localistic case system offers a challenge to the nonlocalistic systems of the type proposed by Fillmore and Chafe. It seems that any semantic domain that can be represented in a nonlocalistic system can be equally well represented in terms of stative and directional locatives. The obligatory theme hypothesis which seems to be common to localistic systems, although not a necessary component of these systems, offers a method by which case systems can be more rigidly defined provided that the model makes use of deletable, lexicalized and coreferential roles. Much can be learned by comparing the localistic case analysis of each verb with the corresponding non-localistic analysis.

Anderson's model is well organized for comparative purposes. Part I: Preliminaries (Chapters 1-2) establishes a grammatical framework for the model. Part II: Nominative and Ergative (Chapters 3-5) uses the Ergative (Agent) and Nominative (Object) cases to establish the basic verb types which require only the Agent and

Object cases. PART III: Locative and Ablative (Chapters 6-9) deals with stative Locative (Location), directional Locative (Goal), and Ablative (Source). Chapter 6 deals with concrete stative location; Chapter 7 deals with abstract stative location including stative experiential and benefactive verbs. Chapter 8 deals with concrete spatial directionals; Chapter 9 deals with abstract directionals and includes process and action experiential and benefactive verbs. PART IV: Interlude (Chapter 10) deals with sequencing and PART V: Local and Nonlocal (Chapters 11-12) concludes the presentation with various suggestions for improving the grammatical model.

Like most early case grammarians, Anderson develops his case grammar within the context of a syntactic model. Fillmore constantly refers to his own model as 'a transformational grammar with a case base' (1975:3). Chafe develops his own case system within the framework of a generative semantics model in which sentences are generated from an initial semantic structure built around a central verb. Anderson develops his case system as part of a dependency grammar (1971:29) in which surface structures are generated from an initial V, with the cases expressed as relations dependent upon the central verb. Although Fillmore has arrived at the conclusion that case grammar is no longer to be considered as 'a general model of linguistic structure' (1977:62) but as a model that deals with 'the semantic nature of the inner structure of a clause' (1977:60), it is useful to consider each case grammar proposal in the context in which it was presented, whether it be interpetive semantics, generative semantics, dependency grammar or tagmemics.

According to Anderson, the problem of placing cases within a grammatical framework is 'to characterize an element which in some sense indicates the function of NPs with respect to what is denoted by the V, but which nevertheless is a terminal category' (1971:29). The constituent approach 'fails to capture the essentially relational character of the cases' (1971:28). Anderson believes that in a dependency grammar in which the cases are represented as dependent upon the verb 'the case elements can be interpreted quite naturally as expressing the relation contracted between their dependent Ns and the governing V' (1971:30). Within this dependency system 'the essentially relational (notional) role of V is contrasted with the basically thing-referential N' (1971:31). Anderson insists that the verb is central in semantic structure, not just in surface structure. 'Verbs are central relationally, they govern the case functions contracted by nouns. Nouns are primary referentially (and perhaps selectionally); they terminate (nonrecursive) dependency trees' (1971:31 fn.1).

The dependency model of Anderson, like the generative semantics model of Chafe, places semantics and not syntax as the basis for the generation of sentences. Within these semantic centered systems the verb is the central element and is the starting point for the formation of semantic structure. Chafe defends verb centrality with syntactic and semantic arguments, such as the verb is always present, verbal inflections modify the whole structure, and metaphorical interpretations keep the meaning of the verb constant. Anderson defends the verb central position with more abstract arguments. The primary function of nouns is to name things; the noun is primary referentially. The function of the verb is to express relations between the nouns in the structure; the verb is central relationally.

This type of argument is similar to the descriptions of some computational analysts who describe the elements of a program as consisting of Names and Relations. The function of a Name (N) is to refer to a specific location in the memory, the function of a Relation (R) is to relate various named locations by giving commands that tell how the various Names are to be used. The computer language can then be constructed using Names and Relations and nothing else.

In Anderson's model the semantic structure is central. This semantic structure is formed by semantic formation rules which include SUBCATEGORIZATION RULES (SRs) which add features to verbs (1971:20) and DEPENDENCY RULES (DRs) which add nouns to verbs in accordance with these features (1971:32). Anderson admits that the semantic formation rules are not strictly necessary since they could be replaced by a set of 'wellformedness conditions on semantic representation' (1971:27).

The semantic structure is converted into a surface structure by TRANSFORMATIONAL RULES (TRs) that relate semantic representations to surface syntactic structures (1971:25). These rules are also called realization rules (1971:15). The syntactic structure then serves as input to PHONOLOGICAL RULES (PRs) which produce the phonetic structure or expression (1971:15). Anderson's model is similar to that of Chafe in placing semantic structure as central with surface structure derived from semantic structure by transformational rules, but Anderson does not separate grammar and phonology by a Chafe-like symbolization process. The Anderson model is illustrated in Figure 4.1.

Figure 4.1 The Anderson 1971 Model.

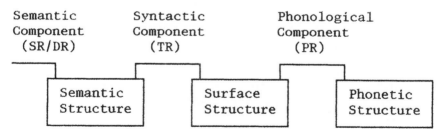

Anderson focuses his attention on the subcategorization rules (SRs) and dependency rules (DRs) which generate the semantic structure and treats the transformational rules (TRs) only to the extent that they account for 'the introduction, interrelation and distribution of the case elements' (1971:33). There is no further development of the phonological rules (PRs) which generate the phonetic representations.

In his development of the model Anderson explicitly excludes the coordination of clauses, sentences containing questions and commands, the modal verbs, and tense and aspect (1971:33). His model then concentrates upon the analysis of simple declarative sentences, including the formation of semantic structures and the realization rules required to derive the surface structure. This treatment is partly syntactic and partly semantic.

One might assume from an abstract description of the model that the semantic structure is formed by subcategorization and dependency rules and that this semantic structure is then transformed into a syntactic structure by postsemantic rules. But this is not the case. Anderson introduces linear sequencing and syntactic features into the semantic rules. First of all, the feature [+stative] is a syntactic feature for Anderson. This feature is not used to distinguish the state verbs [-progressive] from nonstate [+progressive] verbs as in Chafe's model, but is used as a syntactic feature which generates the copula *be*. In working with Anderson's model one must keep in mind that semantically stative verbs are not distinguished by the [+stative] feature. Anderson uses the term 'notionally stative' (1971:94) to describe verbs that are semantically state verbs. Secondly, cases are not merely introduced by features, they are at the same time introduced in proper surface linear order.

The purpose of describing Anderson's 1971 model here is not to present his complete model of language description nor to present the further development given in his most recent work *On Case Grammar* (1977), but rather to concentrate upon the contrast between Anderson's 1971 localistic model and other case models of the period with regard to certain specific issues, including semantic structure, the case system, the verb types, derivation and covert roles.

For contrastive purposes the questions to be asked are as follows: (1) What is the semantic structure framework within which the localistic array of cases is presented? (2) What is the list of cases proposed within that localistic system? Are any cases obligatory? Are any mutually exclusive? (3) What kind of verb types are generated with this list of cases? What are the semantic domains and how are they differentiated? (4) How are the various verb types related? Does Anderson's model have anything corresponding to Chafe's derivational units, namely, the inchoative, resultative, causative and decausative units? And finally (5) to what extent does Anderson make use of covert case roles, such as deletable roles, coreferential roles, and lexicalized roles?

4.1 Semantic structure. The semantic structure of Anderson's dependency model consists of a central verb dominating a series of cases. These cases, in turn, dominate nouns and their case markers. The verb and cases are generated in an SVO order in their proper surface structure position for English. Since the cases are arranged in surface structure order they cannot be arranged according to any subject choice hierarchy. In Anderson's model there is no modality, no higher S node. Although Anderson generally excludes all modal elements, he does suggest, in discussing modal locative phrases, that they are probably derived 'via some type of superordination' (1971:83 fn.1), following Fillmore's suggestion about higher predicates (1968:23 fn.29). A typical semantic structure is illustrated in Figure 4.2.A.

Figure 4.2.A Anderson's dependency structure (1971:30).

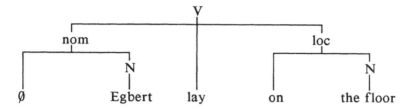

The dependency structure of the Anderson model can be adapted to the Fillmore model by placing the verb in initial position, listing the cases from left to right in subject choice hierarchy order, and changing the case labels to coincide with Fillmore type cases. Fillmore had suggested a kind of dependency structure with one higher V node and one or more case labelled branches. The variable noun phrases under each case then 'represent the entities which bear case relations to the predicator represented at the V node' (Fillmore 1971:55). This Fillmore type dependency structure is illustrated in Figure 4.2.B.

Figure 4.2.B Fillmore type dependency structure.

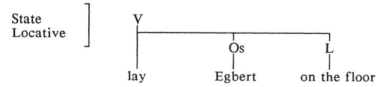

Structures of this type are found in Frances Aid's 1971 *Semantic Structures in Spanish*, in which the semantic structures are composed of an initial V and the cases in right to left order, with the case labels chosen from the Fillmore and Chafe lists. Dependency models have the advantage of representing graphically an absolute verb centrality.

4.1.1 Semantic formation processes. In the Anderson dependency model the semantic structure is generated from an empty V symbol by means of subcategorization rules (SRs), which add features to verbs, and dependency rules (DRs), which add nouns and syntactic features to the structure in accordance with the features generated. The semantic structure in the Anderson model begins with an initial V and without an inital string S, just as it did in the verb centered Chafe model.

Subcategorization rules. SRs are rules that add features to verbs. The most basic subcategorization rules are the rules which add the features [±stative], [±ergative], [±reflexive], and [±oblique] to form the basic verb types which use only ergative and nominative cases.

SR.1. $V \longrightarrow \begin{bmatrix} \pm \text{ ergative} \\ \pm \text{ stative} \end{bmatrix}$ (1971:60)

Read: A verb may be classified as stative or nonstative.
A verb may be classified as ergative or nonergative.

SR.2. +ergative $\longrightarrow$ ± reflexive (1971:60)

Read: An ergative verb, stative or nonstative, may be further subclassified as reflexive or nonreflexive.

SR.3. -reflexive $\longrightarrow$ ± oblique (1971:60)

Read: A verb classified as +stative, +ergative, -reflexive may be further subclassified as oblique.

The stative feature in SR.1 subclassifies verbs according to whether or not they require the introduction of the copula *be*. Consequently, [+stative] forms are adjectives which require the copula and [-stative] forms are verbs which do not require it.

The ergative feature in SR.1 subclassifies verbs according to whether or not they take the ergative (Agent) case. Verbs marked as [+ergative] require an Agent, verbs marked as [-ergative] do not require an Agent.

The reflexive feature in SR.2 distinguishes between ergative verbs marked [+reflexive], in which ergative and nominative cases are coreferential, and ergative verbs marked [-reflexive], in which ergative and nominative cases are not coreferential.

The oblique feature in SR.3 is an optional feature for [+stative, +ergative, -reflexive] verbs. Generally, the nominative noun is chosen as subject and automatically acquires the stative feature as subject of the copula. But for verbs which are marked [+oblique] the stative feature is moved onto the ergative noun which will be chosen as subject of the copula. The oblique feature is an environmental feature which refers only to ergative subjects which are not coreferential with nom, since with coreferential roles the nominative would already be automatically marked with the [+stative] feature.

The verb types generated by subcategorization rules SR.1-3 may be illustrated by a branching diagram. Since the stative and ergative features are introduced simulataneously in SR.1, either may be listed as the primary distinguishing feature. Here stative is considered the primary feature and the ergatives are then listed as reflexive or nonreflexive. Six basic verb types which use only nominative and ergative cases are distinguished, as in Figure 4.3.

Figure 4.3 Basic verb types (1971:61–63)

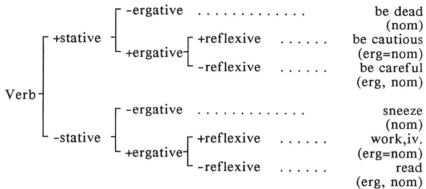

Dependency rules. DRs are rules which add cases to the verb in a particular linear order according to the features generated on the verb. The DRs are developed after the subcategorization rules. The following rules are adapted from Anderson (1971:60).

DR.1. V --> nom $\left\{ \text{// \_\_\_ V} \right\}$

Read: For any verb (V) the nominative case is inserted to the left of and is dominated by the verb symbol (V).

DR.2. +ergative --> erg $\left[\begin{array}{l} \text{// nom /V (+reflexive)} \\ \text{// V \_\_\_} \end{array} \right]$

Read: For any ergative verb the ergative case is inserted on the nom symbol if the verb is reflexive; otherwise it is inserted to the right of and is dominated by V.

DR.3. +stative --> stat $\left[\begin{array}{l} \text{// erg /V (+oblique)} \\ \text{// nom} \end{array} \right]$

Read: For any stative verb the stative feature (+stat) is inserted on the erg symbol if the verb is +oblique (stative, ergative, nonreflexive with erg subject); otherwise the feature (+stat) is inserted on nom.

4.1.2 Surface structure derivation

Transformational rules. TRs are rules that rearrange semantic elements in surface order. Since nom is introduced initially to the left of V in subject position and erg is introduced to the right of V in object position, there must be a rule (TR1) which reverses the order of erg and nom for simple active transitive sentences. For equative sentences or passive sentences there must also be a rule (TR2) for the introduction of the copula. The following rules are adapted from Anderson (1971:60).

>**TR.1.** nom + V + erg --> erg + V + nom
>Condition: stat ≠ nom

Read: The sequence, nom + V + erg, is reversed whenever nom is not marked with the feature [+stative].

>**TR.2.** stat + V --> stat + cop + V

Read: Whenever the case to the left of V is marked +stative the copula is added after the case marked [+stative].

When all of these subcategorization rules, dependency rules, and transformational rules are applied in order they generate the six basic surface structures illustrated in sentences (1-6). Case symbols are given to show case frames in a comparable Fillmore or Chafe model.

(1) Egbert /is /dead. nom=stat + cop + V	be dead	Os
(2) Egbert /is /cautious. nom=erg=stat + cop + V	be cautious	A,*O/A=O
(3) Egbert /is careful /with books. erg=stat + cop + V + nom	be careful	A,O
(4) Egbert /sneezed. nom + V	sneeze	O
(5) Egbert /worked. nom=erg + V	work,iv.	A,*O/A=O
(6) Egbert /read /the book. erg + V + nom	read	A,O

The decision to use stative as a syntactic feature to generate the copula in surface structure prevents Anderson from making a clear distinction between 'notionally stative' verbs like *know, contain* (Anderson 1971:41) which do not take the progressive and notionally nonstative verbs which do take the progressive.

If [+stative] is used as a semantic feature then: (1) stative verbs take neither the progressive nor the imperative, (2) nonstative verbs which take the progressive could be subclassified as [±ergative] to separate process from action verbs, and (3) action verbs would be [+ergative] and could then be subclassified as [±reflexive], depending upon whether erg and nom are coreferential. The rules could then be reconstructed as follows: Every verb in the lexicon is [± stative], nonstative verbs are [± ergative], ergative verbs are [± reflexive]. The verb types produced in this way would then be (1) State [+stative], (2) Process [-stative, -ergative], and (3) Action-process [-stative, +ergative]. Ergatives may also be [+reflexive].

4.2. Anderson's case system. In Anderson's dependency grammar the cases are defined as 'grammatical relations contracted by nouns which express the nature of their participation in the state or process represented in the sentence' (1971:10). The cases are not interpreted as constitutes nor the NPs as constituents; rather, the case 'expresses the function which a particular NP has in a clause' (1971:29). 'The underlying case relations are a universal of language' (1971:14), with the same set of cases applying to all languages.

Case relationships in deep structure are to be distinguished from surface structure relations like subject and object. Following the 1968 Fillmore model, Anderson considers surface grammatical functions like subject and object as 'superficial neutralizations of distinct underlying cases' (1971:10); 'the nominals which come to contract these functions have diverse underlying case relationships' (1971:44). With this distinction Anderson is able to revise the localist hypothesis within a new framework in which localism is applied to semantic structure, not to surface structure.

Anderson's case system consists of four cases: nominative (nom), ergative (erg), locative (loc) and ablative (abl). The nominative is parallel to Fillmore's Object case and the ergative to Fillmore's Agent case. Basic verb types are described in terms of these two cases only. The locative case is used, together with the nom and erg cases, to describe stative location; the locative (as Goal) is used in conjunction with the ablative (as Source) to describe directional locatives.

Here the similarity ends. According to the localist hypothesis, stative and directional locatives are not only applied in the concrete for spatial location and motion but are also applied in the abstract to describe other domains, such as the experiential and benefactive domains. The four cases proposed by Anderson form a localistic system similar to Gruber's system which contained the five cases: Agent, Theme, Location, Source, Goal.

4.2.1 Nominative (nom). Nom is the case required by every verb. Since this case is obligatory to every case frame it is not matched by any feature in the verb. The nominative is 'the notionally most neutral case' (1971:37), the case whose role is 'identified by the semantic interpretation of the verb' (Fillmore 1968:25). With notionally stative verbs this case indicates the object being described; with nonstative verbs nom indicates the noun which 'undergoes the process denoted by the verb' (1971:43).

Anderson's nominative case differs from Fillmore's Object case in that 'nom is the only obligatory case' (1971:37). Unlike Fillmore, Anderson defends 'the unique status of nom as a case element that is universally present in the clause' (1971:50), similar to Gruber's obligatory theme (1976:38).

The nominative case in state or process verbs serves the same function as Fillmore's Object or Chafe's Patient case. However, given the obligatory O hypothesis, there can be no zero place predicates in Anderson's system of the type that Chafe calls 'ambient' (Chafe

1970:101). The solution offered by Anderson in sentences such as *It is hot in this room* is that 'the subject in the former sentence represents an underlying (though perhaps empty) nom' (1971:50 fn.3). The same explanation can be extended to all weather *it* clauses. The so-called ambient verbs would then receive the same analysis as other state and process verbs, requiring the presence of the obligatory nom, as in sentences (7-10).

(7) John /is dead. nom + V	State
(8) It /is hot. nom + V	State (ambient)
(9) John /died. nom + V	Process
(10) It /is raining. nom + V	Process (ambient)

4.2.2 Ergative (erg). Erg is the case required by an ergative verb. All verbs are subcategorized as [±ergative]; verbs which are marked as [+ergative] acquire the erg case through a dependency rule (1971:45). The ergative specifies 'the initiator of the action associated with the V' (1971:40) and answers the question: What did N do? (1971:42). 'The ergative N is typically rather than necessarily animate' (1971:40 fn.1). Ergative verbs take the progressive and the imperative and both adjective and verb forms may be ergative, allowing a class of action adjectives.

With the obligatory O hypothesis there is no distinction between simple action verbs which would take ergative without nominative and action-process verbs which take both ergative and nominative. All simple action verbs are interpreted as action-process verbs; the simple actions are called ergative reflexive with erg coreferential with nom. Other action-process verbs are ergative nonreflexive, as contrasted in sentences (11-14).

(11) John /is cautious. erg=nom + V	Action-process [+reflexive]
(12) John /worked. erg=nom + V	Action-process [+reflexive]
(13) John /is careful /with books. erg + V + nom	Action-process [-reflexive]
(14) John /killed /the duckling. erg + V + nom	Action-process [-reflexive]

Since there is no distinction in Anderson's system between action and action-process verbs, the term ergative (or action) verb will always refer to an action-process verb requiring both the ergative and the nominative cases. There are no simple action verbs in deep structure. Action verbs are either transitive or they have the object case as a coreferential or lexicalized role.

4.2.3 Locative (loc). Loc is the case required by a locative verb. Every verb is subcategorized as [± locative]. Verbs which belong to the [-locative] class are the basic verb types; the [+locative] verbs are further subcategorized as [± directional], with [-directional] for stative locatives and [+directional] for dynamic directional locatives. The locative case is added to the verb by a later dependency rule (1971:83). The locative case is a case 'indicating the spacial location of the nominative' (1971:81). The stative locative case is characteristically marked with stative locative prepositions: *at, in, on*. In *be* + Locative structures Anderson adopts the interpretation that *be* (=be located) is the main verb in the structure (1971:88). State locatives also occur with locative subjects through 'the operation of a permutation rule' (1971:89) which permutes locative and nominative and allows the locative case to appear as the subject, as in sentences (15-16).

> (15) The apples /are /in the box.   O subject
>   nom + V + loc
> (16) The box /contains /the apples.   L subject
>   loc + V + nom

In a localistic case system the stative locative, normally used for concrete spatial location, is extended to abstract location with 'affective verbs' (1971:103) and verbs of 'possession' (1971:107). With both types of verbs the permutation rule can be used to move the locative into subject position, as in sentences (17-20).

> (17) The truth /is known /to many people.   O subject
>   nom + V + loc
> (18) Many people /know /the truth.   L subject
>   loc + V + nom
> (19) The compass /belongs to /John.   O subject
>   nom + V + loc
> (20) John /owns /the compass.   L subject
>   loc + V + nom

In addition, Anderson proposes action [+ergative, -reflexive] and action-process [+ergative, -reflexive] verbs which take stative locative cases, for example, *keep, remain*, in sentences (21-22).

> (21) John /remained /in London.   [+reflexive]
>   erg=nom + V + loc
> (22) They /kept /the money /in a box.   [-reflexive]
>   erg + V + nom + loc

Recent investigation into the nature of aspectual verbs like *keep* and *remain* suggests that these are not simple A-O-L verbs but complex verbs which in their simple intransitive form are one place subject-raising predicates and in their transitive form are two place predicates requiring an equi NP deletion rule.

4.2.4 Ablative (abl). Abl is the case required by a directional verb. Every [+locative] verb is further categorized as [± directional]. The [-directional] verbs are state locatives; the [+directional] verbs are dynamic locatives. The ablative case is introduced to the left of the locative case to form a Source-Goal pattern consisting of the ablative case as Source-from-which and the locative case, now reinterpreted as Goal-to-which. Directional locatives differ from statives in several ways: (1) In every directional clause 'there are two locative phrases either present or implied' (1971:119), namely abl-Source and loc-Goal; (2) the prepositions used are directional not stative prepositions. Abl-Source uses *from*, *out of*, *off of*; loc-Goal uses *to*, *into*, *onto*; (3) the verbs are process or action verbs, not state verbs; and (4) the verb is always 'notionally nonstative'. Exceptions to this generalization include the verbs of extension and verbs of motion used as verbs of extension. The extension verbs are notionally stative, reject the progressive, but require the directional abl-Source and loc-Goal cases. The ablative State, Process, and Action-Process verbs are illustrated in sentences (23-26).

(23) The fog /stretches /from London /to Brighton.   State
      nom + V + abl + loc
(24) The ball / rolled / from Mary / to Jane.   Process
      nom + V + abl + loc
(25) The man / came / here / from London.   Action
      erg=nom + V + loc + abl   [+reflexive]
(26) John / took / the book / to the library.   Action
      erg + V + nom + loc   [-reflexive]

In a localistic system the directional locatives as well as the stative locatives are applied to abstract locative domains. With directional locatives the domain of dynamic affective verbs (process experiential) and the domain of transfer of property verbs (process benefactive) become directional locatives, as in sentences (27-28).

(27) She /learned /Greek /from John.   Process
      loc + V + nom + abl
(28) John /received /a letter /from her.   Process
      loc + V + nom + abl

When ergative is added to the directional structure which contains a nominative moving from ablative Source to locative Goal, the Agent (ergative) may be coreferential with either Source or Goal (1971:131), resulting in the distribution of erg as a feature on abl or on loc, as in sentences (29-30).

(29) John /sold /the book /to Mary.   Action
      erg=abl + V + nom + loc
(30) Mary /bought /the book /from John.   Action
      erg=loc + V + nom + abl

4.3 Anderson's verb types. The verb types in the Anderson model are characterized in terms of four cases, namely ergative, nominative, locative, and ablative. But since the locative case is used both as a stative locative and a Goal locative, the system is equivalent to a five case localistic system consisting of Agent, Object, Location, Source and Goal.

Basic verb types are developed with the nominative and ergative cases but differ from other case systems in that nominative is an obligatory case. Stative locative verb types are developed by adding the Locative case and directional locative verb types are developed by using a combination of the Ablative (Source) case and the Locative (Goal) case.

4.3.1 Basic verb types. Basic verb types are [-locative] and require only the nominative and ergative cases. These basic verb types can be compared to the basic verb types of any other nonlocalistic model, since only the Agent and Object are involved. What makes Anderson's treatment different is the requirement that every case frame must contain the nominative case.

Anderson assumes that 'verbs and adjectives are categorically identical' (1971:38) and he distinguishes them from each other by the [± stative] feature which controls the introduction of the copula *be*. If one ignores the syntactic stative feature in Anderson and replaces it with Anderson's distinction between 'notionally stative' verb types [-progressive] and notionally dynamic verbs [+progressive], then Anderson's verb types can profitably be compared with the analyses of other case grammarians. If nominative with a stative verb is represented by Os, if the nominative case with nonstative verbs is represented by O, and if the ergative case is represented by A, then Anderson's verb types can be translated into Fillmore-type case frames, as in Figure 4.4.

Figure 4.4 Basic verb types.

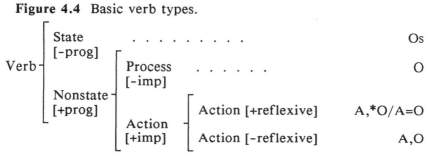

(1) State verbs are one place adjective predicates which do not take the progressive and require only the nominative case. These include *be dead* (1971:60), *be slack* (1971:67), ambient states such as *be hot* (1971:50) with an empty nominative case as subject, and all derived resultative adjectives like *be dipped* (1971:48).

Figure 4.5 Localistic Case matrix (Anderson 1971)

Verb types	Basic types	Locative		Directional	
		Concrete	Abstract	Concrete	Abstract
1. State	0s be cold be dead be hot (w) be slack	0s,L be in stand L,0s contain include	0s,L belong to be known to L,0s have know	0s,S,G go (=extend) stretch	0s,S,G owe be due to
2. Process	0 die sneeze	0,L	0,L	0,S,G move roll	0,S,G learn receive
3. Action +reflexive	A,0/A=0 be cautious work, iv	A,*0,L/A=0 occupy (agt) remain (agt)	A,*0,L/A=0	A,*0,S,G/A=0 come (agt) go (agt)	A,0*,S,G/A=0 ....
4. Action -reflexive	A,0 be careful kill read	A,0,L keep (agt) contain (agt) plant	A,0,L	A,0,S,G bring send take	A,0,S,G buy give teach

1 0s,S,G are anomalous in combining a state object with directional prepositions.
2 A,0,L verbs are anomalous in combining an activity with stative locative prepositions.

(2) **Process verbs** are one place verbal predicates which take the progressive but do not take the imperative; they require only the nominative case. These include: *die, sneeze* (1971:41), and derived inchoatives such as *slacken,iv* (1971:67). Since weather *it* is represented by an empty nominative case, 'action ambient' verbs, such as *rain, snow*, probably belong to this class. Many transitive causative verbs have intransitive counterparts, such as *change,iv/tv*, *grow,iv/tv*, *open,iv/tv*, in which the intransitive verb forms are 'verbs which refer to the same process without mentioning an Agent' (1971:64). The object undergoing the process is subject of the intransitive but object of the transitive verb. Derived inchoatives have corresponding causatives and form transitive/intransitive pairs such as *slacken,iv/tv* (1971:67). These inchoatives 'express the change of state that the causatives effect' (1971:67). In all such pairings the intransitive form is classified as a process verb.

(3) **Action verbs** are two-place predicates which take both the progressive and the imperative. These include action adjectives in which *be* is interpreted as *act*, such as *be (=act) cautious* (1971:56) and *be (=act) careful* (1971:57), as well as a wide range of action verbs. Under the obligatory O hypothesis the nominative O case does not always appear in the surface structure and its existence in the semantic structure of each verb must be explained and justified.

(3a) **Reflexive action:** Some action verbs are reflexive and the ergative case is coreferential with the nominative case, as in the verb *work* (1971:50), in which 'the Agent operates in some way upon itself'. Nominative, as a covert role, does not appear in the surface structure.

(3b) **Deleted objects:** Some intransitive/transitive pairs 'result merely from the deletion of the object' (1971:67), including *paint, dress, drink*. These verbs are transitive in the semantic structure since they contain both ergative and nominative cases but, since they are subject to an optional object deletion rule, they may appear without an object in the surface structure.

4.3.2 Double O case frames. Despite Fillmore's (1968:24) one-instance-per-clause principle which states that 'no case category appears more than once', Anderson suggests that two nominative cases may occur in nominal clauses such as *He was president*, with the case frame Os-Os, and *He became president*, with the case frame O-O. The causative parallel to these verbs is represented by such verbs as *appoint, elect*, which are classed as A-O-O (1971:76). In his later writings on case grammar, Anderson still holds that there are reasons 'for allowing in a single proposition just two of just one specific case relation (namely, nominative)' (1977:38) and there are reasons 'to allow up to two instances per proposition of just nom' (1977:54). Among the examples given in that work are similarity predicates such as *be similar to, resemble, be like*.

4.3.3 Locative verb types. Locative verb types (Chapter 6) are the concrete [+locative, -directional] verbs in which the locative case is used with the ergative and nominative cases. The possible case frames include State Os-L, Process O-L, and Action A-O-L in which L (loc) represents a stative locative phrase marked with the stative locative prepositions, *in, at, on.*

(1) State locative verbs (Os,L) are notionally stative verbs with the locative case added. These include *be at, be in, be on* (1971:85) and *be* + past participle followed by a locative phrase such as *be situated in, be located in.* Flip state verbs such as *contain, include* (1971:89) occur with locative as subject.

(2) Process locative verbs (O,L) are notionally dynamic verbs with stative locative phrases. No examples are given by Anderson but, if aspectual verbs such as *keep, remain* (1971:81) are classed as action locatives, there should be a corresponding process use with inanimate subjects as in *the book remained on the shelf.*

(3) Action locative verbs (A,O,L) are action verbs accompanied by stative locative phrases. The examples are actions derived from state locative predications such as *occupy, plant, contain, strew* (1971:95). The sentence *John planted trees in the garden* could be interpreted as *John caused it to come about that the garden was planted with trees* which would help to explain the common use of stative and not directional prepositions with verbs like *place, put.*

4.3.4 Directional verb types. Directional verbs (Chapter 8) are [+locative, +directional] and use both the ablative–Source and locative–Goal cases. Although Source and Goal may occur alone, the other case is always implied (1971:20); directional expressions that refer to the whole path are listed as loc on abl (1971:170) such as *along, across, around, through.* Possible case frames include State Os-S-G, Process O-S-G, and Action A-O-S-G.

(1) State directional (Os,S,G): Directional prepositions with stative verbs seem contradictory, yet Source and Goal prepositions are common with verbs of extension such as *stretch, extend* (1971:125) and the verb *run* in *Route 95 runs to Richmond.*

(2) Process directional (O,S,G): Process directional verbs denote motion from Source to Goal. Typical verbs are the intransitives *roll, move, come, go* (1971:121) when used with inanimate subjects, as in *The ball rolled from Mary to Jane.*

(3) Action directional verbs (A,O,S,G): Action directional verbs use erg and nom with loc and abl cases. Agent may be coreferential with another case. Examples are *come* and *go* with A = O and *bring, send, take, move* where A does not equal O (1971:121).

4.4 Localism applied. In a localistic system the basic verb types formed from Agent (ergative) and Object (nominative) are the same as in a nonlocalistic system. But in the domains that reach beyond these basic verb types all verbs without exception are described by analogy with physical location. The stative as well as the directional locative case frames developed to describe spatial location and direction are used abstractly to describe all other domains, particularly the experiential and benefactive domains.

4.4.1 Abstract location. The abstract locative verb types given in Anderson's Chapter 7 are [+locative, -directional] verbs used in an abstract sense for domains other than physical location. State experiential (1971:100) and state benefactive (1971:107) verbs are described with the same cases that are used to describe concrete location. The locative case is used in combination with the nominative case. Some verbs have the case frame Os-L with the nominative case as subject but other verbs, by Anderson's permutation rule, have the case frame L-Os with the locative case as subject.

(1) State experiential verbs: There are stative verbs which take neither the progressive nor the imperative and deal with the experiential domains of sensation, emotion, and cognition. The experiencer in whom the experience resides is marked with the locative or L case, generally animate. The exterior object which constitutes the objective content of, or the stimulus for, the experience is marked with the nominative or O case.

(1a) Cognitive verbs: State experiential verbs of cognition with an L subject and an O direct object include *be sure*, *be familiar with*, *believe*, *know*, *think*, and *understand*, while the verbs of cognition with O subject and L indirect object include *be known to* and *seem*, as in sentences (31-32).

(31) Many people /know /the truth.   L subject
     loc + V + nom
(32) The truth /is known to /many people.   O subject
     nom + V + loc

(1b) Emotional verbs: State experiential verbs of emotion with L subject and O object include *be fond of*, *be pleased with*, *hate*, *like*, *love*; verbs of emotion with O subject and L indirect object include *be pleasing to*. State experiential verbs derived from psych movement verbs should be included, such as: *be amusing*, *be amazing*, *be boring*, *be surprising*, as in sentences (33-34).

(33) The audience /liked /the play.   L subject
     loc + V + nom
(34) The play /was pleasing to /the audience.   O subject
     nom + V + loc

(1c) Sensation verbs: Verbs of sensation are not illustrated by Anderson in this chapter but sensation adjectives such as *be cold* (=feel cold) occur with L coreferential with O subject (1971:96). Verbs of sensation with O subjects are suggested by the pairs *see* (L subject) and *look* (O subject) or *hear* (L subject) and *sound* (O subject) (1971:149). The sensation verb types *feel, look, smell, sound, taste,* take an O subject and L object when followed by an adjective or *like* phrase, as in sentences (35-36).

> (35) John /is (=feels) cold.   L subject
>   loc=nom + V
> (36) The music /sounds good /to me.   O subject
>   nom + V + loc

(2) State benefactive verbs: There are stative verbs which denote possession (1971:117). The possessor is the locative case and the object possessed is the nominative case. These verbs may take either the nom case or loc case as subject. Verbs with L subject include *have, own, possess*; verbs with an O subject include *belong to*, or the structure *be* + possessive adjective, as in sentences (37-38).

> (37) John /owns /a car.   L subject
>   loc + V + nom
> (38) The car /belongs to /John   O subject
>   nom + V + loc

4.4.2 Abstract direction. The abstract directional verbs given in Anderson's Chapter 9 are [+locative, +directional] verbs used in an abstract sense for domains other than that of physical motion. Nonstative experiential and benefactive (1971:129) verbs are described with the same cases used for physical motion, namely, the locative-Goal and ablative-Source cases. All nonbasic semantic domains are interpreted by analogy with the motion verbs as having a common underlying structure (1971:131) in which nom is the moving object which moves in some way from ablative-Source to locative-Goal. The Agent case may be coreferential with any of the other three cases, Object, Source, or Goal.

(1) Nonstative experiential verbs: Process experiential verbs take the progressive but not the imperative; action experiential verbs take both the progressive and the imperative. These verbs deal with sensation, emotion, and cognition. Action experiential verbs include the verbs of communication (1971:144) which involve a speaker, the hearer, and what is said.

(1a) Cognitive verbs: Process verbs of cognition use the common cases nom, loc, and abl; action verbs add erg to the structure. The contrast is illustrated in the pair cited by Anderson (1971:138), *learn* (process) and *teach* (action), as in sentences (39-40).

(39) Mary /learned /French /from John.   G subject
    loc + V + nom + abl
(40) John /taught /Mary /French.   S subject
    erg=abl + V + loc + nom

(1b) Emotive verbs: No examples of nonstative verbs of emotion are given by Anderson. However, the psych movement verbs which appear in Anderson (1971:104,106) in present and past participle forms are candidates for process and action emotion verbs. These verbs include *amaze, amuse, annoy, gratify, please, surprise*. The direct object is the experiencer or locative-goal. In process verbs the subject is the stimulus for the experience and is labelled as ablative Source. But if the subject is acting intentionally the subject is both Agent and Source (erg on abl). The problem then arises: where is the obligatory nom case? One possible solution is that the subject is nominative in both process and action verbs and coreferential with the other cases, as in sentences (41-42).

(41) The thunder /annoyed /the baby.   O=S
    abl=nom + V + loc
(42) John (deliberately) /annoyed /the baby.   A=O=S
    erg=abl=nom + V + loc

(1c) Sensation verbs: Anderson (1971:148) describes the process and action verbs relating to the five senses very tentatively. Presumably the sense verbs *feel, hear, see, smell, taste* have action variants as evidenced in the pairs *see /look at, hear /listen to*. Anderson, in a discussion he regards as 'rather inconclusive' (1971:149), interprets experiencer as locative-Goal, the stimulating object as ablative-Source. For verbs such as *smell* he suggests that the noun *smell* (nominative) is lexicalized into the verb so that *smell* = 'receive the smell from' as in the sentence *John* (Goal) *smelled* (nom-lexicalized) *the rose* (Source). When the action is intentional the analysis is the same except that now an Agent is coreferential with the Locative-Goal case in subject position, as in sentences (43-44).

(43) John (unintentionally) /smelled /the rose.   *O,S,G
    loc + V (O-lex) + abl
(44) John (intentionally) /smelled /the rose.   A,*O,S,*G
    erg=loc + V (O-lex) + abl

(1d) Communication verbs: Verbs of communication require a speaker, a hearer, and what is said. In a localistic system the speaker is both Agent and Source, the hearer is the Goal, and what is said is the Object (1971:144). These verbs include *ask, explain, mention, say, speak, talk, tell*, as in sentence (45).

(45) John /spoke /a few words /to Mary.   A,O,*S,G
    erg=abl + V + nom + loc

(2) Nonstative benefactive verbs: Process benefactive verbs take the progressive but not the imperative; action benfactive verbs take both the progressive and the imperative. These verbs deal with transfer of property. In a localistic system the nominative is the Object transferred, the ablative is the Source, and the locative is the Goal. Agent is the instigator of the transfer and is often coreferential with either Source or Goal.'Either locative phrase (loc or abl) can be marked as ergative' (1971:129).

(2a) Process benfactives: These verbs involve no Agent but are concerned with the unintentional receipt or loss of property, such as *acquire, receive* (1971:140) with Goal as subject and *lose* with Source as subject. With verbs of loss the Goal case is unknown   and is deleted. Some verbs, such as *benefit* = 'receive benefit from', have a lexicalized nominative case, as in sentences (46-48).

(46) Mary /received /a book /from John.	G subject
loc + V + nom + abl	
(47) John /lost /his wallet.	S subject
abl + V + nom	
(48) John /benefited /from the change.	O-lex
loc + V (nom) + abl	

(2b) Action benefactives: These verbs involve an Agent. The Agent may be with Source as in *give, lend, sell, send,* or with Goal, as in *borrow, buy, get, obtain, rob, steal.* Verbs like *help* are interpreted as 'reduced clauses' (1971:143) with *help* = 'give help to' with nominative lexicalized. The verb *blame* is also an action benefactive but has an overt nom, as in sentences (49-52).

(49) Mary /bought /the book /from John.	A,O,S,*G
erg=loc + V + nom + abl	
(50) John /sold /the book /to Mary.	A,O,*S,G
erg=abl + V + nom + loc	
(51) Mary /helped /everybody.	A,*O,*S,G
erg=abl + V (nom) + loc	
(52) Harry /blamed /the mess /on Fred.	A,O,*S,G
erg=abl + V + nom + loc	

(2c) Directional state benefactives: These directional state benefactive verbs require Source and Goal cases, similar to the state locatives with the Os-S-G frame such as *owe, be due to.* (1971:140). In a nonlocalistic system these verbs present a problem as they seem to require two benefactive cases, as in sentences (53-54).

(53) John /owes /me /a dollar.	S subject
abl + V + loc + nom	
(54) A dollar /is due /to me /from John.	O subject
nom + V + loc + abl	

4.5 Derivation and covert roles. In Anderson's model the semantic formation rules add syntactic and semantic features to an initial V to generate each lexical predicate. There is no general derivational system to relate similar entries and reduce the number of entries in the lexicon. But Anderson's careful consideration of different forms of the verb indicates the need for a derivational system similar to Chafe's system.

In the area of covert roles Anderson's system is better developed than other systems due to the adoption of the obligatory O hypothesis. If the nominative Object case is present in every deep structure, then the analyst must explain what happens to the O case when it does not appear in the surface structure. This leads naturally to a theory of covert roles.

4.5.1 Derivational system. Although Anderson himself has no derivational system, his investigation of all forms of a verb leads to his exemplifying each of the derivational processes proposed in Chafe (1970), namely, the inchoative, resultative, causative, and decausative derivations.

(1) Inchoative: The inchoative is a derivational unit which, when added to a state verb, produces a process verb. Anderson illustrates the inchoative derivation in the pair *slack/slacken* (1971:67), where the *-en* form is a verbalizing suffix which expresses a change in the state described by the adjective, as in sentences (55-56).

(55) The rope /was slack.   State
   nom + V
(56) The rope /slackened.   Process
   nom + V

(2) Resultative: The resultative is a derivational unit which, when added to a process verb, produces a state verb. Anderson encounters resultative forms in his discussion of the long and short passives (1971:47). Long passives are those forms in which the downgraded subject appears in a *by* phrase; short passives are those in which no *by* phrase occurs. According to Anderson, 'a clause containing a short passive is ambiguous between stative and nonstative, whereas the long passive is unambiguously nonstative' (1971:47). In short passives 'the nonstative version involves a deleted ergative phrase; the stative one is like a simple adjective clause in lacking such' (1971:47). This simple adjective form is a resultative adjective derived from an action or process verb with the meaning 'state as a result of a process' and implies a resultative derivation, as in sentences (57-58).

(57) The lights /were dimmed (=in down position). State
   nom + V
(58) The lights /were dimmed /(by the driver). Action
   nom + V + erg

The ambiguity of the short passive form noted by Anderson is a significant fact about English that is often neglected. Given the statistical fact that the *by* phrase is deleted about 90% of the time, many forms that have traditionally been described as passives are not passives in meaning but derived resultative adjectives.

(1) In the passive interpretation the syntactic structure is NP + V [+Passive]. The passive verb is formed by the addition of the elements *be* + *-en* in which *-en* is an inflectional affix used to form the past participle. Whenever this is the passive of an action verb, an Agent is implied and the verb form may occur with the progressive. In the progressive sentence *the lights were being dimmed* the verb is unambiguously passive. The passive participle fails all the normal adjective tests. It cannot occur with the intensifier *very* nor can it occur after the verb *seem* without an intervening *to be*.

(2) In the nonpassive interpretation the syntactic structure is NP + *be* + Adjective. This adjective is derived from the verb by the addition of a derivational suffix *-en* which has the meaning 'state-as-a-result-of-a-process'. Since this adjective represents a state it is not used with the progressive and it passes all the normal adjective tests. It occurs freely with the intensifier *very* and it may occur after the verb *seem* without an intervening *to be*. Where syntactic tests are inconclusive the ambiguity of the syntactic structure can only be resolved by the meaning of the form in particular contexts.

(3) Causative: The causative is a derivational unit which, when added to a process verb, produces an action verb. In developing his model Anderson introduces the causative feature to explain the difference between certain intransitive /transitive pairs, such as *slacken,iv* /*slacken,tv*, *change,iv* /*change,tv*, *die* /*kill*, the pairs formed from the verbs *blacken*, *decrease*, *increase*, *age*, and phonologically related forms like *lie* /*lay*. In these pairs the process verb is 'the nonverb root intransitive equivalent of causatives, they express the change of state that the causatives effect' (1971:67). This causative feature is also applied to directional verbs such as *move,iv* /*move,tv* (1971:121). In all these examples, the intransitive forms are 'verbs which refer to the same process (as the transitive) without mentioning an Agent' (1971:64). The transitive form, an action verb, is derived from the intransitive form, a process verb, by the addition of the causative feature which adds an Agent to the structure. The direction of derivation is confirmed in the work of Lyons (1968:397), who also claims that the transitive form in these pairs is derived from the intransitive by a causative derivation, as in sentences (59-60).

(59) The landscape /changed.   Process
     nom + V
(60) They /changed /the landscape.   Action
     erg + V + nom

(4) Decausative: The decausative, called deactivative in Chafe (1970), is a derivational unit added to an action-process verb to produce a process verb. Although Anderson recognizes the unique character of these derived process verbs, he states that 'the derivation of such clauses remains something of a mystery' (1971:69). Some examples cited in Anderson are *sell*, *polish*, *wash*, *iron*, *act*, as in sentences (61-62).

> (61) John /polished /the floor.   Action
>   erg + V + nom
> (62) The floor /polishes easily.   Process
>   nom + V

The verb pairs *wash,iv* /*wash,tv* are not related to each other in exactly the same way as *change,iv* /*change,tv*. Anderson notes that 'a clue to this is provided by the obligatory presence of an adverbial with the V which expresses either a qualification of it or a generalization about its feasibility' (1971:68). Lyons (1968:397) suggests that these pseudointransitive verbs are derived from the transitive by a backwards derivation, whereas true transitive verbs are derived from the intransitive form by the causative derivation.

4.5.2 Covert roles. The adoption of the obligatory O hypothesis forces Anderson into a deeper analysis of semantic structures and his text contains examples of deletable roles, lexicalized roles, and coreferential roles. But these examples of covert roles are not united into a coherent theory.

(1) Deletable roles: Deletable roles are those roles which are part of the deep structure but which sometimes occur and sometimes do not occur in the surface structure. In Anderson's model deletable roles occur under the deletable object rule and also in the treatment of the Location, Source, and Goal cases.

In discussing intransitive /transitive pairings of a slightly different kind, Anderson observes that 'there are a large number of surface intransitives that result merely from the deletion of the object' (1971:67) such as *drink*, *kill*, *paint*, *undress*, *change* (for dinner). Since object deletion is a surface phenomenon, it would seem that the deep structure remains unchanged and all such verbs should have objects in the deep structure. Put another way, all verbs that occur sometimes with an object and sometimes without an object are to be classified as containing an object in deep structure but marked as 'deletable object' verbs, as in Fillmore's work (1968:29). Transitive verbs which occur with deleted objects are illustrated in sentences (63-64).

> (63) Egbert /is painting /(something).   Action
>   erg + V +(nom)   (Without object)
> (64) Egbert /is painting /landscapes.   Action
>   erg + V + nom   (With object)

Anderson recognizes that the Locative, Source, and Goal cases may also be subject to surface deletion. In discussing stative locative verbs he states 'the verbs chosen all strongly select loc; i.e., *allowing for deletion*, loc is necessarily part of the frame into which such verbs are inserted' (1971:83). In discussing directional locative verbs he states 'both locational phrases (Source and Goal) may be deleted' (1971:121). Source and Goal always occur in pairs, with the result that if either case is explicit 'the other phrase is implicit' (1971:120). Source and Goal are both present in the deep structure but either or both may be deleted from the surface structure.

(2) Coreferential roles: Coreferential roles are two roles assigned to the same surface NP. The lower ranking role is not evident in the surface structure. These coreferential roles are represented in Anderson as one NP with two or more case labels.

(2a) erg on nom: The Agent is coreferential with the Object case in action reflexive clauses (1971:49) such as *work, be cautious*. The case frame for these verbs is A,*O /A=O. In motion verbs with animate subjects like *come, go*, 'nom is marked as erg' (1971:121), since the subject is both Agent and moving Object. The case frame for these verbs is A,*O,S,G /A=O.

(2b) erg on loc: The Agent is coreferential with the Locative case (1971:99) in sentences such as *his regiment contained the attack*. By analogy with *the box contained the toys*, the *regiment* is at the same time the instigator of the action and forms the containment which holds back the *attack*. The case frame is A,O,*L /A=L.

(2c) erg on loc-Goal: The Agent is coreferential with the Goal case (1971:130) in abstract directional verbs like *buy, get, rob, steal*. The acting subject (Agent) is also the party (Goal) to which the property is transferred. The case frame is A,O,S,*G /A=G.

(2d) erg on abl: The Agent is coreferential with Source (1971:130) in abstract directional verbs such as *give, lend, sell, send*. The acting subject (Agent) is also the party (Source) from which the property is transferred. The case frame is A,O,*S,G /A=S.

(2e) loc on nom: The Locative case is coreferential with the Object case (1971:96) in certain experiential adjectives, called reflexive locatives, in which the adjective indicates a sensation as in *be (=feels) cold*. The case frame for these verbs is Os,*L /O=L.

(2f) abl on loc-Goal: The Source case is coreferential with the Goal (1971:170) in phrases that indicate a complete path such as *along, across, around, through*. The case frame is A,O,S,*G /S=G.

(3) Lexicalized roles: Lexicalized roles do not appear in surface structure because they are lexicalized into the verb. Anderson treats these under the name of 'reduced clauses' (1971:143); 'the underlying nominative phrase is deleted and its lexical content is carried superficially by the verb' (1971:143) as in *help* = 'give help to' with the frame A,*O,*S,G /O-lex,A=S. Other examples are *advise, assure, guide*. The object is lexicalized with A=G verbs such as *benefit*.

4.6 Evaluation of the Anderson model. The case grammar model as proposed by Anderson (1971) in *The Grammar of Case* was an important model in the early history of case grammar that offered significant challenges to the Fillmore model. Inspired by the distinction that Fillmore had made between surface grammatical functions like subject and object and the set of underlying case relationships, Anderson reintroduces the localistic theory and presents the resulting localistic case system within the context of a dependency grammar. This model differs from previous models in (1) the semantic structure, (2) the list of cases, (3) the resulting verb types, (4) the methods for relating verb entries, and (5) the use of covert roles.

4.6.1 Semantic structure. The dependency grammar sets up a new kind of semantic structure in which the case relationships are directly dependent upon a central verb. Verbs are subcategorized by features and then cases are added to the verb in accordance with features generated in the verb itself.

The advantage of this dependency model is that it clearly emphasizes the fact that semantics is the central system of the grammar and that, within semantic structure, the verb is the central element. Since cases are introduced by features first generated in the verb, Anderson's model is a semantic valence system in which cases are elements that in number and kind are directly controlled by the meaning of the verb. Anderson has already adopted the principle, that was to be expressed much later by Fillmore (1977), that the theory of cases offers a semantic valence description of the verbs and adjectives of a language.

The disadvantages of the dependency model as developed by Anderson involve the mixing of syntactic and semantic features in the formation of syntactic structures. Given a dependency model, one would expect that the semantic formation rules, both the subcategorization rules (SRs) that determine verb types and the dependency rules (DRs) that add cases to verbs, would be totally independent of the transformational rules (TRs) that convert semantic structures into surface structures. But this is not the case in the Anderson model. The [+stative] feature appears early as a syntactic feature which introduces the copula. It is used to distinguish adjectives from verbs. This use of the [+stative] feature obscures the semantic stative versus nonstative distinction and makes it necessary later on to speak of 'notionally stative' (Anderson 1971:94) predicates as opposed to syntactically stative predicates. The lack of a semantic stative feature makes it difficult to distinguish semantically stative verbs like *have, own,* from semantically nonstative verbs like *acquire, lose,* when these verbs have the same number and kind of cases. Whatever gain there is to the model from a syntactic stative feature which distinguishes verbs from adjectives is matched by the loss of a semantic stative feature which would be able to distinguish notionally stative verbs and adjectives [-progressive] from notionally nonstative verbs and adjectives [+progressive].

4.6.2 Case system. The localistic case system in Anderson offers a new challenge to case grammarians. The question at issue is whether all case relationships can be described in terms of location and direction. These terms are used in their primary sense for the description of concrete physical location and movement and are applied analogously in their abstract sense to other domains such as the affective and possessive domains. A localistic case system is obviously a notational variant of the nonlocal systems, since one can be easily translated into the other, but it raises deeper questions as to the psychological primacy of these spatial relations, the coherence and completeness of a localistic case system to which no additions are possible, and the explanatory value of the system with regard to the use of similar case markings or prepositions.

Anderson proposes a four case system consisting of nominative, ergative, locative, and ablative cases, but he uses the locative case in two meanings, giving him reductively a five case system. The nonlocal cases, nominative and ergative, are used apart from the local cases to describe basic verb types. Among the local cases, locative is used for both concrete and abstract stative predicates and locative-Goal and ablative-Source are used for both concrete and abstract directional predicates. The five case system is similar to Gruber's 1965 localistic system and Anderson applies it with great consistency.

4.6.3 Verb types. When verbs are described in terms of a local set of cases, the case frames will appear to be different but these cases can easily be translated into nonlocal terms. What makes the verb types in Anderson's model distinctive is the adoption of an obligatory O hypothesis which states that the nominative case is an underlying neutral theme in the case frame of every verb. Gruber (1965), in the model used by Jackendoff (1972), had also proposed a model in which an obligatory underlying theme case must occur in every case frame.

The obligatory O hypothesis, though it occurs regularly in localistic case systems, is not a necessary condition for localism. Localist case systems deal with a set of local cases. The acceptance of the obligatory O hypothesis is a tactical decision regarding the way in which cases are to be used. Consequently, localists need not adopt obligatory O frames and nonlocalists can adopt an obligatory O hypothesis without using local cases.

The adoption of the obligatory O hypothesis has a profound effect on the syntagmatic arrangements of cases. If there is an Object case in every case frame there is no possibility of zero place predicates as proposed in Chafe's ambient verbs which deal with the weather. Also, if there is an Object case in every case frame there is no possibility of an action verb that is not at the same time a process. This hypothesis wipes out Chafe's line of action predicates and forces the investigator to a deeper analysis. Since there is an Object in every case frame, an explanation must be given as to why this Object case does not appear in the surface structure and this involves the use of deletable, lexicalized, or coreferential roles.

4.6.4 Derivation. Anderson proposes no derivational system to link verbs derived from the same morphological root or to link verbs derived from different roots which form suppletive sets like *die /kill*. But his careful study of different forms of each verb leads him to the same sets of forms which Chafe has described as related by the inchoative, resultative, causative, and decausative derivations.

Although Chafe's derivational system was proposed in a non-localistic context, it is equally applicable to localistic systems. Chafe's derivations predict a closer relation between state, process, and action-process, with only a dubious relation to action verbs. Anderson's verb classification, through the obligatory O hypothesis, strengthens the first three verb types while eliminating the action verbs and fits more perfectly into a derivational system.

Chafe's derivational system is language specific and names rather than explains the derivational units, but there is an alternative approach in generative semantics which uses abstract predicates. Process verbs indicating change of state are derived from state predicates by the addition of an abstract predicate COME ABOUT and action-process verbs are derived from process verbs by addition of an abstract predicate CAUSE. This system is a unidirectional system and factors out universal underlying predicates like COME ABOUT and CAUSE. The generative semantics approach is compatible with Chafe's derivational system but differs from it in being unidirectional, language universal, with the state form always as basic. In this system resultative and decausative derivations are explained by the subtraction of the abstract predicates COME ABOUT and CAUSE, respectively. Either system would be compatible with Anderson's model.

4.6.5 Covert roles. Given Anderson's obligatory O hypothesis and given the fact that the obligatory Object case occurs in the surface structure with some predicates only part of the time and never occurs in the surface structure with other predicates, it is not surprising to find that Anderson uses deletable, coreferential, and lexicalized roles. In this context the analyst must reexamine any form which seems to lack the Object case in order to explain the apparent absence of this obligatory case from the semantic structure.

There are no zero place predicates. For Chafe's ambient verbs which use weather *it* as a subject, the pronoun *it*, which 'covers the total environment not just some object within it' (Chafe 1971:101), is the obligatory O case. For Chafe's action completable verbs, which occur sometimes with and sometimes without a direct object, the obligatory O case exists in the deep structure but is a deletable role in surface structure. For action intransitive verbs such as *work* or verbs of motion which occur with animate subjects, Anderson uses coreferential roles with the obligatory O case most often coreferential with Agent. For those cases which occur as lexicalized roles, Anderson recognizes 'reduced clauses' with a lexicalized Object case in verbs such as *help, advise*.

Unique features in Anderson's model include the absence of the Instrumental case and the relaxation of the one-instance-per-clause principle in predicate nominals.

Instrument began as an essential case in Fillmore (1968) and continues to be essential in any Fillmorean list of cases. The notion of Instrument was weakened in Chafe, who lists it as an essential case but one which is not matched by any selectional feature in the verb. Instrument becomes a modal option with action-process verbs. Anderson strongly rejects Instrument as a propositional case, stating that it is never necessary 'to allow for a distinct underlying kind of locational or instrumental case type' (1971:171). If the so-called instrument occurs in subject position, it is an Agent; if it occurs in direct object position, as with the verb *use*, it is an Object; it if occurs in a *with* phrase, it is a manner adverbial outside of the case frame.

Predicate nominals have always been a difficult problem for case grammarians, given the restriction to one instance of a case per clause. Fillmore is hesitant with NP + BE + NP structures (1968:84) and suggests that more than one case may be involved with names such as 'essive' or 'translative'. For structures with similarity predicates such as *resemble*, he later (1971:39) adds that the subject and object should have different cases but suggests no way of characterizing them. Chafe's solution (1970:143) is that the second noun becomes the predicate by a zero marked predicativizer derivation. The resulting predicate then requires only a single noun, its subject. Anderson (1971:76), beginning with causatives which have double objects such as *elect*, postulates that these are derived causatively from underlying NP + BE + NP structures. This would permit state verbs with the frame Os-Os, process verbs with the frame O-O, and action-process verbs with the frame A-O-O. Given the similarity of the two nouns involved and the occasional agreement markings found on predicate nouns, Anderson finds this solution 'not too implausible' (1971:77). Later, in 1977, he strongly insists that the one-instance-per-clause principle must be relaxed to allow two occurrences of just one case, the nominative.

4.7 Conclusion. Anyone who studies Anderson's model seriously will find that it offers substantial challenges to contemporary case models. Should cases be described in localistic or nonlocalistic terms? Is there an underlying obligatory theme object in every case frame? Will the localistic system of cases be necessary and sufficent for the classification of all the verbs of a language? Is this localistic system universal enough to form a descriptive framework for all languages? Can a case system exist without an Instrument case? Is it necessary to relax the one-instance-per-clause principle to explain predicate nominals? Whatever the answers that may be found to these questions Anderson's model forces the analyst to think and choose.

Exercise 4. Write the case frame for the main verb in each of the following sentences. The five cases available are A-O-L-S-G, where A = erg, O = nom, L = loc, S = abl, and G = goal-loc. For the nominative case use Os in notionally stative sentences and O elsewhere. Mark totally covert roles with an asterisk (*) and add the explanation after the case frame, as O-lex or A = O. List the case chosen as subject in first position.

1. Egbert was careful with the vase. _____

2. Egbert was cautious. _____

3. John is (=feels) cold. _____

4. Egbert is dead. _____

5. It is hot (in this room). _____

6. The compass belongs to me. _____

7. Mary bought the book from John. _____

8. The box contains the apples. _____

9. Egbert died. _____

10. John has gone to London. _____

11. We keep the money in a box. _____

12. Many people know the truth. _____

13. John owes me a dollar. _____

14. Egbert read the book. _____

15. He remained in London. _____

16. The ball rolled from Mary to Jane. _____

17. John spoke a few words to Mary. _____

18. The statue is standing on a plinth. _____

19. The fog stretches from London to Brighton. _____

20. John taught Mary Greek. _____

21. Egbert worked hard. _____

Anderson 1971 Lexicon. The Anderson 1971 lexicon is a collection of 80 verbs with the case frames as far as they can be determined from Anderson's *The Grammar of Case*. Totally covert roles, both lexicalized roles and coreferential roles, are marked with an asterisk (*). Verbs in their ergative interpretation are marked as agentive (agt).

abound in	Os,L	kill	A,O
abound with	L,Os	know	L,Os
be + N	Os,Os	learn	G,O,S
be + poss	Os,L	lend	A,O,*S,G
be careful with	A,O	leave	A,*O,S,G
be cautious	A,*O	lie,iv	Os,L
be cold	Os	like	L,Os
be (=feel) cold	Os,*L	march,iv	A,*O,S,G
be dead	Os	move,iv	O,S,G
be due to	Os,S,G	move,iv (agt)	A,*O,S,G
be due from	G,Os,S	move,tv	A,O,S,G
be hot (w)	Os	occupy	Os,L
be in	Os	occupy (agt)	A,*O,L
be known to	Os,L	owe	S,Os,G
be pleased with	L,Os	own	L,Os
be pleasing to	O,L	possess	L,Os
be slack	Os	plant	A,O,L
be strewn on	Os,L	read	A,O
be strewn with	L,Os	receive	O,S,G
become + N	O,O	remain (agt)	A,*O,L
belong to	Os,L	roll,iv	O,S,G
borrow	A,O,S,*G	roll,tv (agt)	A,O,S,G
bring	A,O,S,G	say	A,O,*S,G
build	A,O	sell	A,O,*S,G
buy	A,O,S,*G	send	A,O,*S,G
change,iv	O,S,G	slacken,iv	O
change,tv	A,O,S,G	slacken,tv	A,O
come (agt)	A,*O,S,G	smell	S,*Os,G
contain	L,Os	sneeze	O
contain (agt)	A,O,*L	speak	A,O,*S,G
die	O	stand	Os,L
elect	A,O,O	stretch	Os,S,G
fall	O,S,G	strew	A,O,L
get	A,O,S,*G	take	A,O,S,*G
give	A,O,*S,G	tell	A,O,*S,G
go (=extend)	Os,S,G	teach	A,O,S,G
go (agt)	A,*O,S,G	think	L,Os
have	L,Os	understand	L,Os
help	A,*O,*S,G	walk	A,*O,S,G
keep	A,O,L	work	A,*O

5 Thematic Relations

5.0 Overview. The case-like system of semantic interpretation now called thematic relations was originally introduced by Jeffrey Gruber in *Studies in Lexical Relations* (1965) and later developed in *Functions of the Lexicon in Formal Descriptive Grammars* (1967). These two works were then revised and published under the title *Lexical Structures in Syntax and Semantics* (1976). The system of thematic relations was subsequently developed by Ray Jackendoff in *Semantic Interpretation in Generative Grammar* (1972) and in a later article 'Toward an explanatory semantic representation' in *Linguistic Inquiry* (1976). This system of thematic relations was adopted in Chomsky's *Lectures on Government and Binding* (1982) within the context of the semantic component, or logical form. Jackendoff developed the semantic theory further in *Semantics and Cognition* (1983) and in an article 'The status of thematic relations in linguistic theory' in *Linguistic Inquiry* (1987).

Although Gruber's 1965 thesis was not published until 1976, the original thesis was available to scholars and influenced a lot of work relative to the lexicon, case relations, and the place of semantics in a generative grammar. Working within the context of the standard theory (Chomsky 1965), Gruber states his position as 'a derivational (i.e. generative) semantic theory as opposed to an interpretive one' (1976:1) which concentrates upon 'how the meaning of a kernel sentence and its syntax are related' (1976:1).

Gruber proposes a 'prelexical categorial structure' which is 'deeper than the level of deep structure in syntax' (1976:2). This prelexical structure provides a base for the syntactic structure and at the same time provides the meaning relations between the parts of a sentence. In Gruber's theory of lexical structure, the deeper the syntactic structure is the more semantics will fall within its scope. Within this prelexical structure it is the verb which is the central element. Thus, 'the verb is the principal variable in sentences upon which the syntactic form of a sentence depends' (1976:3). Further, these 'syntactic patterns in a given language are connected to relationships of meaning' (1976:3). Gruber's study therefore deals with the syntactic patterns in sentence structure which are deeper than the level of deep structure and which also give an indication of the semantic structure. The verb is the central element in the structure. Other elements in the structure are noun phrases and prepositional phrases which are given case-like labels associated with particular verbs.

Why should Gruber's work be considered a case grammar? A case grammar model is one that deals with the semantics of a simple sentence. It expresses these semantic relationships in terms of a central verb and a series of case labelled NPs required by the semantic valence of the verb. There is a small list of cases and a set of tactics for using these case roles to express the environments in which a verb occurs. Verbs in the lexicon are related through their case frames and involve the use of deletable, coreferential, and lexicalized case roles.

Gruber's work deals with a prelexical categorial structure which is the basis for both syntactic relationships and semantic relationships within a sentence. The verb is the principal variable upon which the syntax and semantics of a sentence depend. The relationships in a sentence are expressed in terms of this central verb and a series of nouns with case-like labels. The basic case role is the Theme, Fillmore's Object case, which is regarded as 'an obligatory element in every sentence' (1976:38). Other case labels used in conjunction with the Theme are Location (1976:69), Source (1976:78), and Goal (1976:66), to which Agent (1976:157) is added later. Gruber's system then is essentially a five case system consisting of Agent-Theme-Location-Source-Goal, A-O-L-S-G.

These five case roles are used to separate verbs into verb types. In one dimension Gruber classifies verbs as motional, durational, and nondescript (nonmotional, nondurational). In the other dimension he classifies them according to semantic domains as Identificational, Positional, and Possessional. The case system is a localistic one with Location, Source, and Goal used in their concrete meaning to describe positional verbs and in their abstract meaning to describe both possessional and identificational verbs.

Verbs are related to each other through case relationships. For example, the intransitive /transitive forms of the verb *roll* are related as noncausative /causative forms (1976:6); in other words, they differ in that one requires an Agent and the other does not. Coreferential roles are essential to Gruber's analysis for sometimes 'the theme is optionally identified as an Agent' (1976:158). Gruber's use of the incorporation of several lexical categories into a single lexical verb, although it deals primarily with the incorporation of prepositions, opens the way for lexicalized cases. Deletion transformations are also possible within the model, allowing for the possibility of the deletion of some essential case roles from the structure.

With this evidence it is not difficult to understand Anderson's statement that 'we must therefore evaluate the theory of thematic relations as a variant of case grammar' (1977:31). Jackendoff, on the other hand, held that case grammar and thematic relations were two opposing systems. Given a choice between the two systems, he rejects the Fillmore 1968 case model as inadequate to express semantic relationships and adopts Gruber's theory of thematic relations.

According to Jackendoff, the deep and surface structures in Fillmore's 1968 case grammar differ only in word order and the addition of case nodes and case markers. 'The number of NPs in the deep and surface structures is the same; each surface structure noun phrase is assumed to have exactly one deep structure case' (1972:34). The system of thematic relations, however, as proposed by Gruber allows the use of coreferential roles. More than one case label can be applied to the same NP in the surface structure.

It is true that Fillmore does not deal explicitly with coreferential roles in his 1968 model but deletable roles are used as in the sentence *Mother is cooking* (1968:29). If some case roles are deletable then, in those sentences in which the object is deleted, the number of NPs in the surface structure and in the deep structure are no longer the same. Jackendoff is, however, correct in assuming that an adequate case grammar theory requires coreferential roles. Fillmore adds both coreferential roles and lexicalized roles in his 1971 model.

Jackendoff's stated reasons for preferring the system of thematic relations over case grammar are that: (1) 'it provides a way of unifying various uses of the same morphological verb' (1972:33) and (2) it allows us to state certain generalizations for some transformational rules such as Passive, Reflexive, and Equi NP deletion. As for the first reason, it was Fillmore's stated objective to unify different uses of the same verb, such as the intransitive /transitive uses of the verb *break* and the use of this verb with and without the Instrument case. The main difference in unifying uses of the verb comes from the fact that Fillmore did not include the possibility of coreferential roles.

Further, Gruber's system is localistic. It applies concrete locative cases to abstract locative use, whereas Fillmore's 1968 system is nonlocalistic with a different kind of generalization. Although Gruber's localist system has an advantage in relating Positional and Possessional uses of the same verb, Fillmore's nonlocalist system has an advantage in keeping concrete locative verbs distinct from the more abstract domains of possession or mental state verbs.

The second reason that Jackendoff offers, namely that certain generalizations about transformations can be stated more easily in terms of thematic relations, is not so much an argument for thematic relations as opposed to case grammar but an argument for a case grammar /thematic relation approach as opposed to a mere syntactic approach. To whatever extent thematic relations is used to explain transformations, case grammar also can explain them. For example, Fillmore explicitly treats Passive as a subject choice option with transitive verbs which does not change the case relationships. Similar analyses in case grammar could apply to the reflexive rule in which an NP in surface structure is reflexivized without changing the underlying case relationships. In dealing with the semantic relationships, either case grammar or thematic relations will have observable syntactic correlates.

Jackendoff adopts Gruber's system of case-like relations and calls them 'thematic relations' (1972:29), based on the fact that there is an obligatory Theme in every sentence. The other case relations in Jackendoff's system are the same as Gruber's, namely, Location, Source, and Goal (1972:32), to which Agent is later added (1972:32).

Jackendoff arranges these five cases in a thematic hierarchy (1972:43) in the following order: (1) Agent, (2) Location, Source, and Goal, and (3) Theme. He then proceeds to use this thematic hierarchy to explain the passive (1972:43), the reflexive (1972:148), as well as the Equi NP deletion rule (1972:214). As far as the case system is concerned Jackendoff remains faithful to Gruber's original analysis. He clarifies Gruber's system without changing any of the essential details.

The principal difference between Gruber and Jackendoff is the way in which the system is used. Gruber uses thematic relations in a generative semantics system in which these relations are specified at a level deeper than Chomsky's level of deep structure. Jackendoff uses thematic relations in the context of the standard theory as part of the interpretive component. In particular 'the lexical entry of a verb must correlate grammatical and thematic relations' (1972:37).

The lexical entry will contain phonological properties, syntactic properties, and semantic properties. Phonological properties include the phonological form of the verb. Syntactic properties include subcategorization of the verb by selectional features. Semantic properties are given in terms of thematic relations. Subscripts in the syntactic feature are correlated with the subscripts in the semantic representation (1972:40). In simple form the lexical entry for the verb *open,tv* would be given as follows, based upon the analysis of Jackendoff (1972:41). The semantic representation is repeated here to illustrate how case labels are matched with syntactic labels.

/open/
+ V
+ (NP$_1$ ___ NP$_2$)
CAUSE (NP$_1$, CHANGE (NP$_2$, NOT OPEN$_3$ OPEN$_4$))
CAUSE (A$_1$, CHANGE (O$_2$, S$_3$, G$_4$))

Although Jackendoff is faithful to Gruber's list of cases he tends to explain them in terms of abstract predicates. Agent is the subject of the abstract predicate CAUSE and Theme is the subject of the abstract predicate CHANGE. Source and Goal are the initial and final stages of the change (1972:39). When the subscripted cases are correlated with the subscripted NPs of the syntactic structure the verb *open,tv* is described as a verb with Agent as subject and Theme as direct object. In later work Jackendoff (1976) uses the abstract predicates BE, STAY, and GO to represent Gruber's verb types, with the predicates LET and CAUSE to represent the agentive verbs.

5.1 Semantic structure. The grammatical model proposed by Gruber is similar to the standard theory proposed by Chomsky. In the standard theory the base rules, including branching rules, subcategorization rules, and the lexicon, generate the deep structure. Deep structure is the level which is prior to all transformations, at which lexical attachment occurs, and the level which receives a semantic interpretation. In Gruber the branching rules, which are context free

(1976:4), produce a PRELEXICAL CATEGORIAL STRUCTURE which is 'a reflection and representation of the underlying structure of meaning, which is universal' (1976:5). The prelexical structure is then subject to POLYCATEGORIAL LEXICAL ATTACHMENT (1976:4) in which a single lexical item may replace more than one syntactic category. The meaning of this lexical item is semantically specified by its prelexical structure. It is the prelexical categorial structure, a structure deeper than Chomsky's deep structure, which then undergoes semantic interpretation through a SEMANTIC CALCULUS whose function is 'equating or relating nonderivationally connected structures' (1976:2), such as equivalences, implications, and contradictions. Gruber's model is presented in Figure 5.1, adapted from Gruber (1976:5).

Figure 5.1 Gruber's Transformational Model

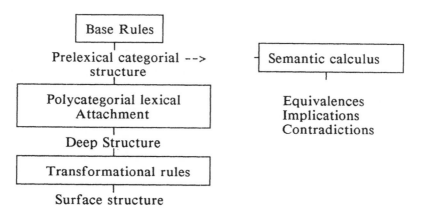

The base rules produce the prelexical categorial structure, a level which is simultaneously the base for syntactic structure and the place where meaning is formalized. Then the process of polycategorial lexical attachment allows a single lexical item to replace several syntactic categories. The replacement process requires the lexical decomposition of surface structure items which are later put together by Gruber's rules of incorporation. The deep structure of this model will then contain some lexical items which were generated directly by the base and some other lexical items, particularly verbs, which were generated by the base as separate categories. Afterwards, the surface structure is derived in the usual way by transformational rules.

5.1.1 Prelexical categorial structure. This model has no need for an interpretive semantic component as described in the standard theory. Part of this interpretation is taken over by the prelexical categorial structure which shows how words are decomposed at a deeper level. The only semantic interpretation needed is to establish equivalences, implications, and contradictions through a semantic calculus. By generating pieces of lexical items rather than whole lexical items and putting them together by polycategorial attachment, many selectional restrictions are already explained.

Evidence for lexical decomposition comes from paraphrases such as *enter* = 'go into'. In Gruber's model what is generated is not the verb *enter* but the verb *go* and the preposition *into* which through lexical attachment become the verb *enter*. But paraphrase must be used with caution. 'All sentences which paraphrase each other do not have the same prelexical structure' (1976:5). They may be reductively the same by the semantic calculus which determines equivalences.

Another kind of evidence for lexical decomposition is found in noncausative /causative variants of the same verb, such as the verb *roll* in *the ball rolled down the hill* (noncausative) and *John rolled the ball down the hill* (causative). Gruber does not believe in homonyms. He would like to consider the verb *roll* as a single verb which is found in both causative and noncausative use (1976:6). The difference between the two uses lies in the fact that in its causative use the verb incorporates the notion of CAUSE.

It is not difficult to see how this theory of incorporation leads naturally to case-like semantic structures. Since most of the elements incorporated are prepositions, or prepositions with a following noun phrase, the prepositions are characterized in their most general form as Locative *in*, *at*, *on*, or as Source and Goal in *from-to* patterns. Once an underlying Theme /Object is postulated as the object which is at a location or which moves from one location to another, Gruber has formed the basis for a localistic case grammar. Later he adds Agent as the subject of CAUSE, which fills out Gruber's five case system of Agent-Theme-Location-Source-Goal. Since the prepositions are generated by the base, their absence from the surface structure is explained by the fact that many prepositions are incorporated into the verb. It is essential to decompose predicates into their prelexical structure in order to reveal the full range of case markings.

According to Gruber, the prelexical structure 'must be set up to adequately characterize the whole set of verbs within a domain' (1976:7). What makes Gruber's model different from other case grammars with similar universal claims is that his prelexical structure is the semantic base characterized by case relationships and also the syntactic base which generates surface structures.

5.1.2 **Incorporation.** The process of incorporation is defined as 'the mapping of categories in a prelexical structure into a lexical item neighboring the one into which it would otherwise be directly mapped' (1976:11), for example, the mapping of a preposition into the verb which is next to it rather than the mapping of verb into verb and preposition into preposition. The essence of incorporation is that two or more categories emerge as one category. Categories must be contiguous in order to be incorporated into a single item. Some samples of typical incorporations are given in Figure 5.2.

Figure 5.2 Lexical Incorporation (Gruber 1976)

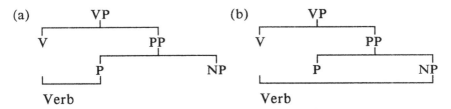

The lexical verb in (a) incorporates only the preposition as in *enter* = 'go into'. The lexical verb in (b) incorporates both the preposition and the following NP as in *cross* = 'go across something'. The verb which has the preposition incorporated will be a transitive verb followed by an NP, while the verb which has the preposition and noun incorporated will be an intransitive verb. There are three possible types of incorporation described in Gruber's model: (1) the obligatory incorporation of an obligatory element, (2) the optional incorporation of an obligatory element, and (3) the optional incorporation of an optional element.

(1) Obligatory incorporation of an obligatory element (1976:15). There are verbs which, given an element which is always present in its environment, must incorporate that element into the verb. For example, the verb *cross* always has the preposition *across* in its environment and must always incorporate the preposition, or the preposition and its object, into the verb. The structure **John crossed across the bridge* is invalid since the preposition *across* is obligatorily incorporated in the verb and cannot be repeated. Various uses of the verb *cross* are illustrated in sentences (1-3).

(1) John crossed the bridge.   cross,tv
    = go + across /___NP
(2) John crossed over the bridge.   cross,iv
    = go + across + NP /___PP
(3) John crossed quickly.   cross,iv
    = go + across + NP /___∅

(2) Optional incorporation of an obligatory element (1976:13). There are verbs which, given an element which is always present in its environment, may or may not incorporate that element into the verb. For example, the verb *pierce* always has the preposition *through* in its environment. But it may or may not incorporate the preposition into the verb and it never incorporates Prep + NP. In sentence (4) the verb incorporates the preposition and becomes a transitive verb. In sentence (5) the preposition is not incorporated and becomes an intransitive verb which is regularly followed by a prepositional phrase. Sentence (6) does not occur.

(4) The pencil pierced the cushion.   pierce,tv
    = go + through /___NP
(5) The pencil pierced through the cushion.   pierce,iv
    = go /___PP
(6) *The pencil pierced.   doesn't occur

(3) Optional incorporation of an optional element (1976:18). There are verbs which, given an element which is sometimes present in its environment, may or may not incorporate that element into the verb. For example, the verb *climb* often has the preposition *up* in its environment but it also occurs in other environments such as *climb down*, *climb along*, as illustrated in sentences (7-9).

(7) John climbed the ladder.   climb,tv
    = go + up /___NP
(8) John climbed quickly.   climb,iv
    = go + up + NP /___∅
(9) John climbed down the ladder.   climb,iv
    = go /___PP

In all three types of incorporation, whenever Prep + NP is incorporated, this is interpreted as an equivalent adverbial incorporation. Thus in sentence (2) *cross over the bridge* = 'go across (adverb) over the bridge'; in sentence (8) *climb quickly* = 'climb upward (adverb) quickly'. Any Prep + NP structure, where the NP is indefinite, is equal to the adverbial use of the preposition.

These few examples of incorporation should indicate how the analyst using Gruber's model must lexically decompose the verbs of the language in order to discover underlying prepositions. These prepositional structures are then sorted out into the categories of Location, Source, and Goal, producing the beginning of a case grammar analysis. When the prepositional phrase as a whole is incorporated into the verb, these Prep + NP structures may include propositional cases lexicalized along with their case markers. The incorporated prepositions may be hidden case markers; incorporated phrases may be hidden cases along with their case makers.

5.2 Nonagentive verb types.

5.2.1 Concrete locatives. The case system in thematic relations consists of five cases: Agent-Theme-Location-Source-Goal. These cases are all defined in terms of specific verb types as typical case notions flowing from the meaning of the verb. Nonagentive verbs are developed by Gruber in Chapters 2-5 (1976:37-156); Agentive verbs in Chapter 6 (1976:157-210). Nonagentive verbs constitute a 3 x 3 verb matrix with State, Durational, and Motional types in one dimension and Positional, Possessional, and Identificational domains in the other. These verb types are summarized in Gruber's first rule (1976:95) for the expansion of the category V.

Rule 1. Nonagentive verb formation (Gruber 1976)

$$V \rightarrow \left[\begin{array}{l} \text{State} \\ \text{Durational} \\ \text{Motional} \end{array}\right] + \left[\begin{array}{l} \text{Positional} \\ \text{Possessional} \\ \text{Identificational} \end{array}\right]$$

State verbs (which Gruber calls 'nondescript' and Jackendoff calls 'punctual') are described negatively as verbs which are nonmotional and nondurational. They are indifferent to durative and point time adverbials but with durative adverbials they 'take on the meaning of the durational' (1976:51). State verbs require a Theme (Os) and a Location (L) and this Location is marked by the stative prepositions *in*, *at*, *on*.

Durational verbs (1976:50) describe a state lasting through time. These verbs are durative states. They accept durative adverbials but not point adverbials. Durational verbs require a Theme (O) and a Location (L) and this Location is marked by the stative prepositions *in*, *at*, *on*.

Motional verbs (1976:37) describe change of state or position. These verbs are process verbs. They require a Theme (O) and a *from-to* pattern indicating the Source (S) and the Goal (G) of the motion. Source is marked by the directional prepositions *from*, *out of*; Goal is marked by the prepositions *to*, *into*.

With these three verb types established, the basic cases of the system (Theme, Location, Source, and Goal) are then defined in terms of the verb types with which they occur.

(1) Theme (O). Theme is 'an obligatory element of every sentence. It is the focus of the construction syntactically and semantically' (1976:38). With state verbs the Theme is the object located, with durational verbs the Theme is the object remaining in a location, with motional verbs the Theme is 'whatever is conceived of as moving' (1976:37), as in sentences (10-12).

(10) The dot /is /inside the circle.   State
     Os   V L
(11) The paper /remained /on the floor.   Durational
     O   V   L
(12) The ball /rolled /down the hill.   Motional
     O   V   S-G

(2) Location (L). Location is the place where the Theme is located. It answers the question: 'Where is the NP (Theme)?' (1976:48). With durational verbs the Location is the place where the Theme remains located. Location, with both verb types, is always marked by stative locative prepositions. Stative location may be expressed with motional verbs but then 'the expression of Location occurs outside the verb-Goal construction' (1976:69). In other words, if stative location occurs with motional verbs the locative expression is a modal locative outside of the basic propositional structure.

In order to resolve the problem of which is the Theme and which is the Location, when neither is marked in the surface structure by prepositions, Gruber asks the question: *Where is the NP Theme?* or *What is the Theme being located?* For example, with the verb *surround* = 'is around' the subject is the Theme because it is being located with respect to the object; with the verb *contain* = 'has inside' the object is the Theme since it is being located with respect to the subject. By the same tests the subject is the Theme for both *precede* = 'is before' and *follow* = 'is after', as in sentences (13-16).

(13) The circle /surrounds /the dot.   O subject
     Os   V   L
(14) The circle /contains /the dot.   L subject
     L   V   Os
(15) The letter C /follows /the letter B.   O subject
     Os   V   L
(16) The letter B /precedes /the letter C.   O subject
     Os   V   L

Given his system of incorporation, Gruber concludes that 'the essential intransitive construction with prepositional phrases may be considered to underlie these forms in the prelexical structure' (1976:50). The preferred prelexical structure seems to be the intransitive structure: BE + prepositional phrase.

(3) Source (S). Source occurs only with motional verbs and indicates the starting point of the motion (1976:39). It is part of an obligatory *from-to* pattern with verbs expressing motion or change.

(4) Goal (G). Goal occurs only with motional verbs and indicates the goal or 'ultimate destination of the motion' (1976:66), the place-to-which the motion or change tends. It is also part of the obligatory *from-to* pattern required with motional verbs.

All motional verbs are associated with prelexical Source-Goal pairs (1976:77), although these patterns may be incomplete in the surface structure. Source or Goal or both may be deleted. The direction of the motion may also appear as a Path (1976:75) along which the Theme is travelling but Path itself 'involves a kind of motion, hence a *from-to* pattern' (1976:77). It describes the complete path from the Source to the Goal and therefore is interpreted as containing a *from-to* pattern. The *from-to* pattern that appears with motional verbs always appears in Source-Goal order. Violations of this order may be a sign that more than one Source-Goal pair is involved (1976:79). Although multiple Source-Goal combinations are permitted with positional verbs, other verb types such as the possessional and identificational may be limited to a single Source-Goal pair (1976:81). The Source-Goal pairs must be homogeneous. In some instances, Source and Goal are marked on the same phrase. These Source-Goal pairs are illustrated in sentences (17-18).

(17) The letter /went /from New York /to Philadelphia.
    O   V   S   G
(18) The horse /galloped /across the bridge.
    O   V   S-G

5.2.2 Abstract locatives. The case system defined for the Positional domain, which deals with true physical location, may be extended to the Possessional and Identificational domains. Location, Source, and Goal are used 'in an abstract sense' (1976:38). The reasons that Gruber gives for extending the use of these cases to abstract domains are: (1) 'the similarity of the senses of what is expressed' and (2) 'the identity of the prepositions used in all these senses'.

(1) Possessional domain. This domain deals with possession and transfer of property. With state verbs the Theme (Os) is 'the thing possessed' (1976:56) and the Location (L) is the possessor. The Theme is the subject with verbs like *belong* (1976:60) but is direct object with verbs like *have, own, possess*. With durational verbs the Theme (O) is the object remaining in one's possession and the Location (L) is the possessor. The Theme is object with verbs like *keep, hold, retain*, but may be subject with phrases like *remain with*. With motional verbs the Theme (O) is the object which undergoes a 'transition of possession' (1976:39). The Source indicates the original possessor and the Goal indicates the later possessor. The Source (S) is subject with verbs like *give, loan, sell, send* and the Goal appears in a *to* phrase. The Goal (G) is the subject with verbs like *borrow, buy, obtain, receive* and the Source appears in a *from* phrase. In those sentences in which agency is involved, the Source or Goal subject may be coreferential with the Agent case to be described later (1976:41). The possessional domain is shown in sentences (19-24).

(19) John /has /a book.   State, L subject
     L   V   Os
(20) The book /belongs /to John.   State, O subject
     Os   V   L
(21) Bill /kept /the book.   Durational, L subject
     L   V   O
(22) The book /remains /with Bill.   Durational, O subject
     O   V   L
(23) John /sent /a book /to Mary.   Motional, S subject
    A=S V   O   G
(24) Mary /received /a book /from John.   Motional, G subject
    G   V   O   S

(2) Identificational domain. This domain deals with the identification of objects. With state verbs the Theme (Os) is the thing identified, the underlying verb is BE + AT, and the Location (L) is the identification expressed as a noun or an adjective. With durational verbs the Theme (O) is the thing continuing to be identified and the underlying verb is REMAIN with AT incorporated. With motional verbs (1976:146) the Theme (O) is the thing changing identification, the Source (S) is the initial identification, and the Goal (G) is the final identification. This abstract domain is shown in sentences (25-30).

(25) The house /is /a shack.   State + noun
     Os   V L
(26) The milk /is /sour.   State + adj
     Os   V L
(27) The house /remained /a shack.   Durational + noun
     O   V   L
(28) Bill /remained /happy.   Durational + adj
     O   V   L
(29) The coach /turned /into a pumpkin. Motional + noun
     O   V   G
(30) The milk /turned /sour.   Motional + adj
     O   V   G

Nonagentive verb types may be summarized in a 3 x 3 matrix with State, Durational, and Motional verbs in one dimension and Positional, Possessional, and Identification domains in the other. The resulting matrix, based on the verbs in Gruber's Table 4 (1976:209) but with the State dimension added, is given in Figure 5.3.

Figure 5.3 Nonagentive verb types (Gruber 1976).

Verb types	Position	Possession	Identification
1.State (Os,L)	be at contain	belong to have	be AT + noun be AT + adj.
2.Duration (O,L)	remain AT stay	hold keep	remain + noun remain + adj.
3.Motion (O,S,G)	come go	receive send	become turn

5.3 Agentive verb types. After developing the nonagentive verb types as state, durational, and motional, Gruber introduces the Agentive verb types in Chapter 6 (1976:157-210). Agentive verbs are of two kinds: (1) those with causative Agents, called C Agent verbs, and (2) those with permissive Agents, called P Agent verbs. The addition of two kinds of Agents expands Gruber's nine basic verb types to twenty-seven verb types, if all nine basic types may occur with both C Agents and P Agents. Jackendoff (1976:93) describes these same verb types in terms of abstract predicates which he calls functions. These include: state BE, durational STAY, and motional GO. These basic functions are combined with C Agents, represented by the abstract predicate CAUSE, and with P Agents, represented by the abstract predicate LET, to form agentive verb types.

Agent (A): Agent is the 'intender of the action' (Gruber 1976:157). The C Agent is the willful entity that is the cause of the event; the P Agent is 'a willful entity, but rather than being the cause, he permits the act' (1976:164). While C Agents cause something to happen, P Agents let something happen. According to Jackendoff, 'causing is bringing about an event' (1976:105). CAUSE (x,e) is a two place predicate relating an Agent and an event. 'Letting is ceasing to prevent an event' (1976:105); LET (x,e) is also a two place predicate. CAUSE and LET are higher predicates which add these Agents to state BE describing 'states of affairs' (1976:96), to durational STAY describing events or happenings (1976:100), and to motional GO describing motion or change of state (1976:93).

In representing the place of Agents in semantic structure, Gruber (1976:197) places agentive as an option parallel to the three basic semantic domains of Positional, Possessional, and Identificational, implying that agentive is an optional choice which is mutually exclusive with these domains. A more exact formulation which coincides with Gruber's practice would be to place both types of agency as an option added to basic verb types. This formulation is given in rule 2:

Rule 2: Agentive verb formation (Gruber 1976)

$$
V \longrightarrow \begin{bmatrix} \text{Nonagentive} \\ \text{P Agentive} \\ \text{C Agentive} \end{bmatrix} + \begin{bmatrix} \text{State} \\ \text{Durational} \\ \text{Motional} \end{bmatrix} + \begin{bmatrix} \text{Positional} \\ \text{Possessional} \\ \text{Identification} \end{bmatrix}
$$

First, depending on the presence or absence of the Agent, every verb is nonagentive, P Agentive, or C Agentive. Next, depending on the situation described, every verb is a state, durational, or motional verb. Finally, depending on the verb's semantic domain, every verb is positional, possessional, or identificational. In Jackendoff's terms, a verb has the predicate CAUSE, LET, or neither; every verb is represented by BE, STAY or GO; and every verb belongs to one of the locational modes (1976:100) of position, possession, or identification. Agentive verbs are represented by basic functions in the scope of agentive functions, such as CAUSE (GO) or LET (GO). Semantic domains are subscripted, such as BE-iden or BE-poss.

5.3.1 Causative Agents. The causative Agent is one who brings about an event. The structure consists of a higher predicate CAUSE which introduces an Agent into the structure. The lower predicate within the scope of CAUSE is either BE, STAY, or GO.

(1a) CAUSE (GO): According to Gruber, in those verbs which are called causatives, a causative Agent can be added to a motional predicate without being coreferential with any other case. Also, 'there are very few verbs which are motional or durational and which cannot be interpreted as being Agentive when the subject is animate' (1976:158). This means that STAY and GO verbs with animate subjects are ambiguous between an unintentional reading with Theme as subject and an intentional reading in which Agent is coreferential with Theme. In other contexts Agent may be coreferential with Source or Goal. The four possible A-O-S-G structures, including coreferential Agents, are illustrated in sentences (31–34).

(31) John /rolled /the ball /down the hill.   A,O,S,G
     A   V   O   S-G
(32) John /went /into the room.   A,*O,S,G /A=O
     A=O V   G
(33) John /sold /the book /to Bill.   A,O,*S,G /A=S
     A=S V   O   G
(34) John /got /the book /from Bill.   A,O,S,*G /A=G
     A=G V   O   S

(1b) CAUSE (STAY): According to Gruber (1976:177), the causative occurs with durational verbs. In some verbs the subject may be identified as only an Agent, but other durational verbs can be interpreted as Agentive with A=O when the subject is animate. Both A-O-L structures are illustrated in sentences (35–36).

(35) John /kept /the dog /in his room.   A,O,L
     A   V   O   L
(36) John /remained /in the room.   A,*O,L /A=O
     A=O V   L

(1c) *CAUSE (BE): Causative agents do not occur with state verbs. State verbs are 'usually necessarily nonagentive' according to Gruber (1976:158). Jackendoff agrees, adding that 'the absence of the configuration CAUSE (BE) I take to be a principled gap excluded by the condition that the final argument of a causative must be an event' (1976:109). But Gruber has problems with verbs that 'seem to be a causative of a stative verb' (1976:161) like the verb *put* in sentence (37). This problem can be resolved if the verb is analyzed as CAUSE (GO), not as CAUSE (BE), with *put* = 'cause O to come to be in L'.

(37) The manager /put /us /in room 206.   A,O,L
     A   V   O L

5.3.2 Permissive Agents. The permissive Agent ceases to prevent an event. The structure has the higher predicate LET introducing the P Agent. The lower predicate representing the event is either BE, STAY, or GO. Opinions differ as to whether these structures are valid.

(2a) LET (GO): According to Gruber *let* as a lexical item 'can be used as a fairly general permissive Agent of motion' (1976:167) with various agentive and nonagentive motion verbs within its scope. Permissive Agents occur in causatives with Agent coreferential with Source or Goal or with Agent not coreferential with any other case, as in sentences (38-41). Apparently there is no problem with LET (GO) structures. But sentences in which the verb *let* has a sentence as its object are complex, and the lower verb may itself be agentive.

(38) John /let /Bill come into the room.   complex
     A   V   O = Sentence
(39) John /released /the bird /from the cage.   A,O,S,G /G-del
     A   V   O   S
(40) John /accepted /the gift /from Bill.   A,O,S,*G /A=G
     A=G   V   O   S
(41) John /granted /Bill /a vacation.   A,O,*S,G /A=S
     A=S   V   G   O

(2b) *LET (STAY): Gruber distinguishes between the verbs *leave* and *permit* in the following way: '*Leave* here means let remain, whereas *permit* means approximately let come to be' (1976:175). Jackendoff (1976:105) considers *leave* ambiguous between LET (STAY) and LET (BE) and concludes: 'I know of no instances of the configuration LET (STAY), but do not know whether the gap is principled or accidental' (1976:109). Possible illustrations of LET (STAY) are given in sentences (42-43) but Jackendoff would prefer to interpret these LET (STAY) verbs as LET (BE). LET (STAY) structures would then be excluded.

(42) John /left /the book /on the table.   A,O,L
     A   V   O   L
(43) John /permitted /the book /on the table.   A,O,L
     A   V   O   L

(2c) LET (BE): While Gruber uses the verb *permit* to illustrate the structure LET (BE), Jackendoff says 'the final argument of LET may be either an event or a state of affairs' (1976:108). Therefore both LET (GO), with the verb *let*, and LET (BE), with the verb *allow*, are possible, as in sentences (44-45).

(44) David /let /Laura /into the room.   A,O,S,G /S-del
     A   V   O   G
(45) David /allowed /Laura /in the room.   A,O,L
     A   V   O   L

Figure 5.4 Localistic Case Matrix (Gruber /Jackendoff)

Verb Types	Non-Agentive			P-Agentive		C-Agentive	
Predicates	BE	STAY	GO	LET(BE)	LET(GO)	CS(STAY)	CS(GO)
Case frames	Os,L	O,L	O,S,G	A,O,L	A,O,S,G	A,O,L	A,O,S,G
Position (concrete)	be+loc contain precede surround	hold keep remain stay	come fall go roll	allow leave let permit	admit drop free release	hold keep prohibit retrain	cause force make push
Possession (abstract)	belong to have own possess	hold keep retain	acquire get lose receive	leave	accept bequeath grant	deprive hold keep retain	get give obtain sell
Identification (abstract)	be+N/Adj cost weigh	keep remain stay	become change grow turn	leave	....	....	change develop make turn

Gruber, Jeffrey S. 1976. *Lexical structures in syntax and semantics*, Table of verbs (1976: 209–210). The first column consisting of nonagentive BE verbs is not included in Gruber's table. Jackendoff, Ray. S. 1976. Towards an explanatory semantic representation in *Linguistic Inquiry*, Volume 7, Number 1, Table of verbs (1976:110).

5.4 Abstract functions. Jackendoff (1976:93) describes all verb types in terms of BE, GO, STAY, CAUSE, and LET. 'This system of semantic functions enables us to express a rich range of semantic information with a rather small set of primitives. The strongest claim one could make is that the five functions presented here are the only functions in semantic theory' (1976:110). But, considering the verb types developed in other grammars, there is some doubt whether these five functions are sufficient for the description of all the verbs of a language since (1) there is no function for simple action verbs, (2) there is no function for expressing the inchoative, and (3) durative STAY should not be considered a lower level function.

5.4.1 Noncausative functions. In the system proposed by Jackendoff all noncausative predications are represented by BE, GO, or STAY, as in Figure 5.5.A. This system is adequate for simple states and processes and for durative states but it provides no way of describing durative process, or simple or durative actions.

Figure 5.5.A Noncausative functions (Jackendoff 1976)

Verb type	Simple	Durative
State	BE	STAY
Process	GO	....

This system should be revised as in Figure 5.5.B. Simple state, process, and action verbs require only the lower level functions BE, GO, or DO. Each of these lower level functions can be converted into a durative by placing them within the scope of the higher level function STAY so as to allow STAY (BE), STAY (GO), or STAY (DO). This revised system is adequate for simple or durative states, for simple or durative process, and for simple or durative action.

Figure 5.5.B Noncausative functions (Revised)

Verb Type	Simple	Durative
State	BE	STAY (BE)
Process	GO	STAY (GO)
Action	DO	STAY (DO)

(1) **State verbs.** State verbs describe a static situation and may be represented by the predicate BE. Durative states, which describe the continuation of a state of affairs over time, should be represented by the combination STAY (BE) and not by STAY alone. The revised simple and durative states are contrasted in sentences (46-47).

(46) The ivory was in Africa.   State
    = BE (ivory, in Africa)
(47) The ivory stayed in Africa.   Durative state
    = STAY (BE (ivory,in Africa))

(2) **Process verbs.** Process verbs describe a nonagentive event or happening and may be represented by the predicate GO. Durative process, which describes the continuing of an event through time, should be represented by the combination STAY (GO). Jackendoff permits this combination by creating 'circumstantial' STAY which locates an individual within an event, expressed as STAY-circ (GO). 'An individual is in a circumstantial location when the location is an event or a state of affairs' (1976:122). But there is no need for this kind of circumlocution if STAY is used only as a higher predicate. Simple and durative processes are contrasted in sentences (48-49).

(48) The ivory was going to Europe.   Process
    = GO (ivory, to Europe)
(49) The ivory kept going to Europe.   Durative process
    = STAY (GO (ivory,to Europe))

(3) **Action verbs.** Action verbs may be represented by the predicate DO but have no representation in Gruber's work, or in Jackendoff until recently. Durative actions are agentive events that last through time. The combination STAY (DO) should not be used, because if the subject of DO is an Agent he will also be the CAUSE of his own activity. Durative actions only exist as causative-durative actions. Simple and durative actions are given in sentences (50-51).

(50) Maria was dancing.   Action
    = DO (Maria, dance)
(51) Maria kept on dancing.   *Durative Action
    = *STAY (DO (Maria,dance))

5.4.2 Causative functions. In the system of semantic functions proposed by Jackendoff, all causative functions are represented by the agentive predicates CAUSE or LET with one of the lower functions, BE, GO, or STAY, within its scope. Within this system *CAUSE (BE) is ruled out because CAUSE requires an event within its scope. *LET (STAY) is ruled out because no clear examples were found (Jackendoff 1976:110). As there is no simple action predicate DO in Jackendoff's system, the causative functions have only states or processes within their scope, as in Figure 5.6.A.

Figure 5.6.A Causative functions (Jackendoff 1976)

Verb Type	Causative	Causative-Durative
State	*CAUSE (BE) LET (BE)	CAUSE (STAY) *LET (STAY)
Process	CAUSE (GO) LET (GO)	. . . .

The predicate DO should be added for simple actions and the predicate STAY should be considered as a mediate level predicate with BE, GO, or DO within its scope. The causative predicates CAUSE and LET are then the highest predicates, with any non-causative function within their scope as in Figure 5.6.B.

Figure 5.6.B Causative functions (revised)

Verb Type	Causative	Causative-Durative
State	*CAUSE (BE) *LET (BE)	CAUSE (STAY (BE)) LET (STAY (BE))
Process	CAUSE (GO) LET (GO)	CAUSE (STAY (GO)) LET (STAY (GO))
Action	CAUSE (DO) LET (DO)	CAUSE (STAY (DO)) LET (STAY (DO))

(1) *Causative States do not occur. The reason for this is that both CAUSE and LET require an event within their scope. CAUSE (BE) should be revised as CAUSE (BECOME (BE)), and LET (BE) should be revised as LET (STAY (BE)), as in sentences (52-53).

(52) John put the book on the table.   A,O,L
     = CAUSE (John, BECOME (BE (book, on table)))
(53) John left the book on the table.   pA,O,L
     = LET (John, STAY (BE (book, on table)))

(2) Causative-durative states describe an Agent who causes a state of affairs to remain in time and is expressed by CAUSE (STAY (BE)) or LET (STAY (BE)). The CAUSE predicate may occur with either like or unlike subjects, as in sentences (54-56).

(54) John stayed out of the house.   A,O + Os,L
    = CAUSE (John (STAY (BE (self, out of house))))
(55) John kept the book on the table.   A,O + Os,L
    = CAUSE (John (STAY (BE (book, on table))))
(56) John left the book on the table.   pA,O + Os,L
    = LET (John (STAY (BE (book, on table))))

(3) Causative process describes an Agent who causes or permits a nonagentive event or process to happen. This is expressed by the predicates CAUSE (GO) and LET (GO), as in sentences (57-58).

(57) John rolled the rock down the hill.   A,O,S,G
    = CAUSE (John (GO (rock,down the hill)))
(58) John let the rock roll down the hill.   pA,O + O,S,G
    = LET (John (GO (rock, down the hill)))

(4) Causative durative process describes an Agent who causes or permits a nonagentive event, or process, to last through time. This notion is expressed by the predicates CAUSE (STAY (GO)) or LET (STAY (GO)), as in sentences (59-60).

(59) John kept the rock rolling down the hill.   A,O + O,S,G
    = CAUSE (John, STAY (GO (rock, down the hill)))
(60) John let the rock keep rolling downhill. pA,O + O + O,S,G
    = LET (John, STAY (GO (rock, downhill)))

(5) Causative actions are double Agent structures in which one Agent causes or permits another Agent to engage in an activity. This is expressed by the combinations CAUSE (DO) or LET (DO), as in sentences (61-62).

(61) John made the men work.   A,O + A,*O
    = CAUSE (John, DO (men,work))
(62) John let the men work.   pA,O + A,*O
    = LET (John, DO (men, work))

(6) Causative durative actions occur with like subjects or unlike subjects. With like subjects causative-durative describes an Agent causing himself to continue an activity and replaces the invalid *durative-action. With unlike subjects these sentences are double Agent structures in which one Agent causes or permits another Agent to continue in an activity, as in sentences (63-65).

(63) Maria kept dancing.   A,O + A,O
    = CAUSE (Maria, STAY (DO (self, dancing)))
(64) John kept the men working.   A,O + A,*O
    = CAUSE (John, STAY (DO (men, work)))
(65) John let the men keep working.   pA,O + A,O + A,*O
    = LET (John, STAY (DO (men, work)))

In summary, Jackendoff's five functions form an incomplete semantic system in which STAY is a primitive and in which there is no place for simple action predicates. The system should be expanded to include BE, GO, DO as basic functions, with STAY and BECOME as mediate functions, and CAUSE and LET as higher functions.

5.5 Locational modes (Jackendoff). Jackendoff (1976:100) adopts Gruber's description of the three locational modes, positional, possessional, and identificational, as 'semantic primitives common to all languages' (1976:104) but suggests that these modes are not the only ones. These locational modes are added as semantic markers to the primitive functions as BE-ident, BE-posit, and BE-poss, to describe the semantic domain in which the verb type is being used.

The identificational mode, 'predicates describing properties', corresponds to the basic verbs of Anderson's model and should be eliminated. But the possessional mode should be extended to all abstract locatives, as Gruber seems to advocate, or supplemented by a new mode to account for 'mental states and intentions', which Jackendoff (1976:124) leaves for future research.

5.5.1 Identificational mode. In Anderson's localistic model the cases are divided into local and nonlocal cases. The nonlocal cases, A and O, are used to describe the basic verb types. The local cases, L, S, and G, are used with A and O cases to describe both concrete and abstract locative verbs. But both Jackendoff and Gruber attempt to force basic verbs into an identificational mode.

(1) Identificational BE (Jackendoff 1976:102). The function BE-ident (Os,L) is a two place predicate in which Os is an object and L is a noun or adjective describing the identifying class. The preposition AT is obligatorily incorporated into the verb *be* (Gruber 1976:145). In other case grammar models adjectives are Os verbs and predicate nouns occur in Os-Os structures, as in (66-67).

(66) The metal was red.   be + adj   Os
   = BE-ident (metal, red)
(67) The coach was a pumpkin.   be + noun   Os,Os
   = BE-ident (coach, pumpkin)

(2) Identificational STAY (Jackendoff 1976:102). The function STAY-ident (O,L) is a two place predicate in which O is an object and L is a noun or adjective describing the class in which the object remains. But if STAY is not a lower level function, it requires no locational mode at all since it will have another function with a locational mode within its scope, as in sentences (68-69).

(68) Nora stayed sick.   stay,iv   O
   = *STAY-ident (Nora, sick)   be + adj   Os
   = STAY (BE SICK (Nora))

(69) Fred remained a doctor.   remain,iv   O
     = *STAY-ident (Fred, doctor)   be + noun   Os,Os
     = STAY (BE (Fred, doctor))

(3) Identificational GO (Jackendoff 1976:102). The function GO-ident (O,S,G) is a three place predicate in which O is an object which changes state, S is the initial state, and G is the final state. Gruber (1976:146) applies this analysis to *change, turn, become*. In other models basic process predicates are one place O verbs and *become* + noun is a two place O-O verb, as in sentences (70-71).

(70) The metal melted.   O
     = GO-ident (metal, solid, liquid)
(71) The coach turned into a pumpkin.   O,O
     = GO-ident (coach, coach, pumpkin)

(4) *CAUSE (BE) /LET (BE). The function CAUSE (BE) does not occur (Jackendoff 1976:109). LET (BE) structure is often ambiguous between LET (BE) and LET (STAY), as in sentence (72).

(72) Henry left Nora sick.   pA,O + Os
     = *LET (Henry, BE-ident (Nora, sick))
     = LET (Henry (STAY (BE SICK (Nora)))

(5) CAUSE (STAY) /*LET (STAY). The CAUSE function may combine with STAY-ident as in sentence (73). LET (STAY) does not occur according to Jackendoff (1976:109), but Gruber (1976:165) says the LET (STAY) structure is possible.

(73) Henry kept Nora healthy.   A,O + Os
     = *CAUSE (Henry, STAY-ident (Nora, healthy))
     = CAUSE (Henry (STAY (BE HEALTHY (Nora))))

(6) CAUSE (GO) /LET (GO). The CAUSE function combines with GO-ident in Gruber (1976:189) for the verbs *change, turn, make*. No examples are given of LET (GO) but Jackendoff considers this gap to be accidental (1976:109), as in sentences (74-75).

(74) Dolly made Martin happy.   A,O + Os
     = *CAUSE (Dolly, GO-ident (Martin, unhappy, happy))
     = CAUSE (Dolly, COME ABOUT (BE HAPPY (Martin)))
(75) John let his son become a lawyer.   pA,O + O,O
     = *LET (John, GO-ident (son, non-x, x))
     = LET (John, COME ABOUT (BE (son, lawyer)))

In summary, the use of Location Source and Goal in basic verbs is an exaggerated localism which, when applied to basic action verbs, produces questionable analyses such as *sing* = 'cause self (O) to GO from not singing (S) to singing (G)'.

5.5.2 Possessional mode (extended). Within the Jackendoff-Gruber model basic verbs are described in the identificational mode, concrete locatives are described in the positional mode, and abstract locatives which deal with possession and transfer of property in the possessional mode. In what mode are the experiential verbs described?

Jackendoff says 'since we have as yet not introduced a formal representation for mental states and intentions, we shall not attempt to deal with such verbs, leaving their analysis for future research' (1976:124). But Gruber develops some of these verbs under the possessional mode in which Theme = information. (1976:125). If the possessional mode is extended in this way, it could be used for all abstract locatives. Since experiential verbs dealing with sensation, emotion, and cognition constitute approximately one verb in every four in running text, their analysis can hardly be overlooked.

(1) Cognitive verbs. There are state, process, and action verbs which deal with cognition and are considered abstract locatives in Anderson's localistic model. For the verbs *learn* and *teach* Gruber considers 'knowledge' as the theme and places these verbs within the possessional mode. By analogy this analysis could be extended to the verb *know*, as in (76-78).

(76) Many people know the truth.   Os,L /L-subject
     = BE-poss (truth, people)
(77) John learned the story from Bill.   O,S,G/ G-subject
     = GO-poss (story, Bill, John)
(78) Bill taught John the story.   A,O,*S,G/ A=S
     = CAUSE (Bill, GO-poss (story, Bill, John))

For communication verbs, Gruber considers 'information' to be the theme and places verbs like *communicate* and *tell* in the possessional mode but *explain*, *say* and *signal* in the positional mode (1976:127-128). Communication verbs *write* and *hear (from)* are possessional, as in sentences (79-81).

(79) John told Bill the story.   A,O,*S,G /A=S
     = CAUSE (John, GO-poss (story, John, Bill))
(80) Mary heard the story from John.   O,S,G /G-subject
     = GO-poss (story, John, Mary)
(81) John wrote the news to Mary.   A,O,*S,G /A=S
     = CAUSE (John, GO-poss (news, John, Mary))

Gruber's choice of the positional domain for verbs like *say* is based on the fact that the information Theme is not necessarily transmitted from Source to Goal. But since the speaker intends that the information be transmitted in all communication verbs, it does not seem inappropriate to consider all communication verbs as belonging to the possessional mode. In any case, it would be simpler to put all communication verbs in one category.

(2) Emotional verbs. State, process, and action verbs which deal with emotion are considered abstract locatives in Anderson's model. Although neither Gruber nor Jackendoff analyzes these verb types, the theory of thematic relations will ultimately have to consider them. These include state verbs such as *want* and *like*, process verbs like *annoy* and *frighten*. The process verbs are also used as action verbs when an Agent is added to the structure, as in sentences (82-84).

(82) The audience liked the play. Os,L /L-subject
    = BE-poss (audience, play)
    where Os = stimulus, L = experiencer.
(83) The thunder annoyed the baby. O,S,G /O-lex
    = GO-poss (annoyance, thunder, baby)
    where O = annoyance, S = thunder, G = baby
(84) John [+Intent] annoyed the baby. A,*O,*S,G /O-lex, A=S
    = CAUSE (John, GO-poss (annoyance, John, baby))
    where John is both Agent and Source.

(3) Sensation verbs. There are state, process, and action verbs which deal with sensation and are considered abstract locatives in Anderson's model, related to the five senses of hearing, sight, smell, taste, and touch. These verbs often occur in contrasting sets like *sound /hear /listen to* in which the subject of the verb can be the Object, Experiencer, or Agent, respectively. These verbs also include all those *be* + adjective structures in which the adjective describes a physical sensation like *be (=feel) cold*, as in (85-87).

(85) John is (=feels) cold. Os,*L /O=L
    = BE-poss (John, cold)
(86) The music sounded good to Mary. Os,L /O-subject
    = BE-poss (music, Mary)
(87) Bill heard the noise. Os,L /L-subject
    = BE-poss (Bill, noise)

In describing the difference between these intentional and nonintentional sensations, Anderson proposes that the sensation is the Theme, lexicalized into the verb. The nonintentional reading is then a process and the intentional reading adds an Agent to the structure coreferential with Goal, as in (88-89).

(88) John (-Intent) smelled the roses. *O,S,G /O-lex
    = GO-poss (smell, roses, John)
(89) John (+Intent) smelled the roses. A,*O,S,*G /O-lex, A=G
    = CAUSE (John, GO-poss (smell, roses, John))

In summary, the elimination of the Identificational mode in favor of nonlocal verb types would eliminate the useless search for non-existent local cases. The extension of the possessional mode to all abstract locatives would make the model complete.

5.6 Evaluation of thematic relations. Thematic relations is a localistic form of case grammar which analyzes the semantics of a clause in terms of a verb and the roles required by the verb. Since Gruber's 1965 model precedes Fillmore's 1968 model, Gruber could be considered the first case grammarian. Gruber proceeds from an explanation of the surface prepositions to a deeper analysis of incorporated prepositions, correlating both visible and invisible prepositional structures into his localistic framework. The revival of Gruber's work by Jackendoff in 1972 and 1976 includes the further development of Gruber's verb types in terms of abstract functions. The significance of Jackendoff's work lies in the fact that he uses thematic relations as part of the semantic component in an interpretive transformational model.

5.6.1 Semantic structure. Gruber (1965) postulates a PRELEXICAL CATEGORIAL STRUCTURE which is deeper than the deep structure of the standard transformational theory. Gruber first decomposes lexical predicates, where possible, into verb and preposition or verb and prepositional phrase. These basic structures, with all prepositions visible, are then generated by the base. Through POLYCATEGORIAL LEXICAL ATTACHMENT Gruber then substitutes single verbs for more than one lexical category. Knowledge of the underlying prepositional structures imposes some selectional restrictions on lexical verbs and leads to a more exact case analysis of the verb in terms of thematic relations. Since the prelexical structure generated contains prepositions which serve as case markers and prepositional phrases which express cases, the array of cases required by the verb is more evident than it would be in a standard type deep structure.

Jackendoff's contribution is to incorporate these thematic relations into the semantic component of a transformational grammar. The lexical entries now include phonological features, syntactic features, and semantic features. The semantic features are expressed in terms of abstract semantic functions like BE, STAY, GO, LET and CAUSE, which represent the verb type, and their accompanying thematic relations expressed in terms of Agent, Theme, Location, Source, and Goal. The noun phrases in the selectional syntactic feature are then correlated with the noun phrases in the semantic feature in order to give them a semantic interpretation. A system of subscripts matches the subjects, objects, and prepositional phrases of the syntactic feature with the thematic case relations expressed in the semantic feature. Through this system every verb in the lexicon is not only subclassified by the type of syntax that it allows but is also categorized in terms of case frames expressed by means of the thematic relations.

5.6.2 Case system. The case system proposed by Gruber and adopted by Jackendoff is a localistic system consisting of five cases: Agent, Theme, Location, Source, and Goal. This is the same as the case system proposed by Anderson (1971). As in the Anderson model, the Theme is an obligatory element present in every case frame. This obligatory O hypothesis encourages a deeper analysis of the case structure and creates the need for covert roles such as deletable, lexicalized, and coreferential roles. But the system of thematic relations, as applied by Gruber and Jackendoff, is an exaggerated localism. Whereas Anderson makes a clear distinction between non-local verb types, which use only the Agent and Object cases, and local verb types, which use the Agent and Object cases in combination with Location, Source, and Goal cases, Gruber and Jackendoff have no basic nonlocal verb types and try to incorporate Location, Source, and Goal into the description of every verb.

This exaggerated localism holds that basic state verbs (Os) must be analyzed as BE (Os,L), that basic process verbs (O) must be analyzed as GO (O,S,G), and that basic action verbs (A,O) can only be expressed by CAUSE or LET combined with GO (O,S,G). For basic state verbs, this system rejects the view that adjectives are predicates and analyzes them as expressions of a Location case; for basic process verbs, Source and Goal must be expressed in the deep structure despite the fact that there is little surface evidence; for basic action verbs, Agent is added to an already formed locational process verb. The system of thematic relations could be considerably improved by introducing basic nonlocal verb types which do not require the Location, Source, or Goal cases.

5.6.3 Verb types. Gruber describes verbs in terms of a set of features which contrast a verb type (state, durational, motional) with a domain (identificational, positional, possessional). Agency is added at a later stage, almost as an afterthought. The verb types are supplemented by the higher predicates CAUSE and LET to express causative and permissive agency.

Jackendoff expresses the verb types in terms of a set of five primitive functions, BE, GO, STAY, CAUSE, and LET, and adds the semantic domain by subscripting the features Ident, Posit, Poss to the lower functions BE, GO, and STAY. The analysis differs from that of Gruber only in the way in which it is expressed. The use of primitive functions is a new development in case grammar, reminiscent of Ikegami's (1965) semological study of English verbs of motion. The distinction between permissive and causative Agent is innovative. But the set of primitive functions might be improved by using BE (state), GO (process), and DO (action). STAY should not be used as a lower function but as a mediate function with BE, GO, or DO within its scope to express the full range of duratives. The predicates CAUSE and LET could serve as higher predicates with either the lower functions, or STAY with a lower function, within their scope.

5.6.4 Derivation. Although neither Gruber nor Jackendoff proposes a derivational system, derivation is implicit in the use of the higher predicates CAUSE and LET. What is required is an inchoative and causative unit to relate sets of state, process, and action verbs, and a durative unit to represent durative state, process, and action.

(1) **Inchoative:** State verbs are represented by BE (Os,L) applied to the three locational modes: identificational for basic verbs, positional for concrete locatives, and possessional for abstract locatives. Process verbs are represented by the predicate GO (O,S,G) in the same modes, but there is no inchoative link between state and process verbs to express the relation between pairs like *thick /thicken*. What is required is an inchoative predicate like BECOME. Jackendoff (1976:129) creates an equivalent predicate, GO-circumstantial, in which the subscript indicates that this verb is a higher function with a sentence, usually the predicate BE, within its scope. Then the inchoative form can be represented as GO-circ (BE (Os,L)).

(2) **Causative:** Process verbs represented by the predicate GO (O,S,G) are easily converted into action verbs by the addition of the predicates CAUSE or LET which introduce Agents into the structure. The problem here is not with actions derived from process but with basic actions, for which there is no simple representation. Without a predicate DO for simple activity every action verb receives a forced causative analysis, whereas many action verbs are not causatives. In the Gruber-Jackendoff analysis there is no Agent which is not the subject of CAUSE. Jackendoff (1987:394) suggests the use of an 'action tier' to express for agent-patient relations, which might serve as a temporary solution to this problem.

(3) **Durative:** The notion of duration is prominent in Gruber's verb classification and becomes one of the five basic semantic functions in Jackendoff's adaptation, where it is represented by the function STAY (O,L). The problem is whether STAY is a lower level primitive with concrete arguments or a higher level function with only predications within its scope. Since state, process, and action can all last through time, it would seem that the durative must apply to all three. STAY as a basic predicate applies only to durative state. Jackendoff creates a STAY-circumstantial which acts as a higher predicate with BE within its scope to express durative process. Since there is no simple action predicate, durative action can only be described in terms of CAUSE or LET with lower predicates. What is required here is a system in which STAY is a higher predicate occurring in the combinations STAY (BE), STAY (GO), STAY (DO).

(4) **Causative-durative:** Not only do state, process, and action last through time but there are also causative variants of the durative in which an Agent causes or lets the state, process, or action last through time. What is required to express these relationships is a higher predicate CAUSE or LET, an intermediate predicate STAY, and a set of lower predicates including BE, GO, and an added lower predicate DO. In the Jackendoff system state and process can be expressed by the combinations CAUSE (STAY-circ (BE)) or CAUSE (STAY-circ (GO)) but would have no realization for the type of predicate which is causative and durative.

5.6.5 Covert roles. Covert case roles are case roles that are sometimes or always missing from the surface structure. In any case system which holds the obligatory O hypothesis, like that of Gruber and Jackendoff, the use of deletable, lexicalized, and coreferential case roles becomes all the more necessary.

(1) **Deletable roles:** In Gruber's system deletable roles are often expressed in terms of the optional incorporation of an element. An obligatory element that is optionally incorporated is an element that is present in the deep structure but which may or may not be present in the surface structure. Deletable roles include deletable objects as well as deletable Source and Goal cases, which always appear in pairs.

(2) **Lexicalized roles:** Since lexical decomposition is the foundation stone of Gruber's analysis, both the prepositional markers which indicate case relationships and cases with their markers are often lexicalized or incorporated into the verb. Gruber's model generates deep structures in which these cases and markers are clearly evident, which, by his polycategorial lexical attachment, reach the surface as single lexical items.

(3) **Coreferential roles:** Gruber's use of coreferential roles was dictated by the fact that all basic verbs were described before the addition of the predicates CAUSE and LET which introduce Agents. The Agent case could often only be explained as coreferential with an existing case in the basic structure. It was this use of coreferential roles that motivated Jackendoff to adopt Gruber's thematic relations with coreferential roles rather than Fillmore's 1968 case grammar analysis which lacked coreferential roles.

5.7 Conclusion. The system of thematic relations proposed by Gruber was the first case grammar ever proposed but it did not become prominent until it was adopted by Jackendoff in 1972. In many ways Gruber anticipates Fillmore, describing verbs in terms of case relationships, and also anticipates Anderson, proposing a localistic system with an obligatory Theme. Jackendoff accepts Gruber's basic classification of verbs in terms of a set of thematic relations, reducing Gruber's verb types to primitive semantic functions with semantic domains specified by locational modes. He then incorporates this analysis into the interpretive semantic component of the grammar. The system of thematic relations proposed by Gruber and Jackendoff raises many serious issues for case grammar theory. Given a localistic case system, should local cases be excluded from basic verb types? Is durative a lower level semantic primitive or a higher function with lower semantic functions in its scope? Can the system be successfully applied to experiential verbs? Given the importance of the Gruber-Jackendoff contributions to case theory, these questions should be answered in a context that compares thematic relations with the case grammar models of Fillmore, Chafe, and Anderson.

Exercise 5. Write the case frame for the main verb in each of the following sentences. The cases available are A-O-L-S-G, where A = Agent, O = Theme, L = location, S = Source, G = Goal. Use A for causative Agent and pA for permissive Agent; use Os for stative Themes. Mark totally covert roles with an asterisk (*) and add the reason after the case frame. Lexicalized roles are marked as O-lex, coreferential roles as A = O. List the case chosen as subject first.

1. Bill is a cook. _____

2. The weather is bad. _____

3. John allowed the cat on the sofa. _____

4. The book belongs to John. _____

5. The coach became a pumpkin. _____

6. The circle contains the dot. _____

7. John dropped the dishes onto the floor. _____

8. Henry entered the house. _____

9. John granted Bill a trip home. _____

10. John kept the dog in the room. _____

11. John learned from Bill that the earth is flat. _____

12. John left the book on the table. _____

13. Mary received a book from John. _____

14. John released the bird from the cage. _____

15. The house remained a shack. _____

16. John [+Intent] remained in the room. _____

17. John said to me that he was through. _____

18. Bill sold a book to John. _____

19. Bill [-Intent] stayed happy. _____

20. John taught Bill the story. _____

21. The milk turned sour. _____

Gruber 1965 Lexicon. The Gruber 1965 lexicon is a collection of 80 verbs with the case frames as far as they can be determined from Gruber's *Studies in Lexical Relations*. Totally covert roles are marked with an asterisk (*). Distinguish permissive Agent (pA) from causative Agent (A). The subject case is listed first.

accept	pA,O,S,*G	keep	A,O,L
acquire	G,O,S	kill	A,O,*S,*G
admit	pA,O,S,G	know	L,Os
allow	pA,O,S,G	lead	A,O,S,G
be + adj	Os,L	learn	G,O,S
be + loc	Os,L	leave (behind)	A,O,L
be + N	Os,L	let (go)	pA,O,S,G
become + adj	O,*S,G	lose	S,O,G
become + N	O,*S,G	make	A,O,S,G
belong to	Os,L	obtain	A,O,S,*G
bring	A,O,S,G	open, tv	A,O,*S,*G
buy	A,O,S,*G	own	L,Os
cause	A,O,*S,*G	permit	pA,O,L
change,iv	O,S,G	pierce	O,S,G
climb	A,*O,S,G	possess	L,Os
coerce (into)	A,O,*S,G	precede	Os,L
come	O,S,G	prohibit	A,O,L
contain	L,Os	push	A,O,S,G
continue	Os,L	put	A,O,L
cross	O,S,G	raise	A,O,S,G
deprive	A,O,L	receive	G,O,S
develop (into)	O,S,G	release	pA,O,S,G
drop	pA,O,S,G	remain	Os,L
elect	A,O,L	restrain	A,O,S,G
enter	A,*O,S,G	retain	A,O,L
fall	O,S,G	rise	O,S,G
float	O,S,G	roll	O,S,G
fly	A,*O,S,G	save	A,O,L
follow	Os,L	say	A,O,*S,G
force	A,O,*S,G	sell	A,O,*S,G
free	A,O,S,G	send	A,O,*S,G
get	A,O,S,*G	sink	O,S,G
give	A,O,*S,G	smell (bad)	L,Os
gallop	A,*O,S,G	stay	Os,L
go	A,*O,S,G	surround	Os,L
grant	pA,O,*S,G	take	A,O,S,G
grow	O,S,G	teach	A,O,*S,G
have	L,Os	throw	A,O,*S,G
hold	A,O,L	transport	A,O,S,G
insert	A,O,*S,G	turn (into)	O,*S,G

6 Case Roles in Tagmemics

6.0 Overview. In the early seventies, in a paper entitled *Crucial Issues in the Development of Tagmemics*, Kenneth Pike stated 'The need for further study of the relation between the implications of tagmemics and of case grammar comprises a major topic of concern for the seventies; at this point, tagmemics should benefit greatly from the work of the case grammarians' (Pike 1976). After more than ten years of development, although there seems to be a general agreement that case roles are a useful addition to tagmemic analysis, there is widespread disagreement as to how case theory is to be incorporated into a tagmemic grammar.

Typical attempts to incorporate case grammar into tagmemics include: Conjoining in a tagmemic grammar of English (Becker 1967), Case grammar as a deep structure in tagmemic analysis (Cook 1970), *Grammatical Form and Grammatical Meaning: A Tagmemic View of Fillmore's Deep Structure Case Concepts* (Platt 1971), On the systematization of box 4 (Hale 1972), The tagmemic-case grammar model: A review of Platt's *Grammatical Form and Grammatical Meaning* (Cook 1973), *An Anatomy of Speech Notions* (Longacre 1976), and *Grammatical Analysis* (Pike and Pike 1977). Although this list cannot be considered to be exhaustive, it is sufficiently representative to understand the different ways of approaching a case grammar–tagmemic model.

There is a general agreement about the compatibility of case grammar and tagmemics and a general feeling that case roles should be incorporated as part of the tagmeme unit. One trend, which is represented by Hale (1972) and Pike and Pike (1977), attempts to link case assignment to the transitivity system, with the result that the assignment of cases becomes almost automatic. The deep case inventory in these systems tends to be minimal and therefore highly abstract. The other trend, represented by Becker (1967), Platt (1971), Cook (1979), and Longacre (1976), views the case system as an independent system not linked to transitivity. Within this trend the case inventories tend to be larger, five to ten cases, and vary according to whether the author prefers a more concrete system with a larger number of cases or a more abstract system which makes greater use of the principle of complementary distribution.

Case grammar as it is understood today (Fillmore 1977) is a semantic valence system in which the number and kind of cases is dependent upon the meaning of the verb. Case grammar is not a full grammar; it describes one level of organization of the clause. Cases are semantic relations which elements of a clause have in context with a particular verb. This set of semantic relations can be incorporated into any form of syntax. Fillmore's models (1968, 1971) attempted to establish a transformational grammar with a case base, Chafe (1970) used cases in a form of generative semantics, Anderson (1971) used a case system as a base for establishing a dependency grammar, and Jackendoff (1972) used a case system called thematic relations in the interpretive component of a transformational grammar.

6.0.1 Tagmemic analysis. There is no reason why the system of tagmemic analysis cannot be furnished with a case base. As a matter of fact, the system of tagmemic analysis seems to be particularly suited for adding deep structure cases. Tagmemic analysis posits a correlation of function and form called the tagmeme as its basic unit. The tagmeme is defined as 'a correlation of a grammatical function or slot with the class of mutually substitutable items that fill that slot' (Cook 1969:15). In working with unknown languages, Pike discovered that an analysis made in terms of function alone (subject-predicate-object) or in terms of form alone (noun phrase-verb phrase-noun phrase) was inadequate. He proposed that function and form be combined into a single grammatical unit which would express both function and form, such as subject slot filled by a noun phrase. In this way both the functional information, that the noun phrase acts as subject, and the form information, that the form acting as subject is a noun phrase, could be retained.

Tagmemics differs from traditional structuralism in several significant ways. (1) Traditional Immediate Constituent analysis was in terms of form alone; tagmemics uses a combined function-form unit. (2) Immediate Constituent analysis was a binary analysis in which each construction was divided successively into two parts; tagmemics is a multiple branching type of analysis in which each construction is analyzed into as many parts as the linguistic analyst perceives. (3) Immediate Constituent analysis had no predetermined number of levels since the number of levels was determined by the number of binary cuttings; tagmemics accepts a series of natural levels, sentence, clause, phrase, and word levels, and analyzes the construction into its relevant parts at each level.

At the sentence level the intonation is stripped from the sentence and complex-compound sentences are broken down into single clauses. At the clause level clauses are broken down into phrases that express functions such as subject, predicate, object and various adverbial adjuncts. Phrases are then broken down into words in prepositional, coordinate, or head-modifer constructions. Finally words are broken down into stem and affix in the analysis of inflected, derived, and compound words. The resulting morphemes are entered in a lexicon.

In tagmemics the analysis usually begins at the clause level since this is the level at which the subject-predicate structure of simple sentences is determined. The clause level provides a convenient 'entrance point into understanding the methodology' (Pike & Pike 1977:xvii). The clause is defined as 'a string of tagmemes that consists of or includes one and only one predicate or predicate like tagmeme in the string' (Cook 1969:65). Besides the predicate the string would normally have subjects, objects, and various adjuncts of time, place, and manner. But while subject and object functions are grammatically determined by subject marking and subject-verb agreement, the various adjuncts of time, place, and manner have to be analyzed according to semantic criteria. The resulting analysis, though descriptively accurate, is a mixed bag of grammatical and semantic relations.

6.0.2 Case grammar. It was suspected very early that grammatical notions such as subject and object could be further distinguished according to meaning. Pike (1967:196) proposed distinguishing the different types of subject such as subject-as-actor, subject-as-undergoer, subject-as-item-described in order to indicate the various meanings possible in the notion of subject. Terms like subject and object refer only to the grammatical constructions in a language, terms like actor and undergoer refer to the real world. There appeared to be no level in tagmemics which dealt exclusively with semantics and that represented the elements of a clause and their semantic relation to each other, despite the fact that adverbial elements were determined semantically. Tagmemics was a surface structure analysis in search of a deeper level of semantic analysis.

Why case grammar? Tagmemic clause analysis is based on verb centrality with the predicate as the only obligatory element. Combined with this predicate are various tagmemes that can be nuclear or peripheral to the structure. Only tagmemes which are essential to the diagnosis of clause types are nuclear. Subject, predicate, and object are generally nuclear while time, place, and manner are peripheral. Nuclear elements can be obligatory or optional, peripheral elements are always optional.

Case grammar considers the verb to be central, all other clause elements being analyzed with relation to the verb. The cases are either propositional cases required by the meaning of the verb or modal cases not required by the meaning of the verb. The propositional cases are obligatory or optional in the surface structure, since essential cases might be deleted in a given sentence, but modal cases are always optional. Like tagmemics, case grammar is a multiple branching system. Case grammar analyzes a clause into a verb and as many cases as the meaning of the verb requires. There are also similarities in the use of tagmemes and cases. Fillmore claims that only like cases are conjoined; in tagmemics only like tagmemes are conjoined. Fillmore (1968:24) suggests that cases can not be repeated in the same clause; in tagmemics like tagmemes can not be repeated in the same clause. The surface structures of tagmemics at the clause level and the deep structure of case grammar are essentially compatible. These similarities are outlined in Figure 6.1.

Figure 6.1 Tagmemics and case grammar.

Tagmemics	Case Grammar
Multiple branching	Multiple branching
S,P,O,L,T,M	V + cases
Essential tagmemes	Propositional cases
Obligatory P	Central V
Nuclear S,IO,DO	A,E,B,O,L
Peripheral tagmemes	Modal cases
L,T,M...	L_m, T_m, M_m...
Restrictions	Restrictions
Like units joined	Like cases joined
No units repeated	No cases repeated

In order to use case grammar as a deep structure in tagmemic analysis the grammatical functions of subject and object must be respecified in terms of cases. But peripheral elements, being semantically determined, already have semantic case labels. In order to add the deep case relationships to a tagmemic analysis: (1) mark the verb as central; (2) add new case labels to the grammatical units subject and object but retain the semantic labels for time, place and manner tagmemes; and (3) group the cases required by the meaning of the verb into a case frame, excluding those cases which are peripheral to the structure. In some instances a phrase labelled on the surface as peripheral will turn out to be essential to the meaning of the verb and must be included in the case frame. The tagmemic-case grammar analysis is illustrated in the following sentence.

Sentence: John /took /the book /to the library /yesterday.

Tagmemics: +S:np +P:tv +O:N +L:RA ±T:av

Case grammar: A   V   O   L T_m

The surface sentence is analyzed as a clause containing a subject slot filled by a proper noun, a predicate slot filled by a transitive verb, an object slot filled by a noun phrase, a locational slot filled by a prepositional or relater-axis phrase, and an optional time slot filled by an adverb. But in deep structure the clause is centered around a motion verb which requires an Agent subject (A), the Object (O) that is taken, and the Location (L) to which the object is taken. The expression of Time is not required by the verb and is listed as a modal case. The case frame of the verb *take* is +[___ A,O,L]. It should be obvious even from the analysis of simple sentences that case grammar adds a new dimension to tagmemics, a semantic dimension based on the meaning of the verb and the roles noun phrases play in the state or event described by the verb. Case roles, by specifying the meaning of the noun phrases in the clause, relate grammar to the real world.

6.1 The four-part tagmeme. Assuming that surface tagmemic analysis is compatible with the semantic analysis of case grammar and assuming the desirability of adding this semantic dimension to the tagmemic system, the question then arises: How are case roles to be incorporated into the tagmemic theory? Since case roles seemed to apply to units, particularly at the clause level, there was a general feeling that case belonged as a separate cell within the traditional two-part tagmeme. This led to the proposal that the tagmeme should be considered a four-part unit and include case role.

The first suggestion for a four-part tagmeme was made by Alton Becker (1967). He suggested that the two-part surface structure tagmeme consisting of function and form be supplemented by two other parts referring to deep structure. Surface slot and class should be supplemented by deep role and features. Slot and role were assigned to the grammar, class and features were assigned to the lexicon. The four-part tagmeme is given in Figure 6.2.

Figure 6.2 The four-part tagmeme (Becker 1967:116).

Tagmeme unit	Grammar	Lexicon
Form (surface structure)	A (slot)	C (class)
Meaning (deep structure)	B (role)	D (feature)

Example: John sang.   Subject-actor: Noun-human

ASPECT A (slot) is surface grammatical form and refers to the functional slot, such as subject or object. ASPECT B (role) is deep grammatical meaning and refers to the case role, such as Agent, Object, Location. ASPECT C (class) is surface lexical form and refers to the class of items that fill the grammatical slot, such as noun phrase, verb phrase. ASPECT D (features) is deep lexical meaning and refers to the features inherent in the class filler.

Becker's plan is a sound one which contrasts deep and surface structure in one dimension and grammar and lexicon in the other. His choice of labels, however, is unfortunate. Grammatical form (GF) is really grammatical function or relation. Grammatical meaning (GM) is not grammatical at all but meaning independent of the grammar. These two terms are taken over in John Platt's work *Grammatical Form and Grammatical Meaning* (1972), in which surface grammatical functions are described as GFs and the deep structure cases are described as GMs. Becker's plan and Platt's later development could be considerably improved by omitting all reference to grammatical form and meaning and simply referring to case as the deep structure counterpart of surface grammatical function and inherent features as the deep structure for surface filler classes.

Austin Hale (1972) includes case role as part of a nine-cell tagmeme in a matrix with grammatical, sememic, and phonological hierarchies in one dimension and function, systemic class, and item in the other. Case role occurs in box 4 of the matrix, as in Figure 6.3.

Figure 6.3 The nine-cell tagmeme (Hale 1972).

Tagmeme unit	Function	Systemic Class	Item
Grammatical	1.Focus	2.Category	3.Citation
Sememic	4.Role	5.Concept	6.Gloss
Phonological	7.	8.	9.

If the phonological level and the item column are deleted then Hale's nine-cell tagmeme is similar to Becker's four-part tagmeme with (1) focus for Becker's grammatical slot, (2) category for Becker's lexical class, (3) role for Becker's grammatical role and (4) concept for Becker's lexical features. In both models role means case role.

Pike and Pike (1977) return to the four-part tagmeme with the first three cells similar to those of Becker and Hale but with the fourth cell filled with elements of cohesion. 'The tagmeme is a constituent of a construction seen from the point of view of its four general features: slot, class, role, and cohesion' (1977:35). Although Pike and Pike give no labels to their rows and columns, the labels used in earlier models are given for comparison in Figure 6.4.

Figure 6.4 The four-part tagmeme (Pike and Pike 1977:35).

Tagmeme unit	Function	Form
Surface structure	SLOT	CLASS
Deep structure	ROLE	COHESION

There is a tendency to move from a two-part slot-class tagmeme to a four-part tagmeme with case roles, allowing classifications like subject-as-actor, subject-as-undergoer, as in Pike's earlier work. 'The class fills a slot which performs a specific role in the stream of speech' (Pike and Pike 1977:35). But tagmemicists disagree as to whether the fourth cell should deal with semantic features (Becker, Hale) or cohesive elements (Pike and Pike).

6.1.1 Slot. Slot deals with grammatical functions such as subject, predicate, object, and adjunct, which Chomsky called grammatical relations (1965:68). In tagmemics these have been used as a universal set of grammatical relationships dealing with the surface structure of language. Terms such as subject describe grammatical relationships within the sentence; they do not deal directly with referential meaning and by themselves have no relation to the real world. Subjects are recognized by case markings, by subject-verb agreement, or by position, and take on a grammatical meaning relative to the predicate with which they are associated. But no referential or semantic meaning is attached to the notion of subject as subject.

A subject may be actor, undergoer, item described, or item identified. But the subject function adds only grammatical meaning. In the active sentence *the hunter killed the bear* one knows that the hunter does the killing and that the bear gets killed because the hunter is the subject. But in the passive sentence *the bear was killed by the hunter* the reader knows that the bear was killed because the bear is the subject. Subject only has meaning relative to its grammatical relation to the verb. There is no adequate definition of the term 'subject' independent of a particular language. Since the term is relational, it only has meaning relative to a subject-predicate combination. The relational realities of the grammar cannot be described in absolute terms.

6.1.2 Role. Role deals with semantic relations such as agent, object, undergoer, based upon the meaning of the verb, which Fillmore has described as deep structure cases. Role is independent of grammatical relationships such as subject. According to Hale, 'given only the grammatical function of an item, it is not in general possible to determine the sememic function, and vice versa' (1972:59). Given a noun as subject, one cannot tell what case role it fulfills; and given a noun filling a definite case role, one cannot tell what surface grammatical function it will perform. Slot and case role are independent of each other. For example, an Agent noun may fill the subject slot in an active sentence but this same Agent is found in a *by* phrase adjunct in the passive sentence.

If the case role is to add some meaning not contained in the grammatical function slot, then it is essential that case roles be viewed as 'underlying relationships which move in and out of positions in the surface structure patterns' (Longacre 1976:26). Slot and role must be viewed as independent systems. Slot deals with the surface grammar, case role deals with the underlying deep structure meaning. It is the correlation of these two independently motivated systems which can add to traditional tagmemic analysis an entirely new semantic dimension. The original slot-class analysis which was designed to analyze only surface function and form can now be described in terms of semantic reality. When case roles are added to the tagmemic surface analysis, the grammatical slot of the surface grammar can be further specified according to its deep case role meaning.

6.1.3 Class. Class deals with the class of lexical items that fill a grammatical slot. Predicate slots are typically filled by verbs or verb phrases. Subject and object slots are typically filled by nouns or noun phrases and occasionally by embedded sentences. Adjunct slots are more generally filled by adverbs, adverbial phrases, or prepositional phrases. Nouns as they occur in the lexicon have neither grammatical function slot designations nor do they have, in the lexicon, the semantic relationship denoted by case role. Thus class is independent of both slot and role. Hale claims 'neither grammatical nor sememic function are in general predictable in terms of the identification of a citation form' (1972:59).

Nouns will assume a grammatical relation or function slot only when they are placed in the context of a clause as its subject, object, or object of a preposition. Likewise nouns in the lexicon do not have case roles but rather are candidates to express a variety of case roles. Nouns will assume a case role within a semantic structure only when they are placed in context with a particular verb. The case role does not spring from the noun; it is read onto the noun from the verb.

6.1.4 Features. Features are the inherent semantic features of the lexical item. In emphasizing the independence of the four cells of the tagmeme, Hale criticizes Fillmore's 1968 practice of assigning features to cases. Cases are relational notions, not categorial notions, yet 'Fillmorean cases appeared to incorporate a great deal which is, from our point of view, nonrelational' (1972:60). However, by 1971 Fillmore had rejected the notion that cases should be defined by features and later describes cases as relational, not categorial notions (1977:65). Hale believes that Agent can be animate or inanimate and defines Agent as a noun 'capable of the actions named by the accompanying verbs' (1972:61).

If role is a relational notion dependent upon the verb used and features are independent of the case role, then features form an independent cell. Features will, however, be almost completely determined by class, since a noun in the lexicon out of context will have its own set of inherent features. Despite this relative dependence of class and feature, the fourth cell as described by Becker and Hale is consistent in that role provides semantic subclasses for grammatical slots, while features provide semantic subclasses for grammatical classes.

The more recent suggestion of Pike and Pike that cohesion fill the fourth cell is not as well motivated as that of Becker and Hale. Cohesion is an important element in construction but is questionable as part of the grammatical unit. Pike and Pike state that cohesion is illustrated by 'the number and kinds of tagmemes in the clause...with a subset of verbs within the predicate' (1977:35). The principal problem with cohesion is the independence of the cells in the four-part tagmeme. Since slot deals with grammatical function, it already has its cohesiveness as part of a relational system. The use of features seems to be a better development for the four-part tagmeme.

6.2 Case systems in tagmemics. Most tagmemicists agree that the tagmeme should be supplemented by a system of case roles to be added within the third cell of a four-part tagmeme. But the lists of cases proposed are different, ranging from three to ten cases. In general, these lists conform to Fillmore's suggestions that the list of cases be (1) small in number, (2) adequate for the classification of verbs in the language, and (3) universal across languages.

Case systems may be local, nonlocal, or mixed systems. All case systems have the two basic cases in common. Each system has the equivalent of a neutral object or theme case and each system has an agent or actor case. These two basic cases are sufficient for the classification of basic state, process, and action verbs. Beyond these two cases the systems differ considerably.

6.2.1 Local case systems. These systems consider physical location as the prime analogate for the description of all other semantic domains. According to Anderson, 'a localist theory holds that the members of the category of case are opposed to each other in terms of (combinations of) the directional notions source, goal, and resting point' (1977:111). Verbs of stative location and verbs of motion are treated as concrete locatives, described in terms of Location, Source, and Goal cases. Verbs from other domains are considered to be abstract locatives. The same cases, Location, Source, and Goal are used in an abstract sense to describe mental state verbs and verbs of possession and transfer of property.

Austin Hale (1972) proposes three cases: Actor, Undergoer, and Site. Actor conforms to Fillmore's Agent and Undergoer to the Object case. Site includes the three local cases, Location, Source, and Goal. 'Under the heading of Site are grouped three kinds of locative expressions that subcategorize the verb: goal-to-which, source-from-which, and place-in-which' (1972:66). Hale's case system is then reductively the same as that used by John Anderson and Jeffrey Gruber. The only difference is that Source, Goal, and Location are combined under a single case label called Site. By combining these cases under a single label Hale has lost the ability to discriminate between stative location on the one hand and directional Source and Goal concepts on the other. If he follows the one-instance-per-clause principle, information that distinguishes locative cases will be lost.

Pike and Pike (1977) propose only four cases: Actor, Item, Undergoer, and Scope. Their system is similar to Hale's except for the fact that Item is introduced as a special case for the subject in equative sentences and Site is renamed Scope. This new Scope case, like Hale's Site case, includes the notions of Location, Source, and Goal. According to Pike and Pike, Scope is 'the direction or Goal toward or (Source) away from which the action is directed' (1977:43) That Scope also includes stative location is indicated in the examples used to illustrate this case, such as *John lives in New York* (1977:45). Scope is subject to the same objections as Hale's Site case, namely, the loss of the stative /directional dichotomy.

Figure 6.5 Case Systems Compared

	Hale 1972	Pike 1977	Gruber 1965	Cook 1979	Fillmore 1968	Chafe 1970	Fillmore 1971	Platt 1971	Longacre 1976
	+Local 3	+Local 4	+Local 5	-local 5	-local 6	-local 7	Mixed 8	-local 9	Mixed 10
	Actor	Actor	Agent	Agent	Agent	Agent	Agent	Agent	Agent
	Undgoer	Undgoer Item	Theme	Object	Object Fact	Patient Compl	Object	Neutral Aff Fact	Patient Range Measure
	Site	Scope	Loc Source Goal	Loc	Loc	Loc	Loc Source Goal	Loc	Loc Source Goal Path
	.....	.....	.....	Exper Ben	Dative	Exper Ben	Exper	Part Ben	Exper
	.....	.....	.....	.....	Instr	Instr	Instr	Instr	Instr
	.....	.....	.....	.....	.....	.....	Time	Purpose	.....

6.2.2 Nonlocal case systems. These systems restrict the locative cases to physical location and introduce cases like Experiencer and Benefactive to describe the domains of mental state verbs or the verbs of possession and transfer of property. In nonlocal systems Source and Goal cases are usually omitted. Location, Source, and Goal are considered to be in complementary distribution. All three cases are regarded as manifestations of a single locative case, following Fillmore's argumentation: 'There is a certain amount of evidence that locational and directional elements do not contrast, but are superficial differences determined either by the constituent structure or by the character of the associated verbs' (1968:25). According to this principle, the locative case is interpreted as stative location with state verbs but is interpreted as directional Source and Goal with motion verbs, which are either process or action verbs. Since Location is not applied in an abstract sense to domains other than physical location, these domains must be described in terms of other cases, such as the Experiencer case for mental state verbs and the Benefactive case for verbs of possession or transfer of property.

Platt (1971) proposes a typical nonlocal system largely based upon Fillmore (1968). Platt lists nine cases: Agent, Neutral, Affective, Factitive, Participative, Benefactive, Locative, Instrumental, and Purposive (1971:72). If compared to Fillmore's 1968 list, Neutral, Affective, and Factitive seem to be subtypes of the Object case. The neutral object is used with state verbs for an object being described, the affective object for objects affected by the verbal action, and the factitive for objects created by the verbal action. The Participative case is Platt's version of the Experiential case, which is evident from his definition: the 'animate being or human institution (not itself an Agent) which is emotionally, mentally or sensually involved in the state or action' (1971:61). The inclusion of a Purposive case is an innovation and its status as a propositional case is doubtful. Although Platt lists it among his cases, he admits that this case occurs only in adjunct tagmemes and never in subject position. Finally, when Platt lists his verbs classified by case frames, the Purposive case never occurs (1971:154–155). It would seem that Purposive is a modal case and should not be included in the list of propositional cases.

6.2.3 Mixed case systems. These systems contain the Source and Goal cases like the localist systems but do not apply them abstractly to all nonlocal domains. Consequently, Source and Goal occur side by side in the case system with the Experiencer or Benefactive cases. Fillmore (1971) uses this type of mixed system. In most instances Location, Source, and Goal are applied to the possessive domain but not applied to the experiential domain of sensation, emotion, and cognition. The disadvantage of the mixed case system is that although localism is applied to some domains, the full advantage of the localist system for describing all domains in local terms is lost. Mixed systems are by their nature inconsistent in the way in which they use local terms.

Longacre (1976) proposes a mixed case system consisting of ten cases: Agent, Experiencer, Patient, Range, Measure, Locative, Source, Goal, Path, and Instrument (1976:27). Within the scope of Fillmore's Objective case, Longacre uses three cases: Patient, Range, and Measure. Range (1976:29) is similar to Chafe's complement case and includes the factitive case and cognate objects. Measure (1976:29) is defined as a quantifying complement and corresponds to Chafe's complement in analyzing the direct objects of the verbs *weigh*, *measure*. Longacre's Measure and Range cases are subject to the same criticism as Chafe's complement case. Since by definition they are syntactic verbal complements, they never occur as subjects and therefore cannot be listed in a subject choice hierarchy. Any case that can not move freely in and out of the subject position should be suspect as a propositional case. Then there is the Path case. Fillmore had considered it in 1971 but came to no definite conclusions about it. Localists such as Anderson reject the notion of a separate Path case, preferring instead to consider it as a combination of Source and Goal under a single phrase that describes movement from Source to Goal as with the prepositions *across*, *through*. Longacre not only includes Path in the concrete locative sense but applies it to transitory ownership in some transfer of property verbs. The rest of Longacre's case system conforms to Fillmore's 1971 cases.

What is the status of the instrument case among tagmemicists? One would suspect that those using a surface syntactic system like tagmemics would naturally tend to include the instrument case, since they are used to labelled instrumental tagmemes in surface grammar. But inclusion of the instrumental case depends more upon whether the case system is local or nonlocal. Both Hale's system and that of Pike and Pike are local, and therefore both reject the instrument case. Platt's system is nonlocal, Longacre's is mixed, so both include the instrument case.

The principal problem with these proposed case systems is whether the system is overdifferentiated or underdifferentiated. Hale, as well as Pike and Pike, tend to underdifferentiate when they include the three basic local notions under a single label such as Site or Scope. Most local systems use five cases: Agent, Object, Location, Source, and Goal. On the other hand, Platt and Longacre tend to overdifferentiate, particularly with regard to the Object case. In the context of nonlocal or mixed systems the principle of complementary distribution should be invoked to reduce the number of cases in the case system.

In conclusion, all of the above case systems, whether local, nonlocal or mixed, are viable case systems if they are applied consistently. Individual preferences may determine the number and kind of cases but the case system remains a paradigmatic set of case roles that divides the continuum of reality into the segments that the arguments of the various predicates denote. As long as the cases are relational notions that arise from the meaning of the verb and not categorial notions, they will be useful in the semantic description of simple predications.

6.3 Case frames (syntactic view). When a list of cases is applied to the classification of verbs, the case grammarian must have a set of tactics which guide him in arranging the cases into case frames. A case grammar system must be evaluated not only in terms of the cases used but in terms of the case frames permissible in the system.

6.3.1 Nuclear roles. In tagmemics two points of view have emerged as to how the nuclear roles are to be arranged in case frames. (1) The syntactic view, adopted by Pike and Pike (1977) following Hale (1972), sees the case role system as tied to the verb transitivity system and therefore completely dependent upon surface syntax. In this view, slot and role do not form independent systems. Rather, case role is completely predictable once the slot and verb type are known. (2) The semantic view, adoped by Longacre (1976) and Platt (1972), following Becker (1967), sees the case system as a semantic system independent of syntax. In this view, slot and role form independent systems and role is not predictable from the slot and verb type.

Hale (1972) uses his three cases, Actor, Undergoer, and Site, as verb features. A verb is classified first as [±Actor], then as [±Undergoer], then as [± Site]. These types are tied together in a system which 'explicitly links (case) features to the notion of relative transitivity' (1972:63), as in Figure 6.6.

Figure 6.6 Hale's verb types (1972).

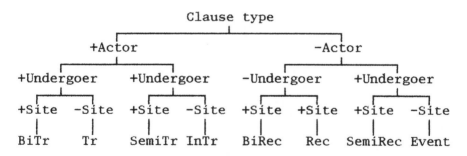

Among the agentive verbs, (1) bitransitive verbs are three-place predicates with the frame A–U–S, in which U is the direct object and S an indirect object; (2) transitive verbs are two-place predicates with the frame A–U, in which U is the direct object; (3) semitransitive verbs are two-place with the frame A–S, in which S is an adjunct; (4) intransitive verbs are one-place predicates with the frame A and no object or adjunct. Among the nonagentive verbs, (5) bireceptive verbs are two-place predicates with the frame U–S, in which S is an adjunct; (6) receptive verbs are one-place predicates with the frame U, a form of process verb; (7) semireceptive verbs are one-place predicates with the frame S, similar to Fillmore's use of the L case for *It is hot in the room*; (8) eventive verbs are zero-place predicates similar to Chafe's state ambient verbs.

Pike and Pike (1977) also use cases as features linking the case system to the verb system. 'The first choice is between Actor and no Actor. This distinguishes between transitives and equatives. For the transitive set the next choice is between Undergoer and no Undergoer. Those which have no Undergoer are intransitive; those which have either an obligatory or an optional Undergoer are the transitives' (1977:46). Equative verbs are assigned the Item case. All verb types are further subclassified as to whether or not they require the Scope case. This feature analysis results in six case frames, as Figure 6.7.

Figure 6.7 Pike and Pike's verb types (1977).

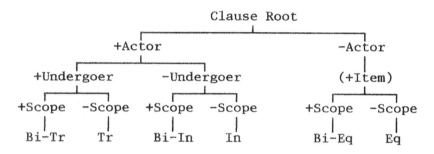

In the case system of Pike and Pike, clause types with Scope are distinguished from clause types without Scope by the prefix Bi-. 'To those types with either an obligatory or an optional Scope, we add the prefix Bi-. Those verb types which have no scope at all are: transitive, intransitive, and equational' (1977:47). There are six verb types.

(1) Bi-transitive verbs (A-U-Sc). These verbs are three-place predicates with Agent as subject, Undergoer as direct object, and Scope (Sc) as required adjunct. For example *give, say.*

(2) Transitive verbs (A-U). These verbs are two-place predicates with Agent as subject and Undergoer as direct object but with no Scope (Sc) as adjunct. For example *know, read.*

(3) Bi-intransitive verbs (A-Sc). These verbs are two-place predicates with Agent as subject and Scope as adjunct. For example *arrive, run.* The structure *be* + locative is considered bi-intransitive, not equational. For example *be in, be at, be on* are bi-intransitive.

(4) Intransitive verbs (A). These verbs are one-place predicates with Agent as subject but with no Scope. For example *cook,iv, die.*

(5) Bi-equative verbs (It-Sc). These verbs are two-place predicates with Item subject and Scope. For example *be hot (w), seem.* The sense verbs, followed by an adjective or *like* phrase, belong to this class. For example *sound good, taste like.*

(6) Equative verbs (It). These verbs are one-place predicates with Item as subject and no Scope. For example *mean, resemble,* and also any structure with *be* or *become* + noun /adjective /adverb. Only non-locative predicate adverbials belong to the equative class.

The basic verb types conform to the traditional tagmemic position that there are three types of clauses: transitive, intransitive, and equational. Transitive clauses are defined as those which have the capacity to take an object (Cook 1969:70). Even clauses with optional objects are treated as transitive. Intransitive clauses are those which never take an object and equational clauses are those which include an optional linking verb as predicate and an obligatory predicate attribute slot.

Pike and Pike (1977) double the number of clause types by distinguishing between those clauses which may take a Scope adjunct and those which never take this adjunct. Clauses with Scope have the prefix BI-, such as Bi-transitive, Bi-intransitive, and Bi-equational. In all six types of clauses there may be deletable case roles. Due to the definition of transitive, the direct object may be optional on the surface but obligatory to the clause type. Likewise, the Scope adjunct may be optional on the surface but obligatory to the clause type. In practice, Pike and Pike are reaffirming the principle stated by Hale (1972:65) that a verb must be classified according to its 'full complement of case roles', even when one or more of these roles is missing in a particular surface structure.

Pike and Pike begin by defining the roles semantically: 'ACTOR is that which does the action of the verb; the UNDERGOER is the item on which the actor acts; and the SCOPE is the direction or goal toward or away from which the action is directed' (1977:43). ITEM is not defined but presumably means 'item described or classified'. However, once these roles are tied to the transitivity system, they acquire a new operational definition. ACTOR is the subject of a nonequative verb, ITEM is the subject of an equative verb, UNDERGOER is the direct object of transitive verbs, and SCOPE is any other essential nominal.

The discrepancy between the semantic definition of the roles and the practical definitions that actually govern the choice of case roles is explained in terms of 'central meaning' (1977:43). Though Actor has the central meaning of 'one who does the action', there are contexts in which Actor, defined as the subject of any nonequative verb, does not have that central meaning. Pike and Pike assert: 'We consider *we* as emic Actor in *we owe him a debt of gratitude* even though it does not carry the central meaning of Actor' (1977:43). In practice, Pike and Pike advise the analyst to use double labels involving both slot and role, such as S-A for subject as Actor, Ad-U for adjunct as Undergoer, or Ad-Sc for adjunct as Scope (1977:50). Undergoer never occurs as subject except with passive verb forms.

But if case role is always associated with the same grammatical slot, even when the case role does not have its 'central meaning', then the case role follows automatically from the slot designation. There is no reason to consider case role at all except as an extra label applied to certain slots in the transitivity system. In this interpretation, since slot and role are no longer independent of each other, it is impossible for the case role to move in and out of the various grammatical slots to add a new semantic dimension.

6.3.2 Marginal roles (ClMar). These roles are used in the system as fillers of slots which are peripheral to the clause analysis. Among the marginal roles are included: Location (Loc), Time (Tm), Manner (Man), Instrument (Inst), Benefactee (Ben), Associated Actor (AA), Associated Undergoer (AU), and Purpose (Pur). These are used in a combined slot-role notation, ClMar-Man = 'clause margin as manner'. All clause margins are peripheral tagmemes and are assumed to be optional to the structure. These marginal roles conform to what other case grammarians call 'modal cases'. Instrument is always treated as a marginal role, at least in English (1977:36), as in *He eats with his fingers.* Marginal locatives differ from Scope locatives in Figure 6.8.

Figure 6.8 Inner and outer locatives.

Scope Locative (inner)	Marginal Locative (outer)
1. Essential to predicate meaning	1. Not essential to predicate
2. Phrase not normally moveable	2. Phrase freely moveable
3. Actor not located entirely within the location.	3. Location as setting: Actor within location
4. Location is directional, uses *to* / *from* patterns	4. Location not directional, uses *in, at, on.*

NONPARTICIPANT ROLES are used in the system in addition to the nuclear and marginal case roles. 'Complement (Co-) usually has the nonparticipant role of character-of-subject (COS) and occasionally character-of-undergoer (COU); only rarely does it have the participant role of Item' (1977:46). The label Co-COS is applied to predicate adjectives after *be, become, turn, remain,* and also to adjectives following *feel, look, smell, sound, taste,* and *seem.* It is used for predicate nouns after *become, be,* and for the objects of *resemble* and *mean.* Co-COU occurs in such phrases as *paint the house white, burn the toast black.* Co-It is assigned to the true subject in *There are birds (Co-It) in the attic.*

Complement is a surface syntactic position and it should be filled by some role essential to the meaning of the predicate. The use of Co-COS for predicate adjectives contradicts most linguists who consider adjectives to be predicates requiring no case label at all. The use of Co-COS for predicate nouns denies to these nouns a proper case label in the structure. The same applies to the use of Co-COs for the object of the verbs *resemble, mean.* Other case grammarians consider these as O-O predicates. Adjectives after *seem* and the five sense verbs are generally assumed to be separate predicates which, by subject-raising operations, become complex predicates on the surface. Structures such as *paint the house white* are usually handled as a type of causative construction with the underlying meaning: 'cause-by-painting the-house-become-white'. In sentences where extraposition or *there* insertion has applied, the case analysis is the same as the underlying sentence. Elements introduced transformationally have no case status.

6.4 Case frames (semantic view). Even as a case system linked to the transitivity system Pike and Pike's system could be improved by making the distinction that Hale (1972) makes between those intransitives with Actor as subject like *laugh, dance, sing*, and those intransitives with Undergoer as subject like *break, change, melt*. Hale calls the former intransitive and the latter receptive verbs. Receptive verb is an intransitive verb with the subject as Undergoer. This establishes a link between those transitive /intransitive pairs such as *melt,iv/tv* in which the subject of the intransitive verb is identical to the object of the transitive verb, as in *the butter melted* and *the sun melted the butter*. It is an obvious advantage to be able to treat *butter* as Undergoer in both the transitive and intransitive structure. Such an analysis is amenable to treating *melt,tv* as the causative of *melt,iv*. The amended system would then contain eight case frames rather than the six case frames that Pike and Pike propose, as illustrated in Figure 6.9.

Figure 6.9 Transitivity system (amended).

Verb type	Without Scope	With Scope
Transitive	Actor-Undergoer	Actor-Undergoer-Scope
Intransitive	Actor	Actor-Scope
Receptive	Undergoer	Undergoer-Scope
Equative	Item	Item-Scope

To create this system by a feature analysis: First, the verbs classed as [+Actor] are subclassified as [+Undergoer] or [-Undergoer]. Next, the verbs classed as [-Actor] are also subclassified as [+Undergoer] and [-Undergoer]. Finally, those verbs which fall in the category [-Actor, -Undergoer] are given the Item label. But the analysis of verb types does not have to be linked to the transitivity system. It can be linked instead to the semantic verb types developed in the work of Chafe (1970) such as action-process, action, process, and state. Each of these four verb types is then considered as a basic verb type and may occur with or without Scope. The Scope case would then be consistent with the other relations of noun to verb in Chafe's work, namely, the experiential, benefactive, and locative. Without the transitivity link, verb types would be determined by semantic considerations, not by surface syntax. In such a system slot and role would be independent of one another and case roles could move freely in and out of the various syntactic slots. In Figure 6.10 these eight verb types are listed in a branching diagram, with the various branches of the transitivity tree tied to semantic verb types.

Figure 6.10 Clause Types (Semantic)

Clause Type

- +Actor
  - +Undergoer
    - +Scope — (1) Action Process 3-place
    - -Scope — (2) Action Process 2-place
  - -Undergoer (=Item)
    - +Scope — (3) Action 2-place
    - -Scope — (4) Action 1-place
- -Actor
  - +Undergoer
    - +Scope — (5) Process 2-place
    - -Scope — (6) Process 1-place
  - -Undergoer
    - +Scope — (7) State 2-place
    - -Scope — (8) State 1-place

(1)	(2)	(3)	(4)	(5)	(6)	(7)	(8)
Actor Undergoer Scope	Actor Undergoer	Actor Scope	Actor Scope	Undergoer Scope	Undergoer	Item	Item
say,tv give,tv put,tv	break,tv dry,tv kill,tv	go,iv run,iv walk,iv	dance,iv laugh,iv sing,iv	enjoy,tv lose,tv move,iv	break,iv die,iv dry,iv	be in have,tv know,tv	broken,aj dead,aj dry,aj

6.4.1 Platt's analysis. Platt (1971), following Becker (1967), advocates case as the third cell in a four-part tagmeme. Using Becker's terminology, Platt labels surface function slots as grammatical forms (GFs) and underlying case roles as grammatical meanings (GMs). The slots used in Platt's system are: subject, predicate, object (direct or indirect), adjunct, and complement. The case roles he uses are taken from Fillmore (1968) with some minor variations. Dative is split into participative (experiencer) and benefactive, and Object is split into neutral, factitive, and affective. The list of cases then includes: Agent, Participative, Instrument, Object (3 kinds), Benefactive, Locative, and Purposive.

Platt's slot and role are mutually independent systems. Role classifications are not tied to the transitivity system. In his strongly verb-centered approach the meaning of the predicate filler determines the number and kind of case roles required by the verb. Platt states his position as follows: 'It is likely that all languages have the same set of GMs (case roles)...and the cooccurrence of the GMs (roles) with GFs (slots) differs considerably from language to language' (1971:145). In practice it is necessary for the analyst to consider carefully the meanings of the various verbs in a particular language and list in formula form (in case frames) 'the GM (role) implications of predicate fillers' (1971:85). Platt applies this principle to thirty typical predicate fillers for English in the appendix.

The classification presented by Platt has the advantages and the disadvantages of Fillmore's early case model. There is no distinction between state and process verbs since stativity is not marked in the case frame. The direct objects of *kill*, *murder* are listed as experiencer, although Fillmore later changes this case to Object (affected). The *spray-paint* verbs are listed as A-I-L as in Fillmore 1968 but Fillmore later changes these to A-O-L in 1969. Following Fillmore's 1968 model, Platt does not consider the possibility of coreferential case roles.

In a few places Platt anticipates future developments. His establishment of a neutral object case is similar to that of Gruber (1965) and his treatment of action adjectives reflects Lakoff (1966) and anticipates Anderson (1971). Platt correctly interprets the subject as Agent, not Object, in sentences such as *Joe is being nasty* (1971:111). Finally, Platt's use of double O frames anticipates later developments in Anderson (1976). For example, Platt analyzes *resemble*, *look like* as containing two neutral object cases in *Jack resembles his brother* (1971:107). He also analyzes *change* as containing two object cases, affective and factitive, in *the liquid changed to gas* and in combination with an Agent in *Jones changed the liquid into gas* (1971:108). In the examples with *change* Platt does not violate the one-instance-per-clause principle since for him affective and factitive are different cases, but in the example with *resemble* he certainly violates that principle. In Platt's work at least one case, the neutral case, may occur twice in the same case frame. In taking this position, Platt is ahead of his time.

6.4.2 Longacre's analysis. Robert Longacre (1976), like Platt, advocates a case role system which is not tied to the transitivity system. Slot and role are completely independent. As Longacre states: 'Surface structure categories of language mark functional slots of a rather high level of abstraction; and these functional slots correlate only roughly with underlying categories (roles) which are the primary linguistic encoding of the real world' (1976:23) After illustrating the various different roles that may occur in the subject slot, he adds: 'there are not only surface structure relationships (slots), but there are also certain underlying relationships (roles) which move in and out of positions in the surface structure patterns' (1976:26). This freedom of movement is essential to propositional cases.

The particular case system advocated by Longacre is based upon Fillmore (1970), Chafe (1970), Anderson (1971), and others. From Chafe's work he accepts the division into the verb types: State, Process, Action, and Action-Process, adding the types Chafe has described as Ambient, some of which are zero place predicates. The list of cases is very close to Fillmore (1970), with Patient in place of Object. Longacre's Range and Measure replace Chafe's Complement. The terms used to describe location such as Locative, Source, Goal, and Path are also used abstractly to describe possessives and transfer of property. There is no inner Benefactive case. The final list of cases then includes ten cases: Agent, Patient, Range, Measure, Experiencer, Instrument, Location, Source, Goal, and Path.

In arranging these cases into case frames, Longacre proposes an irregular matrix, 48 verb types with 45 cells filled (1976:42). He sees the cases as part of a case system: 'Case frames should constitute some sort of system, i.e. they are not a mere list or inventory but a system of intersecting parameters' (1976:38). Longacre makes a clear distinction between nuclear cases which are 'necessary components of the predication' and peripheral cases which are not necessary components. In the assignment of nuclear cases Longacre, like all tagmemicists, uses deletable roles such as deletable objects (1976:58). Unlike Platt and early Fillmore, Longacre does have coreferential roles. At least 'Agent may be coreferential with other roles' (1976:28). This coreference is illustrated in *Tom listened to the owl*, with A=E (1976:63) and *Tom gave Bill the book*, with Agent coreferential with Source (1976:78). All locomotive predicates have Agent = Patient, since 'the Agent moves himself from one place to another' (1976:76). Coreference is also used to disambiguate the intentional and non-intentional readings of *John amused me*, in which *John* is Agent and Instrument in the intentional reading but considered to be Instrument alone in the nonintentional reading (1976:55).

With the adoption of Chafe's four basic verb types, Longacre recognizes 'there is considerable regularity of the patterns of derivation' (1976:43) which carry across State, Process, and Action-Process verb types. Longacre's model, with its basic verb types, coreferential case roles and derivational patterns, seems to be a more powerful model that the earlier one of Platt.

6.5 Case roles: syntactic or semantic? In order to demonstrate the fact that it is not the particular list of cases but the link to the transitivity system that nullifies the semantic character of the case roles, syntactic and semantic views are contrasted here, using the same list of case roles. In the syntactic view, Actor is the subject of every nonequative verb, Undergoer is the direct object of every transitive verb, Item is the subject of every equative verb, and Scope is every other essential nominal. In the semantic view, using the same list of cases, Actor is the subject of an action verb, Undergoer is the subject of a process verb or the object of an action-process verb, Item is the subject of a state verb, and Scope is every other nominal.

6.5.1 State verbs. These are verbs which describe a semantically static situation in which there is no change or movement. In English, state verbs do not take the imperative or the progressive. The following examples illustrate the ways in which the syntactic view and the semantic view differ in interpretation.

(a) For BE + Adjective structures, the syntactic view calls the verb *be* Equative and the subject Item. The adjective has the 'non-participant' role of character-of-subject (COS). In the semantic view, the adjective is a State predicate and the subject is Item. For BECOME + adjective structures, the syntactic view calls the verb *become* Equative and the subject Item; in the semantic view, the BECOME + adjective structure is a Process verb and the subject is Undergoer of the process, as in sentences (1-2).

(1a) John /is /ill. It (Eq) COS?	Syntactic
(1b) John /is ill. It (St)	Semantic
(2a) John /became /ill. It? (Eq) COS?	Syntactic
(2b) John /became ill. U (Pr)	Semantic

(b) For BE + locative structures, the syntactic view calls the verb Bi-intransitive, the subject Actor, and the locative Scope, but after the rule of *there* insertion has applied, the verb is Equative and the subject Item. The semantic view calls the verb State, the subject Item, and the locative Scope, as in sentences (3-4).

(3a) Birds /are /in our attic. A? (BI) Sc	Syntactic
(3b) Birds /are /in our attic. It (St) Sc	Semantic
(4a) There /are /birds /in our attic. It (Eq) Co-It? Sc	Syntactic
(4b) There /are /birds /in our attic. ∅ (St) It Sc	Semantic

(c) For state locative verbs such as *hold*, *contain*, *include*, the syntactic view calls the verb Transitive, the subject Actor, and the object Undergoer. The semantic view calls the verb State, the subject Scope (locative) and the object Item. These verbs are the flip version of *be* + locative structures. Only in the semantic view is the Item located treated consistently, as in sentences (5-6).

(5a) The toys /are /in the box.   Syntactic
     A?   (BI)   Sc
(5b) The toys /are /in the box.   Semantic
     It   (St)   Sc
(6a) The box /contains /the toys.   Syntactic
     A?   (T)   U?
(6b) The box /contains /the toys.   Semantic
     Sc   (St)   It

(d) For position verbs such as *lie*, *sit*, *stand*, the syntactic view calls the verb Bi-intransitive, the subject Actor, and the locative phrase Scope. In the semantic view, position verbs may describe a stative situation in which the verb is State, the subject Item, and the locative phrase Scope. But if the verb means getting into that position, the verb is an Action, the subject Actor and Undergoer, and the locative phrase Scope. Only in the semantic view is there a contrast between the location of physical objects, and an Actor placing himself in a location, as in sentences (7-8).

(7a) The book /stood /on the table.   Syntactic
     A?   (BI)   Sc
(7b) The book /stood /on the table.   Semantic
     It   (St)   Sc
(8a) John /stood /on the table.   Syntactic
     A?   (BI)   Sc
(8b) John /stood /on the table.   Semantic
     A=U (Ac)   Sc

(e) For motion verbs used as verbs of extension, the syntactic view calls the verb Bi-intransitive, the subject Actor, and the locative phrase Scope. The semantic view calls the verb a State. The subject is Item and the locative is Scope. Contrast this with Action locatives in which an Actor is moving, as in sentences (9-10).

(9a) The path /led /to the bay.   Syntactic
     A?   (BI)   Sc
(9b) The path /led /to the bay.   Semantic
     It   (St)   Sc
(10a) John /ran /to town.   Syntactic
     A?   (BI) Sc
(10b) John /ran /to town.   Semantic
     A=U (Ac) Sc

(f) Anderson, in order to illustrate how cases reverse position in pairs such as *be in /contain*, *be in /include*, uses the verb *abound* as a single lexical item in which the cases appear in either order. In the syntactic view, the verb *abound* is Bi-intransitive and the subject is always Actor. In the semantic view, the verb is State and either Item or Scope may appear as subject, as in sentences (11-12).

(11a) Wild life /abounds /in this area.			Syntactic
A?	(BI)	Sc	
(11b) Wild life /abounds /in this area.			Semantic
It	(St)	Sc	
(12a) This area /abounds /in wild life.			Syntactic
A?	(BI)	Sc	
(12b) This area /abounds /in wild life.			Semantic
Sc	(St)	It	

(g) State experiential verbs are verbs which denote sensation, emotion, or cognition, such as *know*, *want*, *like*. In the syntactic view, the verb is Transitive, the subject Actor, and the object is Undergoer. In the semantic view, the verb is a State verb, the subject is Scope (experiencer), and the object is Item, reflecting the stative content, or stimulus for, the experience, as in sentences (13-14).

(13a) Mary /knows /the story.			Syntactic
A?	(T)	U?	
(13b) Mary /knows /the story.			Semantic
Sc	(St)	It	
(14a) The story /is known /to Mary.			Syntactic
U	(T-Pass)	A?	
(14b) The story /is known /to Mary.			Semantic
It	(St)	Sc	

(h) State benefactive verbs are verbs denoting possession. Verbs like *have*, *own*, *possess*, contrast with the flip counterparts *belong to*, *be* + possessor. None of these takes the progressive. In the syntactic view the verb *own* is a Transitive verb, the subject Actor, and the object Undergoer, but *belong to* is Bi-intransitive, with subject as Actor and the *to* phrase as Scope. In the semantic view, both verbs are State but *own* has Scope, the possessor, as subject and *belong to* has Item as subject, as in sentences (15-16).

(15a) She /owns /the horses.			Syntactic
A?	(T)	U?	
(15b) She /owns /the horses.			Semantic
Sc	(St)	It	
(16a) The horses /belong /to her.			Syntactic
A?	(BI)	Sc	
(16b) The horses /belong to /her.			Semantic
It	(St)	Sc	

6.5.2 Nonstate verbs. These may be process, action, or action-process. Process verbs are nonagentive events which take the progressive but not the imperative. Process verbs have inanimate noncausative subjects or animate subjects acting involuntarily.

(a) For motion verbs, the syntactic view considers the verb to be Bi-intransitive, the subject Actor, and the locative Scope. But the semantic view distinguishes between process verbs with Undergoer as subject and action verbs with Actor as subject.

(17a) The letter /arrived /at the office.   Syntactic
     A?   (BI)   Sc
(17b) The letter /arrived /at the office.   Semantic
     U   (Pr)   Sc
(18a) Joe /arrived /at the office.   Syntactic
     A? (BI)   Sc
(18b) Joe /arrived /at the office.   Semantic
     A=U (Ac)   Sc

(b) For many transitive /intransitive pairs, the transitive verb is the causative of the intransitive verb. In the syntactic view, the intransitive verb has Actor as its subject; the transitive verb has Actor as its subject and Undergoer as its object. In the semantic view, the intransitive verb is a process verb with Undergoer as subject; the transitive has Undergoer as object.

(19a) The bottle /broke.   Syntactic
     A?   (I)
(19b) The bottle /broke.   Semantic
     U   (Pr)
(20a) John /broke /the bottle.   Syntactic
     A   (T)   U
(20b) John /broke /the bottle.   Semantic
     A   (Ac)   U

It should be obvious from the examples given that the syntactic view and the semantic view are totally different, not merely notational variants. In the syntactic view, in which case role is tied to the transitivity system, all of the case designations are predetermined by the verb type. One need not even look at the sentence to be analyzed or reflect on its content. If the verb is not an equative verb, the subject is Actor, no matter what the meaning may be; if the verb is an equative verb, the subject is Item. The Undergoer only occurs as the direct object of transitive verbs and Scope is used for any other essential role. In such a system there is no semantic analysis, only a second labelling of items in the syntax that are already well defined in the grammar. In the semantic view, however, in which case is not tied to the transitivity system, all of the case roles move freely in and out of subject and object positions. The underlying set of case roles is totally independent of the functional slots of syntax.

6.6 Evaluation of the tagmemic-case grammar model. Models incorporating case grammar are useful if they add a new semantic dimension to tagmemic analysis. Tagmemics provides a methodology for surface structure analysis using as a basic unit a tagmeme which specifies both grammatical function and filler form class. This surface structure analysis can be supplemented by a case analysis which adds the semantic role manifested by the surface function-form unit.

6.6.1 Semantic structure. Every case grammar model is presented in the context of a syntactic system which specifies the order of constituents in the surface structure. The system of tagmemic analysis provides a set of formulas from the sentence to the word level which taken together give a picture of the underlying structure. From these surface formulas trees can be drawn which express the branching relationships which begin with sentence level and end with the individual morphemes. What case grammar can add to this structure is a set of case designations for the elements of each clause. These cases are added to the normal subject, object, and other clause level slots to give semantic information about these constituents.

6.6.2 Case system. The case systems proposed for use in the tagmemic system include local, nonlocal, and mixed systems. Hale as well as Pike and Pike use a local system, Platt uses a nonlocal system, and Longacre uses a mixed case system.

(1) Typical local systems, as used by Anderson (1971), Gruber (1965), and Jackendoff (1972) have five cases: Agent-Object-Location-Source-Goal. Agent and Object are used for basic verb types and the three locative cases are used to express both concrete and abstract locative domains. Hale (1972) uses a single Site case in place of Location, Source, and Goal. Pike and Pike (1977) use Scope to replace Location, Source, and Goal and add an Item case as the subject of stative equational verbs.

(2) Typical nonlocal systems, as used by Fillmore (1968), Chafe (1970), include Agent-Experiencer-Benefactive-Instrument-Object-Locative. In Fillmore (1968) Experiencer and Benefactive are combined under a Dative case and in Chafe (1970) the Object case is represented by Patient and Complement. Platt (1971) follows this tradition but expands Object into affective, effective, and neutral cases. He also adds a Purpose case but does not use it.

(3) Typical mixed systems, as used by Fillmore (1971), include Agent, Experiencer, Instrument, Object, Location, Source, and Goal, with abstract Location, Source, and Goal cases used to represent the benefactive domain and Experiencer used to represent mental state verbs. Longacre (1976) follows this tradition but expands the Object case into Patient, Range, and Measure, and adds Path as a supplement to the three locative cases.

6.6.3 Case tactics. It is not the particular list of cases used but the way in which cases are assigned to clauses that can make the incorporation of case roles useful in tagmemic analysis. Any system that is tied to the transitivity of the verb will fail to add any new semantic dimension; the case roles will be automatically assigned by the surface structure. But any system that depends only upon the meaning of the verb will demand of the analyst a new insight into semantics and in this way will contribute to the overall completeness of the tagmemic analysis.

Once the independence of slot and role is established, the way is open to a more sophisticated view of case roles which takes into account the history and development of case grammar models. If tagmemics is to profit from the work of case grammarians, as Pike has suggested, then tagmemicists have to be familiar with these models in detail in order to extract from them what will constitute the most efficient role system for tagmemics.

The best defense of the role system described in Pike and Pike (1977) is that it is not, and is not intended to be, a case grammar analysis. Role is simply another, and perhaps useful, way of describing surface grammatical functions. Within their descriptive framework role is not case as understood by Fillmore. On the other hand, both Platt (1971) and Longacre (1976) have made serious attempts to incorporate case role, as understood by case grammarians, into tagmemic analysis. By incorporating semantic case into the tagmemic grammatical system there is some hope of discovering the semantic /syntactic correlates which link the deep meaning of sentences to surface expression.

6.6.4 Derivation. Pike and Pike use the terms basic and derived in their analysis but not in the sense of semantic or morphological derivation. 'Basic' means the basic sense of the verb and 'derived' means other senses in which the verb is used. The choice of the basic sense seems to be a matter of the analyst's intuition. For example, *change,tv* is considered basic but *change,iv* is considered derived; *leave* = 'go away from' is basic but *leave* = 'let x remain in a place' is derived. It is necessary to differentiate between the different uses of a verb but this does not constitute a derivational system.

Longacre alone seems to be aware of the need to relate various verb types, particularly those derived from the same lexical root. In any semantic analysis the similarities and differences between *broken* /*break,iv* /*break,tv* and similar sets should become obvious. Longacre is aware of Chafe's (1970) derivation system which links state, process, and action-process in one direction by the inchoative and causative derivations and in the other by the decausative and resultative derivations. The state verb *broken* becomes the process verb *break,iv* by the addition of the inchoative derivation which adds the notion of change-of-state. The process verb *break,iv* becomes the action-process verb *break,tv* by the causative derivation which adds an Agent to the structure. Surely such derivations are needed.

6.6.5 Covert case roles. In developing a system of case roles, much more attention should be paid to the theory of covert case roles, including deletable, coreferential, and lexicalized roles. Although all tagmemicists make use of deletable case roles as optional tagmemes, only Longacre uses coreferential roles. Coreference is a necessity for any case grammar model and is used by Fillmore after 1968, and by Anderson, Gruber, and Jackendoff. Only early Fillmore and Chafe lack coreferential roles.

None of the tagmemicists seems to be aware of the possibility of lexicalized case roles. Lexicalized roles occur in most case grammar models and seem to be fairly prevalent in English. It is difficult to analyze surface expressions semantically without the realization that *water* = 'put water on' or *skin* = 'remove the skin from' with the object lexicalized into the verb. If these lexicalized roles are not noted, then it is impossible to analyze a verb according to its full complement of case roles. In sentences like *John watered the lawn* the main verb would be analyzed as A-L rather then as A-O-L with O lexicalized, making it impossible to compare this sentence with its paraphrase *John put water on the lawn*, which must also analyzed as A-O-L. Any analysis that uses lexicalized roles would give the same A-O-L case frame to both sentences with the added comment that the O case is lexicalized in one sentence but not in the other.

An ideal tagmemic-case grammar model is one in which tagmemic surface analysis and deep case grammar analysis constitute two independent but compatible systems. The tagmemic analysis then depends upon surface syntax while the deep case analysis depends upon the semantic valence of the verb. In an ideal combined model, case roles would move freely in and out of surface positions.

The assignment of case roles is only possible at the clause level of analysis. It is at the clause level that the verb is inserted into the predicate slot and it is the verb alone which determines the case roles. If only clause level tagmemes have case roles, then it is doubtful that tagmeme units, which exist at all levels of the grammar, should include a third cell for case role in a four-cell tagmeme unit.

Another possible interpretation of role within a tagmemic grammar is that role is a dimension which provides allounits of a tagmeme at the clause level. Tagmemes which differ by form or by distribution may be considered as allotagmas of the same tagmeme. If the case role is considered to be such a dimension then the tagmeme could be described in terms of concrete allotagmas differing in meaning, form, or distribution.

For example, the subject of a clause is universally called subject but it may express the role of agent, experiencer, benefactive, object, or locative. The respective allotagmas could then be described as subject-as-agent, subject-as-experiencer, subject-as-benefactive, subject-as-object (described), subject-as-location, in much the same way as Pike described subject variants in his original work. The tagmeme would still be a function-form surface unit but its variants would be described in terms of case roles.

The tagmemic model traditionally describes the surface structure in terms of subject, predicate, object, location, time, and manner tagmemes. This list is a mixed bag of syntactic and semantic labels. If the surface analysis were restricted to only syntactic labels, it might consist of such universals of surface structure as subject, predicate, object, and adjuncts with no semantic specification for the various adjuncts. Deep role structure would then consist of two parts: the propositional roles and the modal roles. The propositional roles are those required by the verb and generally fill subject and object positions, though occasionally they fill an adjunct position. The modal roles of Time, Place, Manner, Instrument, Purpose, Cause, and Result would fill only clause marginal adjunct slots.

In Longacre's analogy, the clause level is like a drama. The predicate slot indicates the plot; the subject, direct and indirect object slots generally express the characters; the adverbial adjuncts represent the setting or scenery; and adjectives and relative clause are relegated to the costume department. Generally subject, predicate, and object slots are nuclear and are diagnostic of the type of clause used. Adjuncts tend to be peripheral slots which only add to the setting and are independent of clause type.

In a case role analysis the nuclear slots would absorb the essential cases but occasionally there would be adjunct slots containing a propositional role. In particular, the adjunct of location is often propositional when the locative is an inner locative, as with a verb like *put* or in motion verbs with directional locatives. Sometimes there are characters lurking in the shrubbery.

For predicate attribute structures where the surface structure consists of subject, predicate linking verb, and an obligatory predicate attribute slot filled by noun, adjective, or adverbial, certain cautions are necessary. If the predicate attribute is an adjective, then the logical predicate is BE + adjective and the adjective receives no role label. The same principle holds true for BE + adverbial. Only in the case of BE + noun structures are two case labels to be assigned, one to the subject noun and another to the predicate noun. In many systems the subject noun and the predicate noun will receive the same case label.

Case grammar is applied only to simple active predicates. Case assignment is not dependent upon (1) whether the sentence is a statement, question, or command, (2) whether the verb is used in the active or passive voice, (3) whether *there* insertion, *it* extraposition, or any other transformation has applied, (4) whether the verb is used in a main clause or a subordinate clause. Case deals with semantic verb valence and semantic valence does not change with verb use.

With these cautions in mind, it should be possible to assign case roles and to use case grammar as an effective instrument in the description of language, adding a new semantic dimension to the surface structure description already complete in terms of function-form units or tagmemes.

Exercise 6. Write the case frame for the verb in the following sentences. The four cases are A = Actor, U = Undergoer, Sc = Scope, and It = Item. Complements which are nonparticipant roles are listed as COS (Character of Subject), COU (Character of Undergoer). The case frames are those of Pike and Pike (1977). Using the same cases, rewrite the case frame for each verb but with A = Agent, U = process Object, It = stative Object, and Scope = any other essential case.

1. Wild life abounds in this area. (A,Sc) _____

2. The letter arrived at the office. (A,Sc) _____

3. John is tall. (It,COS) _____

4. The toys are in the box. (A,Sc) _____

5. The liquid became gas. (It,COS) _____

6. The bottle contained the medicine. (A,U) _____

7. The chicken cooked slowly. (A) _____

8. He found the dolphin. (A,U) _____

9. He got (= procured) a car. (A,U) _____

10. He had apples. (A,U) _____

11. I know the legends. (A,U) _____

12. The body lay sprawled on the floor. (A,Sc) _____

13. The path led to the bay. (A,Sc) _____

14. A dozen means twelve. (It,COS) _____

15. An accident occurred. (A) _____

16. She owns the horses. (A,U) _____

17. It rained. (A) _____

18. The book stands on the table. (A,Sc) _____

19. That tasted like an apple to me. (It,Sc,COS) _____

20. He underwent surgery. (A,U) _____

21. He just watched the waves. (A,U) _____

Tagmemic lexicon. The tagmemic lexicon is a collection of 80 verbs with the case frames as described in *Grammatical Analysis* (Pike & Pike 1977). The cases used are Actor, Undergoer, Item, and Scope. Nonparticipant roles are listed as COS (Character of Subject) and COU (Character of Undergoer).

abound (in)	A,Sc	live (in)	A,Sc
arrive	A,Sc	look + adj	It,Sc,COS
be + adj	It,COS	mean	It,COS
be + adv	It,COS	meet	A,U
be + loc	A,Sc	melt,iv.	A
be + N	It,COS	melt,tv.	A,U
become + adj	It,COS	need	A,U
become + N	It,COS	occur	A
belong to	A,Sc	owe	A,U,Sc
break, iv	A	own	A,U
break,tv.	A,U	paint + adj	A,U,COU
bring	A,U,Sc	play	A
buy	A,U	pour	A,U,Sc
change,iv.	A	put	A,U,Sc
change,tv.	A,U	rain	A
contain	A,U	read	A,U
cook,iv.	A	receive	A,U,Sc
cost	A,U,Sc	remain + adj	It,COS
cough	A	require	A,U
cure,tv.	A,U	resemble	It,COS
die	A	run	A,Sc
drink	A,U	say	A,U,Sc
eat	A,U	see	A,U
empty,tv.	A,U,Sc	seem + adj	It,Sc,COS
feel + adj	It,Sc,COS	sell	A,U,Sc
find	A,U	sing	A,U
fix	A,U	sit	A,Sc
fly	A,Sc	sneeze	A
get	A,U	stand	A,Sc
give	A,U,Sc	swallow	A,U
go	A,Sc	sweep	A,U
hand	A,U,Sc	take (from)	A,U,Sc
have	A,U	taste (like)	It,Sc,COS
hold	A,U	throw	A,U,Sc
keep	A,U,Sc	try	A,U
know	A,U	undergo	A,U
last	A,U	watch	A,U
lead (= extend)	A,Sc	want	A,U
leave	A,U,Sc	win	A,U
lie (down)	A,Sc	write	A,U

7 The Case Grammar Matrix Model

7.0 Overview. Case grammar theory is a theory that deals with sentence semantics. Within a general theory of semantics case grammar is not concerned directly with the semantics of discourse nor with the componential analysis of words. Case grammar deals only with the internal structure of a single clause. And even within the clause case grammar does not deal with all elements of meaning; it deals only with the essential predicate-argument structure. Case grammar is a theory that attempts to describe the meaning of a clause in terms of a central predicate and the arguments required by that predicate.

In this study of semantic structure all nonessential elements are excluded such as negation, tense, aspect, mood and optional adverbials. The resulting case grammar is essentially a labelled predicate logic in which the arguments required by the predicate are described in terms of the roles these arguments play in the situation described by the predicate.

Case grammar models are particular applications of the theory at a given point in time. In the preceding chapters a series of case grammar models have been described as illustrations of how case grammar theory has been applied in practice. These included the original Fillmore model (1968), his revised model (1971), the verb centered model of Chafe (1970), the localistic model of Anderson (1971), the system of thematic relations proposed by Gruber (1965) and Jackendoff (1972), and several of the case grammar models proposed by tagmemicists.

The principal points investigated in the study of each of these case grammar models were: (1) What type of logical structure is proposed? (2) What is the list of cases used? (3) How do these cases combine to form case frames? (4) What means are provided for deriving one verb type from another verb type? and (5) To what extent is covert role theory developed to explain the occasional or total absence of required cases from the surface structure? On each of these points the models investigated provided a series of alternate and often contradictory choices for the construction of an ideal case grammar model.

(1) Logical structure. What type of logical structure should be adopted for a case grammar model? The logical structure selected should describe the semantic content of the sentence in terms of a predicate and its case labelled arguments. Logical structure ought to be independent of any particular syntactic system and universal enough to apply to all languages. If case grammar is regarded as an independent semantic model, then it is not necessary to use the logical structure of the case grammar model as a base for the generation of sentences.

All of the case grammar models proposed describe the semantic content of the sentence but they also attempt to incorporate this structure into a model for the generation of sentences. Fillmore (1968, 1971) proposes a transformational grammar with a case base, Chafe (1970) develops case structures in a generative semantics system, Anderson (1971) uses his case system in the context of a dependency grammar. Jackendoff (1972, 1976) prefers to match his set of thematic relations with syntactic selectional features in the interpretive component of a generative grammar. The tagmemicists want to use case roles as an added dimension for the syntactic tagmeme unit.

The issue raised here is whether the purposes of case grammar are not better served by developing the model independent of any syntax. Its only objective would be the semantic representation of sentences. All syntactic systems could use the same model while all users could contribute to the structure of the model. Such a model would then be universal, independent of particular languages, and independent of any syntactic system. Its sole purpose would be to describe the logical form of sentences.

(2) Case system. What list of cases should be adopted? The list, according to Fillmore, should be small, universal, and adequate for classifying all the verbs of a language. There should be one list of cases, not different lists for different verb classes or different lists for different languages.

In the models proposed there are many different lists of cases. There are localist and nonlocalist systems. The pure localist systems such as Anderson, Gruber, and Jackendoff seem to resolve into five cases: Agent, Object, Location, Source, and Goal, though Hale and Pike and Pike reduce Location, Source, and Goal to a single case. The nonlocalist systems include some common elements such as Agent, Experiencer, Benefactive, Object, and Locative. The other cases proposed seem to be variants of the Object case such as effected and affected objects or variants of the Locative case such as Location, Source, Path, and Goal. Some case systems are mixed in the sense that they used the Source and Goal cases abstractly for other domains.

Two solutions seem to be the most realistic. The first alternative is to accept the localist system and use their five cases: Agent, Object, Location, Source, and Goal. This is a viable alternative and is applied effectively by Anderson. The other alternative is to adopt a nonlocalist system with the common elements: Agent, Experiencer, Benefactive, Object, and Locative. The other proposed cases are then explained as variants of the Object and Locative cases or retained separately as essential cases. The case grammar matrix model adopts this second alternative but its nonlocalist system can be readily translated into the localist system.

(3) Case frames. What combinations of cases should be permitted in a case frame? If the case grammar model is to be explicit in its formulation, it requires an explicit set of tactics by which cases are to be combined into case frames. Some of the principal tactical questions to be answered are: How many cases may occur in a case frame? In what order are they to be listed? Which cases may cooccur? Can cases be repeated in a single frame?

In the models proposed, the case tactics had to be determined more by the author's practice than by his explicit statement of principles. How many cases may occur in a case frame? Most of the nonlocalists used one, two, or three cases while localists admitted four cases. Chafe alone proposed caseless case frames under the title 'ambient verbs'. In what order should the cases be listed? Both Fillmore and Chafe suggest that the cases should be listed in subject choice hierarchy order; Anderson generates cases only in surface structure order. Which cases may cooccur? Anderson and all localists require an obligatory O case but none of the nonlocalists proposed an obligatory Object because the various splittings of the Object case made this impossible. For the nonlocalistics the Experiencer, Benefactive, and Locative cases are mutually exclusive, as evident in Chafe. In practice Fillmore also treats the experiential and locative verbs as belonging to separate domains. Can cases be repeated in the same frame? Most analysts accept the Fillmore one-instance-per-clause principle but some analysts, like Anderson, allow multiple occurrences of the O case.

(4) Derivation. Should the model require a derivational system? A priori it would seem that case grammar models do not have to have a derivational system to relate the verbs in the lexicon but once the verbs are classified according to case frames the relations between different forms from the same root become obvious. It is not sufficient simply to classify individual verbs. What is required is a set of lexical redundancy rules that would make the relations between the various verb forms explicit.

Fillmore stated as one of his original goals the organization of the lexicon but this organization is not as strong as it could be in the Fillmore models. In his early model he proposes such methods as adding cases, substituting cases, and different subject choice as a means for relating verb entries. Chafe alone proposes a coherent derivational system which links the State, Process, and Action verbs by explicit derivational units such as inchoative, causative, resultative, and decausative. Anderson's model contains the elements for a derivational system because of his close attention to various uses of the verb but no explicit system is developed. Jackendoff, by representing the principal verb types in terms of abstract predicates, is involved in the problem of derived inchoatives and causatives. These are represented by the abstract predicates BECOME and CAUSE and serve to relate verb entries within the lexicon. Although none of the systems proposed relates all verbs in the lexicon, those relations which can be made explicit should be made explicit.

(5) Covert roles. To what extent should the model make use of covert role theory? Without some theory of covert roles, it seems impossible to classify each verb according to the full complement of case roles that the verb demands. Analysis will vary from sentence to sentence and reflect surface structure configurations rather than the essential semantic structure which is the goal of the model. When one considers all of the options provided for covert role theory it seems logical to find cases wherever they are hidden and to distinguish partially covert roles like deletable roles which are seen on the surface some of the time from totally covert roles like the coreferential and lexicalized roles which are never seen on the surface. These three ways in which a case may be overlooked constitute covert role theory.

Most of the models under investigation developed some theory of covert roles. Fillmore introduced deletable roles in 1968 but coreferential and lexicalized roles were added to the model only in 1971. Chafe is the weakest in the use of covert roles, adapting his case frames more to what occurs on the surface. Anderson also has deletable roles and introduces coreferential roles as double labels on a single noun, postulating a wide range of possible coreferential roles. Lexicalized roles occur in Anderson as 'reduced clauses'. Gruber and Jackendoff use coreference as an essential in a system with an obligatory Theme or Object case. Deletion is also used in the system and case roles are subject to lexical incorporation.

(6) Modality. Aside from the questions of what constitutes the essentials of the model, an important issue is the distinction between propositional cases and modal cases. For unless a clear distinction is made between the cases which make up part of the proposition and the cases that belong to the modality, there will be confusion as to what is part of the essential logical structure required by the predicate and what is not.

Propositional cases are essential to the proposition while modal cases are optional adjuncts of virtually any predication. Modal cases are not treated explicitly in many models since the object of the model is to illustrate only the essential cases. But the knowledge that modal elements also occur is useful in text analysis to explain the other phrases which will inevitably occur in text analysis. Fillmore in 1968 made a distinction between those cases which belong to the proposition and those cases which belong to the modality; he also distinguished between inner locatives required by the verb and outer locatives not required by the verb. In 1969 he explicitly describes Time, Place, and Frequency as cases which belong to the modality. Tagmemicists, accustomed to separating nuclear and peripheral elements in their syntactic analysis, are careful to exclude modal elements such as manner, purpose, place, time, instrument as outside of the essential proposition. Case grammarians have to approach the analysis of essential logical form with a clear idea of what is part of the proposition and essential to the meaning of the verb, and what belongs to the modality and is not essential to verb meaning.

7.1 Logical structure. Logical structure is the representation of the semantic content underlying a sentence. The object of a case grammar analysis is to discover and represent logical structures. The logical structure should properly represent the meaning of the sentence, it should be in a form that can be related to the surface syntactic structure, and it should be in a form which is universal across languages.

The case grammarian seeks to find (1) the simplest way to characterize logical structures, (2) the simplest way to relate logical structure to syntactic structure, and (3) a system of representing logical structures that is universal.

A simple sentence is a surface syntactic form which contains a single proposition if the sentence is unambiguous. Ambiguous sentences will have more than one underlying proposition. The logical structure of a sentence is the logical structure of the proposition underlying the surface sentence.

Propositional logic is the analysis of a proposition into the elements which constitute its logical structure. Propositional logic deals with the relation between elements of a proposition. These elements are called predicates and arguments. Each proposition has one and only one predicate, represented in the surface structure by a verb or predicate adjective. The proposition may have one or more arguments, represented in the surface structure by nouns or other nominals. The predicate is the relational element; it ties together the arguments in a proposition. Arguments are referring elements; they refer to objects in the real world. Both predicates and arguments can be further analyzed into features, as illustrated in Figure 7.1.

Figure 7.1 Logical structure (Leech 1974:133).

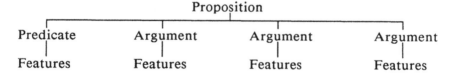

The analyst first extracts the predicate which is the key to the logical structure and places it in initial position in the structure. Next, he determines the number of arguments that are required by the predicate and adds these to the structure. Finally, both the predicate and all the arguments can be further analyzed in terms of features.

An argument may be represented by an embedded sentence, as when a clause is embedded as the subject or object of the verb. Clauses also occur as downgraded propositions (Leech 1974:149), acting as features for both predicates and arguments. Relative clauses may occur as features of nouns and adverbial clauses may occur as features of verbs. Tense and modality elements may also be included as features of the predicate.

Generative semantics represents the content underlying the sentence in terms of logical structure. In place of the terms proposition, predicate, and argument, generative semantics uses the syntactic labels sentence (S), verb (V), and noun phrase (NP). The verb is placed in initial position in a VSO order. The arguments required by the verb are placed after the verb, usually in the order subject, indirect object, direct object. This logical structure is then used as a base from which surface structure is derived by lexical insertions and meaning-preserving transformations. The structures of generative semantics (Langacker 1975) consist of a series of layers: (1) a performative layer which distinguishes between statements, questions, and commands, (2) a tense-aspect-modality layer which adds tense-aspect-mood, and (3) a propositional layer which contains the predicate and the arguments required by that predicate.

Case grammar is a system of semantic analysis which represents the internal semantics of a single clause (Fillmore 1977). Each clause has a single predicate which has a valence or propensity for a set of arguments. These arguments are given case role labels to indicate the part they play in the situation described by the verb. The verb is central and the number and kind of case roles is fully determined by the verb's semantic valence.

Logical structure is the best way to represent the results of a case grammar analysis. As in logic, there is one central verb which is the relational element and determines the number of arguments. Case grammar differs from logical representation only in that the arguments are given names or case roles. This labelled logical structure is simply a case labelled generative semantic structure. It differs from generative semantics in three ways: (1) the arguments have case role labels, (2) the arguments are ordered according to a subject choice hierarchy, and (3) the case analysis is limited to the propositional content of the sentence and excludes modal elements. A typical logical structure is given in Figure 7.2.

Figure 7.2 Logical structure with cases.

The verb is the central element which determines the number and kind of cases that occur. The S is simply a bracketting device which groups together the verb and its cases. This structure is mirrored exactly in the form of the case frame + [___A,B,O] with the verb in initial position and the required cases in subject choice hierarchy order after the verb. There is no simpler or more direct way of representing case structures.

One advantage of using a logical structure that conforms to the principles of logic is that it makes case frame structures intelligible to the logician. Instead of creating new forms for representing the meaning, the adoption of logical structures uses a system that has been tested over many years. These basic logical structures can then be expanded to include the modal elements, the features, and the downgraded propositions which make up a complete logic.

The advantage of using a system that conforms to the practice of generative semantics is that a way is provided for relating underlying logical structures to surface syntactic structures. Even though case grammar concentrates upon the propositional content of a sentence, the way is open to expanding the system to include performative and modality layers to express all the elements which enter into the literal meaning of a sentence, not just the basic predicate and arguments.

Modal cases are cases not required by the meaning of the verb and are therefore not part of the basic logical structure. In a logical analysis these modal cases could be represented as higher predicates with the whole proposition within their scope, as suggested by Fillmore (1968). This practice is also followed with various types of adverbials in generative semantics. These adverbials include expressions of time, place, manner, cause, result, and purpose when these are not part of the essential underlying proposition. Instead of being simply ignored, these modal cases would then have a part in a more fully developed logical structure, as represented in Figure 7.3.

Figure 7.3 Logical structure with modal cases.

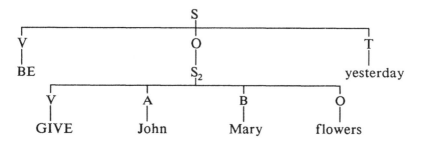

In the sentence *John gave Mary flowers yesterday* the verb *give* is a three-place predicate which requires a giver (A), a receiver (B), and the object given (O). The verb does not require an expression of time. The expression of time here is a modal case which is outside of the proposition. This modal case can be represented in a higher predication using the verb *be* = 'occur' with the event (O) and the time expression (T) as its arguments. The sentence is then translated as *It was yesterday that John gave Mary the flowers*. Even if all of the modal case can not included in the structure by this particular method, a rational way is provided to account for at least some of these modal cases.

Another advantage of this type of logical structure is that predicates can readily be decomposed into atomic elements. The derivational system proposed for the case grammar model is made stronger by the causative analysis of generative semantics. For example, the factoring of the predicate *thicken,tv* into CAUSE, COME ABOUT, BE THICK confirms the case analysis of stative adjectives, inchoative forms, and causative forms. Given the stative form as Os, the inchoative form indicates a change of state and is therefore a process with the case frame O. The causative form introduces the Agent as the subject of CAUSE. What the Agent causes is the change of state of the object so that the resulting case frame is A,O. These forms have been consistently analyzed by case grammarians in this way. Lexical decomposition of these predicates leads to an explanation of why the case frames must be the way they are.

Case grammar habitually decomposes predicates in the search for incorporated propositional cases which are part of the case frame. Generative semantics, following techniques initiated by Gruber (1965), look for a more complete lexical decomposition which includes the uncovering of all essential prepositions, atomic predicates, and both propositional and modal cases. For example, if *enter* = 'go into', its object is recognized as a locative governed by the lexicalized preposition *in* and the verb is analyzed as a motion verb which takes a locative case as its direct object. With the preposition governing the object manifest by decomposition, it is easier to establish the Locative case as essential to the case frame.

The logical structure proposed here is substantially that proposed by Fillmore (1970) and reported in Cook (1979:18). It is the simplest of the structures proposed by case grammarians and most directly reflects the case frame. It has a higher S as in Fillmore (1968) but has no separate modality component. It does not have a higher V as in Anderson (1971) or Chafe (1970). It is not part of an interpretive component as in Jackendoff (1972) nor is it tied in any way to syntactic structure as in Pike and Pike (1977). It is an independent structure which represents only the logical content of a proposition, a single level of the grammar. Yet it is adaptable to expansion by the addition of modal elements such as tense, aspect, negation, and the performative verbs.

The logical structure which represents the semantic content of a proposition in a case grammar model should be characterized in the simplest way possible, it should provide the simplest way to relate this structure to syntactic structure, and this logical structure should be universal across languages. This structure should be independent of any particular syntactic model but at the same time be adaptable for use in any syntactic system such as transformational generative syntax, generative semantics, dependency grammar, or tagmemics. The simple logical structure adapted from propositional logic and used elsewhere in linguistics in generative semantics seems to have all of these qualities and consequently seems to be the best way to represent a case grammar analysis.

7.2 The case system. In order to determine the list of cases required for the model, the case grammar matrix model makes a distinction between propositional and modal cases. Propositional cases are cases that are required by the semantic valence of the verb; modal cases are optional elements that are not required by the semantic valence of the verb. Verbs are classified according to the set of propositional cases with which they occur; modal cases do not enter into this classification. Modal cases are optional adverbials that may occur in virtually any predication. Fillmore (1975:7) claims that the basic questions about the list of definite cases remain unanswered: (1) What is the correct list of cases? (2) How are the cases to be defined? (3) How do we know, in principle, when the list of cases is complete?

7.2.1 The correct list of cases. What is the correct list of cases? Anderson (1971) lists four cases, Gruber (1965) five, Fillmore (1968) six, Chafe (1970) seven, Fillmore (1971) eight, Platt (1972) nine, Longacre (1976) ten. These different lists indicate different ways in which the analyst chooses to divide the continuum of reality. There is no absolutely correct list of cases. Each list must be defended on its own merits.

Fillmore (1975:5) suggests that the list of deep cases should be (1) small in number, (2) adequate for the classification of all the verbs in a language, and (3) universal across languages. Fillmore rejects the opinion that different lists of cases might be used for different areas of the language or that different lists of cases will be needed for different languages. All the proposed lists of cases are small, all claim to be adequate for the classification of verbs, and all claim to be universal across languages.

First, local systems have to be distinguished from nonlocal systems. For a localist, physical location is used as a prime analogate for the description of nonlocal semantic domains. The localists tend to agree on a system of only five cases: Agent, Object, Location, Source, and Goal. Some localists, such as Hale and Pike and Pike, group Location, Source, and Goal under a single case.

Next, the nonlocal systems should be examined. In comparing nonlocal systems, it is evident that certain cases are common to all systems. The cases which are not common to all systems are suspect and usually result from splits or mergers of other cases. The matrix model uses, as a common denominator, the five cases of Agent, Experiencer, Benefactive, Object, and Location.

The Instrument case is included in all of Fillmore's models but rejected by virtually everyone else. Chafe includes Instrument but has no matching feature in the verb. In effect his claim is that no verb by its valence requires the Instrument case. If so, Instrument is merely a modal option which may occur with any action verb. Anderson (1970) and localists in general reject the Instrument case.

The Object is the case that is most frequently split into subcases. Fillmore (1968) uses both Factitive and Object to distinguish the affected from the effected object. Chafe (1970) has Patient and

Complement cases, with Patient serving as a general theme for states and processes and Complement serving as the case for factitive and cognate objects. Chafe also has ambient verbs with no object at all. Platt (1972) splits Object into affective, effective, and neutral, with neutral more proper to states, and affected and effected objects distinguished with process and action verbs. Longacre (1976) uses Patient in Chafe's sense, supplemented by Range and Measure similar to Chafe's Complement.

The argument against this proliferation of subcases for the Object is not a semantic but a distributional one. The semantic distinctions observed by these analysts certainly exist. The question is whether it is better to represent this distinction by separate case labels or to consider these cases to be in complementary distribution and leave them under a single case label. No one doubts the distinction between affected and effected objects. But the distinction is already clear from the type of verb used. Creative verbs take effected objects and noncreative verbs take affected objects.

Localistic systems never split the Object case. As a result they are able to maintain an obligatory Object or theme in every case frame. It seems that the underlying obligatory theme is a useful generalization that will be missed whenever the Object case is split into subcases. The obligatory theme hypothesis severely restricts the classificatory power of the case model, making it a more efficient and tightly constrained model.

The Locative case is also frequently split into subcases such as Location, Source, Goal, and Path. For localist systems the split in the locative cases is necessary since these cases are the basis for all classification. For nonlocalist systems it is not necessary to split the locative. Fillmore (1968) was the first to advance the arguments for the unity of the locative case, namely, that stative and directional locatives are in complementary distribution. Stative locatives occur with states; directional locatives occur with motion verbs. No one doubts that stative locatives are different from directional locatives. The point at issue here is whether the model is better served by grouping these under one case label. For nonlocalist case systems this move has the tactical advantage of describing a set of locative verbs and defining the whole locative domain as one that involves the locative case.

If the Object case is considered to be a single unified case including affected, effected, and neutral objects, if Locative is considered to be a single unified case, including both stative and directional locatives, and if Instrument is considered to be a modal case, then the nonlocal case systems are reduced to a system of five cases: Agent, Experiencer, Benefactive, Object, and Locative. The unified Object case now allows the analyst to hold the obligatory O hypothesis. This is the case system used in the case grammar matrix model. Agent and Object cases are used to define the basic verb types and the Experiencer case, the Benefactive case, and the Locative case are used to establish verbs within their respective semantic domains.

7.2.2 The cases defined. How are the cases to be defined? According to Fillmore (1977), cases are relational, not categorial, notions and are not to be defined in terms of features such as [±animate]. Cases spring from the meaning of the verb; they are attached to features in the verb. If so, then cases are already assigned to a verb before that verb is put into context, that is, before any noun is present. On the other hand, nouns are not cases but case candidates. In the lexicon nouns have no cases assigned to them but once they are put into context the case roles are read onto the nouns from the verb. The cases of the case grammar matrix model are as follows:

Agent (A). Agent is the case required by an action verb. Although Agent is the typically animate performer of the verbal action, inanimate nouns may also occur as Agents. These include physical objects, machines, communities, and natural forces, anything capable of producing the action described by the verb.

Experiencer (E). Experiencer is the case required by an experiential verb. Experiencer is the person experiencing sensation, emotion, or cognition. In verbs of communication the experiencer is the hearer. Experience deals only with the inner life of man, not with experience in its more general sense.

Benefactive (B). Benefactive is the case required by a benefactive verb. Benefactive is the possessor of an object or the nonagentive party in the transfer of property. Benefaction may be either positive or negative and the benefactor may be a gainer or loser.

Object (O). Object is an obligatory case found with every verb. Object is the neutral underlying theme of the state, process, or action described by the verb. With state verbs the Object is the thing being described. With process or action verbs the Object is the moving object or the thing undergoing change.

Locative (L). Locative is the case required by a locative verb. Locative is restricted to physical location in space and includes both stative location with state verbs, and directional source and goal locatives with process and action verbs.

Modal cases. Modal cases do not enter into the classification of verbs and therefore are not defined within the system. However, these cases should be recognizable if only to be discarded for they occur in context with the essential cases required by the verb. A list of the modal cases should include: Time, Manner, Instrument, Cause, Result, Purpose, outer Locative, and outer Benefactive. Outer locative is generally recognized as a stative locative expression which occurs with an action or process verb. Since locatives essential to process or action verbs are directional, stative locatives can only be interpreted as setting the location for the whole process or action and not as part of the verb's propositional structure. Outer benefactive is generally signalled in English by *for* = 'for the sake of'. This outer benefactive is distinct from one who participates in the transfer of property.

7.2.3 The complete list of cases.

How do we know in principle when a list of cases is complete? Case systems are always submitted with the implicit claim that this given list of cases is necessary and sufficient for the classification of all the verbs of a language and that it will be so for any language. 'Necessary' means that every case in the list is needed, that none can be omitted. 'Sufficient' means that no other cases are needed.

The first argument for completeness of a case system is a comparison with all other proposed case systems. Since these systems revolve around illustrative examples with particular attention to problem areas, a proposed case system must be able to handle these areas in an efficient way. If a particular case system has been designed with a knowledge of all the current case systems, it can presumably make an honest claim at completeness.

The second argument for completeness is extensive use of the model in text analysis. Although comparison with other models is useful, it is possible that all the models have missed essential areas of semantic reality which will only be discovered in the analysis of texts. The matrix model has been extensively tested in this way with the complete text of Hemingway's *The Old Man and the Sea*, consisting of roughly 5000 clauses. Each verb was given a case frame based upon the meaning of the verb in context. Although many interesting problems were encountered, there was no verb that could not be classified using the five-case system.

A final argument for completeness is a philosophical one. Since philosophers have already attempted analyses of all of semantic reality, their classifications are pertinent to the completeness of a case system. Aristotle lists ten categories which may be predicated of a subject: substance, quality, quantity, relation, action, passion, time, position, place, and circumstances. Predicate nouns are obvious candidates for the substance category. Quality, quantity, and relation probably occur in predications that attribute these to an underlying Object or theme. Agent and Patient are obvious case candidates, as are position and place grouped under Location. Time and circumstances would probably occur only as modal cases.

Lexicographers have also attempted to classify all of semantic reality. Peter Roget in his thesaurus lists the following semantic categories: abstract relations, space, physics, matter, sensation, intellect, volition (including possessive relations), and affections. Basic relations would be handled by the Agent and Object cases; sensation, intellect, and volition fall under the Experiencer case; space would fall under the Locative case; and possessive relations under the Benefactive case. There is no semantic domain described in Roget's thesaurus that cannot be handled by a model which includes the five cases: Agent, Experiencer, Benefactive, Object, and Locative.

7.3 Case frames. A case system is not just a list of cases but a paradigmatic set of oppositions between contrasting semantic roles. The case frames, on the other hand, are the syntagmatic arrangements in which case roles occur. The value of a case system depends in large part upon the case tactics which are used to arrange case roles into case frames. In a phonological system it is not just the list of phonemic oppositions that gives a picture of the sound system of the language but the phonemes in combination with the phonotactics by which these phonemes are arranged in morphemic structures.

7.3.1 Case tactics. The tactics by which the five cases of the matrix model are arranged into case frames have been developed from many sources. If these tactics are followed, then the number and kind of case frames possible within the model are severely limited. These tactics are summarized in the following set of statements:

(1) Each frame consists of a verb and one, two, or three cases.
(2) The Object case is obligatory to every case frame.
(3) The secondary cases E, B, and L are mutually exclusive.
(4) No case except O occurs more than once in a case frame.
(5) Cases are listed left to right by subject choice hierarchy.

(1) Each case frame consists of a verb and one, two, or three cases. This means that the model includes one-place, two-place, and three-place predicates. Zero-place predicates are excluded as are multiplace predicates with more than three arguments.

Although this is not stated in any model as a principle, it is followed in practice in Fillmore (1968) and, except for the zero-place ambient verbs, by Chafe (1970). Nonlocalist case systems generally operate with the three-place limit, that is, they do not postulate case frames with more than three cases. Localistic systems, however, with their distinction between Source and Goal cases, regularly use four-place predicates. A mixed case system that includes Source and Goal cases will also regularly use four-place predicates.

(2) The Object case is obligatory to every case frame. This obligatory O hypothesis was first introduced by Gruber (1965) and followed by Anderson (1971) and Jackendoff (1972). Other case grammarians appear to be close to this hypothesis and the several examples that they give without the O case can easily be explained with the use of covert role theory.

The principal objection to the obligatory O hypothesis is the existence of the so-called ambient verbs proposed in Chafe (1970). Those who hold zero-place predicates claim that in sentences dealing with meteorological conditions the subject pronoun *it* has no content and therefore has no case label. Anderson's answer to this objection is that even if the content of this pronoun is vague it can be represented by an underlying 'though perhaps empty' (1971:50 fn.3) nominative (Object) case.

(3) The secondary cases, Experiencer, Benefactive, and Locative, are mutually exclusive. Only one of these may occur in a given case frame. This is a principle practiced by Chafe (1970). The reason for this is that the primary cases, Agent and Object, are first used to develop the basic state, process, and action verbs. Then these basic verb types are all tested one by one with the Experiencer, the Benefactive, and the Locative cases to determine whether such verb types exist. In effect each secondary case establishes a separate semantic domain, resulting in a class of experiential verbs, benefactive verbs, and locative verbs. These domains are mutually exclusive domains and a verb can belong to only one of these semantic areas.

(4) No case occurs more than once in a single case frame. This principle is stated in Fillmore (1968) and in Fillmore (1971) and is accepted as a necessary principle in case analysis. In general, this principle is followed in the matrix model but an exception is made for the O case, following Anderson (1976), who claims that the model should accept more than one occurrence of only the Object case. These double O structures are necessary to account for predicate nominals after *be* and *become* and certain three place predicates with object and object complement, such as *elect* in *they elected him president.*

(5) Cases are listed in a left-to-right order according to a subject choice hierarchy. Cases that are favored as the subject choice are ranked higher in this hierarchy. Although some models have used right to left order, including Fillmore (1968) and Chafe (1970), the preferred order is left to right. The subject choice hierarchy is considered an essential of the case grammar model (Fillmore 1971). The subject choice hierarchy is merely a convenient generalization about the order of cases which enables the analyst to state within the case frame which case will be subject and to note exceptions to this generalization. Without this generalization subject choice would have to be stated for each individual verb.

7.3.2 The matrix of case frames. If the above tactics are followed, then the number and kind of case frames is severely limited. The verb types used are state, process, and action verbs, expressed in terms of one-, two-, and three-place predicates. These verb types are arranged into specific semantic domains. There are basic verb types which exclude the experiencer, benefactive, and locative cases, and use only the Agent and Object cases. There are experiential, benefactive, and locative verb types which use the Agent and Object cases in combination with the Experiencer, Benefactive, and Locative cases, respectively. The possible case frames can then be arranged in a 3 x 4 matrix with state, process, and action verbs in one dimension and the basic, experiential, benefactive, and locative semantic domains in the other. The matrix of possible case frames described in this model is given in Figure 7.4.

Figure 7.4 Case frame matrix.

Verb types	Basic	Experiencer	Benefactive	Locative
1.State	Os be tall	E,Os like	B,Os have	Os,L be in
2.Process	O die	E,O enjoy	B,O acquire	O,L move,iv
3.Action	A,O kill	A,E,O say	A,B,O give	A,O,L put

The verbs of a language are first analyzed as state, process, or action verbs. If the verb is a state, it belongs on the first line of the matrix and the O case is marked as Os to indicate stativity. If the verb is a process, it belongs on the second line of the matrix and no Agent is present in the case frame. If the verb is an action, it belongs on the third line of the matrix and has an Agent case in the case frame.

(1) **State verbs** express a notionally stative situation. In English, state verbs do not take the progressive aspect nor the command imperative. In any conflict between the stative meaning and the syntactic tests, the stative meaning takes precedence.

(2) **Process verbs** express a dynamic nonagentive event. In English, they freely take the progressive aspect but do not take the command imperative. Process verbs include motion verbs with inanimate subjects and involuntary human activities.

(3) **Action verbs** express a dynamic agentive event. In English, action verbs take both the progressive aspect and the command imperative. Action verbs refer to an Agent who may be said to be performing the action indicated by the verb.

Verbs are next classified within a specific semantic domain. Verbs that use only the primary cases, Agent and Object, are classed as basic verbs. Verbs which also use one of the other three cases, the Experiencer, the Benefactive, or the Locative case, are listed within the experiential, benefactive, or locative domains. The Experiencer, Benefactive, and Locative cases are mutually exclusive and never occur together in the same case frame.

(1) **Basic verbs** use only the Agent and Object cases. These are verbs which do not belong to the experiential, benefactive, or locative domains and include basic state, basic process, and basic action verbs.

(2) Experiential verbs use the Experiencer case along with the Agent and Object cases. These verbs describe the semantic domains of sensation, emotion, and cognition proper to the inner life of man. Experiential verbs are also used to describe human communication, which always involves a speaker, a hearer, and what is said.

(3) Benefactive verbs use the Benefactive case along with the Agent and Object cases. These verbs describe the semantic domains of possession and transfer of property. State verbs describe possession while action and process verbs are used to describe voluntary and involuntary transfer of property.

(4) Locative verbs use the Locative case along with the Agent and Object cases. These verbs describe the semantic domains of location and direction. State verbs describe static location in a place, marked with stative prepositions. Process and action verbs describe directional motion, marked with directional prepositions.

7.3.3 Extension of the matrix. The suggested case frame matrix is established with the claim that the twelve case frames of the matrix are necessary and sufficient for the classification of all the verbs of the language in all their meanings. This claim has to be modified in at least the following ways. (1) Double O case frames are to be allowed, (2) some special verbs will require an essential Time element, and (3) verbs with the same case frame may differ in regard to the case to be chosen as subject.

(1) Double O case frames. Special problems arise with the analysis of predicate nouns, those two-place predicates in which the subject and predicate nominal are somehow equated. The simplest solution is to relax Fillmore's one-instance-per-clause principle and allow double-O case frames, for example *be* + N as + [___Os,Os], *become* + N as + [___O,O], and verbs with the meaning *make become* as + [___A,O,O].

(2) Essential Time case. There are verbs in the language which require an essential Time case. For example, Time is predicated of an event as in *the meeting is on Wednesday*, classified as + [___Os,T]. Process verbs may occur such as *last*, classified as + [___O,T], and action verbs occur such as *spend (time)*, classified as + [___A,O,T].

(3) Subject choice. Verbs with the same case frame often differ by subject choice such as *have* + [___B,Os] and *belong to* + [___Os,B]. The frame is identical in the number and kind of cases but the abnormal subject choice is indicated by writing the case frame with the cases in reverse order. If these exceptions are taken into account, then the case frame matrix must be revised to include double O frames, that is, frames with a Time case and frames that differ in subject choice. The revised matrix is shown in Figure 7.5.

Figure 7.5 Revised case frame matrix.

Verb Types	Basic	Experiential	Benefactive	Locative
1.State	Os be tall Os,Os be + N	E,Os like Os,E be boring	B,Os have Os,B belong to	Os,L be in L,Os contain
2.Process	O die O,O become	E,O enjoy O,E amuse	B,O acquire O,B	O,L move,iv L,O leak
3.Action	A,O kill A,O,O elect	A,E,O say A,O,E amuse(agt)	A,B,O give A,O,B blame	A,O,L put A,L,O fill

7.4 Derivation. Once the verbs of a language have been classified into case frames and placed within definite cells of the matrix, it is clear that there are related sets of verbs based upon the same lexical root. These related verbs often include state, process, and action forms. What is needed is a derivational system which, given one verb in the set is basic, will explain how other verbs are derived from it.

7.4.1 Unidirectional derivation. The derivational system proposed in generative semantics is a unidirectional system which assumes the state form is always the basic form. This system is independent of the morphology and syntax of any particular language. Process and action forms are derived from the state form by adding abstract predicates. State forms become process forms by adding the inchoative predicate BECOME (McCawley 1968) or COME ABOUT (Lakoff 1970). COME ABOUT is defined by Dowty (1972) in Von Wright's logical terms as $-p$ T p, where p = a proposition, $-p$ = the negative of that proposition, and T is a dyadic operator meaning 'and next'. A sentence such as *the door opened* is interpreted as COME ABOUT + *be open* and is read as 'the door was not open AND NEXT the door was open'. Process forms become action forms by adding the predicate CAUSE, a two-place predicate with an Agent or event as its subject and an event, not a state, as its object (McCawley 1968). A sentence such as *John opened the door* is interpreted as CAUSE (John, COME ABOUT (BE OPEN (door))) and is read as *John caused it to come about that the door is open*. The unidirectional derivational system is given in Figure 7.6.

Figure 7.6 Unidirectional derivation

State + Inchoative = Process + Causative = Action

The advantage of the unidirectional system is that no decision has to be made about the basic form. The state is the basic form no matter what the language. The disadvantage of this system is that backwards derivations are not as easily represented. In many languages there is a backwards derivation from process to state called resultative and there is a backwards derivation from action to process in which the notion of Agent and the abstract predicate CAUSE are deleted. These must then be represented by subtracting the abstract predicate CAUSE to derive a process from a state and by subtracting the abstract predicate COME ABOUT from a process to derive a state.

7.4.2 Bidirectional derivation. Chafe (1970) proposes a bidirectional derivational system for English using four derivational units: inchoative, resultative, causative, and decausative (which he calls deactivative). The basic form may be a state, a process, or an action verb. If there is a set of forms derived from the same morphological root, these forms may be related by the bidirectional system. This derivational system is represented in Figure 7.7.

Figure 7.7 Bidirectional derivation.

$$\text{State} \begin{bmatrix} >\text{Inchoative} \\ \text{Resultative}< \end{bmatrix} \text{Process} \begin{bmatrix} >\text{Causative} \\ \text{Decausative}< \end{bmatrix} \text{Action}$$

(1) A State verb may become a derived process verb by adding the inchoative derivation. In logical structure this is represented by adding the predicate COME ABOUT to the state verb.

Rule 1.   State + Inchoative = derived Process
be thick,adj + inchoative = *thicken,iv*
thicken,iv = COME ABOUT (BE THICK)

(2) A Process verb may become a derived state verb by adding the resultative derivation. In logical structure this is represented by subtracting the predicate COME ABOUT from the process verb.

Rule 2.   Process + Resultative = derived State
break,iv + Resultative = *be broken,adj*

The direction of derivation between State and Process forms is determined by morphological criteria, with the simplest form as the basic form. Given the forms *thick /thicken*, the State form is the simpler form and is considered the basic form; but given the forms *broken /break*, the Process form is considered the basic form.

If the State and Process forms seem to be equally simple, then other criteria must be used. Given the pair *hot* /*heat*, either form could be the basic form. If there is another State form *heated*, which is a resultative form, then it is probable that, since a separate resultative form already exists, the State *hot* is not a resultative form and therefore must be the base form. The Process form *heat* is then derived from the adjective *hot* by the inchoative derivation. If there is no other State form, as with the adjective *cut*, this form is assumed to be the resultative form derived from the process *cut,iv* by the resultative derivation. According to the norms established here, the adjective *tired* is derived from the verb *tire,iv*, contrary to Chafe, who claims that *tired* is the base form despite the fact that morphology 'perversely suggests the opposite' (Chafe 1970:122).

(3) A Process verb may become a derived Action verb by adding the causative derivation. In logical structure this is represented by adding the predicate CAUSE to the process verb.

Rule 3.   Process + Causative = derived Action
                break,iv + Causative = *break,tv*
                break,tv = CAUSE (BREAK)

(4) An Action verb may become a derived process verb by adding the decausative derivation. In logical structure this is represented by subtracting the predicate CAUSE from the action verb.

Rule 4.   Action + Decausative = derived process
                wash,tv + Decausative = *wash,iv*

The direction of derivation between Process and Action verbs is determined by syntactic criteria first suggested by John Lyons (1969). If the process is a true intransitive which may occur in a simple subject-predicate structure without manner adverbials, the direction of derivation is from process to action. Given the pair *break,iv* /*break,tv*, the direction of derivation is from process to action. The process form is the base form since *the window broke* is a grammatical sentence without adding manner adverbials. But if the process verb is a pseudointransitive which may only occur in subject-predicate structures when accompanied by manner adverbials, the direction of derivation is from action to process. Given the pair *wash,iv* /*wash,tv*, the transitive *wash,tv* is the base form since **the sweater washes* is not a grammatical sentence without the addition of manner adverbials.

The disadvantage of the bidirectional derivational system is that the norms for choosing a base form depend upon the morphology and syntax of a particular language. The results are language particular, not universal. It cannot be assumed that, if the Process form is the base form in English, it will be the base form in some other language. When using bidirectional derivation, the whole system of basic and derived forms will depend on the morphology and syntax of the language under consideration and the relation between the forms must be reconstructed for each language.

The advantage of the bidirectional system is that derivations do in fact occur in both directions. For example, the resultative derivation occurs in English and is often confused with the passive form of the verb. This ambiguity can only be resolved in context when the analyst realizes that these resultative adjectives exist. In a similar way the decausative derivation is common in English and creates a special class of psuedointransitive verbs that exclude the notion of Agency, are generic in meaning, and require special manner adverbials. The use of pseudointransitive verbs such as *wash* and *sell* is easily explained in a system that includes a decausative derivation.

7.4.3 Other derivations. The causative paradigm which links State, Process, and Action verbs is not the only system of derivations in a language. The derivations in a language are as widespread as the derivational endings provided for the verbal and adjectival systems, since both verbs and adjectives may occur as predicates. For example, in English, psych movement verbs have a derivational system of their own. Psych movement verbs are defined as process verbs which take the Object case as subject and the Experiencer case as direct object. Each of the Psych movement verbs has two derived adjectives, one with the Experiencer case as subject and the Object case in a prepositional phrase, and another which takes the Object case as subject and the Experiencer case as indirect object. Typical derived forms are given in Figure 7.8.

Figure 7.8 Psych movement derivations.

O subject	Basic verb	E subject
be amusing	amuse	be amused at
be boring	bore	be bored with
be interesting	interest	be interested in

The adjective with the O case as subject is a derived adjective formed from psych movement verbs with the derivation ending *-ing*. That this form is a true adjective and not the progressive form of the verb can be seen by contrasting the derived adjective with progressive forms. The progressive verb takes the E case as direct object; the derived adjective takes the E case as indirect object and may be modified by the intensifier *very*, as in sentences (1-2).

(1) The story /was amusing /me.
    O   V   E
(2) The story /was very amusing /to me.
    Os   V   E

The adjective which takes the E case as subject is a derived adjective and not a passive form of the verb,as can be seen by contrasting the adjective form with the passive form. The verb in its passive form takes the preposition *by* with a downgraded subject. The adjective form takes a variety of prepositions and therefore cannot be considered a passive. It can also be modified by the intensifier *very*, as in sentences (3-4).

(3) John /was bored /by the story.
    E   V   O
(4) John /was very bored with /the story.
    E   V   Os

Although the *-ed* forms might be called resultative with the meaning 'state as a result of a process', there is no convenient term for the *-ing* forms with the meaning 'quality of an object to induce a certain psychological experience'. Surely many other derivational sets can be found in language which are independent of the inchoative and causative paradigms.

7.5 Covert roles. In case grammar verbs must be classified according to their full complement of case roles but in the analysis of particular sentences one or more cases required by the meaning of the verb may be missing from the surface structure. What is needed is a covert role theory which will explain the partial or total absence of essential cases in the surface structure.

Case roles are either overt or covert. OVERT CASE ROLES are roles that are always present in the surface structure of simple active sentences. COVERT CASE ROLES are roles that are sometimes or always absent from the surface structure. Covert roles may be partially covert or totally covert. PARTIALLY COVERT ROLES are sometimes present and sometimes absent and are called DELETABLE ROLES. TOTALLY COVERT ROLES are roles that are never present in the surface structure despite the fact that they are part of the verb's valence. Totally covert roles include both COREFERENTIAL ROLES and LEXICALIZED ROLES. The various kinds of case roles, classified according to their occurrence in surface structure, are given in Figure 7.9.

Figure 7.9 Case roles in surface structure.

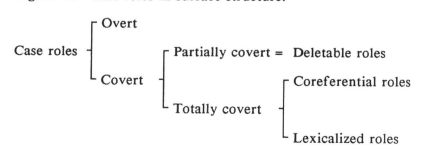

7.5.1 Deletable roles. Deletable roles are case roles that are present in some occurrences of the verb but not present in others. When a case role required by the verb's semantic valence occurs sometimes but not always in the surface structure, it is called a deletable role. These roles must occur at least in some sentences. The most common deletions are the direct object with A-O verbs and the indirect object with Os-E verbs, as in sentences (5-6).

(5) Mary /is cooking /(something).   A,O/O-del
     A   V   O-del
(6) Mary /seems /(to me) /to be happy.   Os,E/E-del
     Os   V   E-del   Os = Sent

Deletable roles occur with three-place predicates. The most common deletions are the E case or the O case with communication verbs, the deletion of the B case with A-B-O verbs, and the deletion of either the O case or the L case with A-O-L verbs, as in sentences (7-11).

(7) Harry /told /me /(something).   A,E,O/O-del
     A   V   E   O
(8) Harry /said /something /(to me).   A,E,O/E-del
     A   V   O   E
(9) Dick /sold /the car /(to somebody).   A,B,O/B-del
     A   V   O   B
(10) Tom /filled /the glass /(with milk).   A,O,L/O-del
      A   V   L   O
(11) Tom /poured /the milk /(into the glass).   A,O,L/L-del
      A   V   O   L

Deletable case roles are not to be confused with the syntactic deletions which are recoverable from the context. Case analysis deals with the semantic structure of simple sentences. Before a case structure can be determined the text has to be broken into single clauses and each clause rewritten as a simple sentence. All recoverable syntactic deletions must be restored before any determination is made about deletable roles. A simple discovery procedure for deletable roles is to test the verb by constructing sentences with each of the cases in turn omitted from the sentence. If the sentence is acceptable without a particular case role, then that role is a deletable role. The subject is never a deletable role, as in sentences (12-15).

(12) Harry /told /me /that he was sick.   A,E,O
      A   V   E   O
(13) Harry /told /me.   A,E,O /O-del
      A   V   E
(14) *Harry /told /that he was sick.   E is not deletable
      A   V   O
(15) *Harry /told.   E + O not deletable
      A   V

7.5.2 Coreferential roles. Coreferential roles are two case roles that are applied to a single noun. The lower ranking of these two cases is called a totally covert role because, despite the fact that it is part of the verb's valence, it can never appear in the surface structure. Coreferential roles may occur with A-O and E-O verbs and also with A-E-O, A-B-O, and A-O-L verbs. Most coreferential roles involve the Agent case. Coreferential roles also occur with E-O verbs in experiential adjectives in which E=O. They may occur with A-O verbs in action adjectives in which A=O. These types of adjectives are different from simple descriptive adjectives. Coreferential roles may occur when an Agent is added to an involuntary human process that would normally be an O verb, as in sentences (16-19).

(16) The boy /is tall.   Os
BE = is tall
(17) The boy /is hungry.   E,*Os /E=O
BE = feels hungry
(18) The child /is being kind.   A,*O /A=O
BE = acts kindly
(19) He /rested for a while.   A,*O /A=O
REST = cause self to rest

Coreferential roles occur with A-E-O verbs. The Agent case is coreferential with the Experiencer case in the active form of verbs of sensation, emotion, and cognition. The Agent case is coreferential with the Object case in the active form of psych movement verbs, as in sentences (20-21).

(20) Adam /looked at /the sunset.   A,*E,O /A=E
Adam = Agent + one who sees
(21) John /frightened /the baby.   A,E,*O /A=O
John = Agent + cause of the fright

Coreferential roles occur with A-B-O verbs. The Agent case is coreferential with the Benefactive case in the active form of verbs of deliberate acquisition, as in sentence (22).

(22) They /caught /three good fish.   A,*B,O /A=B
CATCH = acquire for self

Coreferential roles occur with A-O-L verbs. The Agent is often coreferential with the moving object in active verbs of motion. In a few rare examples the Agent may be coreferential with the location, as in sentences (23-24).

(23) John /went /to Chicago.   A,*O,L /A=O
John = Agent = moving Object
(24) The army /contained /the attack.   A,O,*L /A=L
army = Agent = container

Coreferential roles are different from surface reflexives. Coreferential roles deal with identity of reference at the semantic level; a single noun fills two semantic functions. Reflexivization is a surface syntactic rule which states that, when two NPs in the same clause are identical in form and reference, the second may be changed into a reflexive pronoun.

Reflexive pronouns are prima facie evidence that there are no coreferential roles. If two case roles are coreferential at the semantic level, then the lower ranking role is deleted and does not reach the surface. Coreferential roles are applied to a single noun in surface structure; reflexives, on the other hand, require two nouns in the surface structure. If the reflexive pronoun fills an argument position in the structure, it will receive its own case label despite the reflexive form. For example, when the reflexive form occurs in object position it has a different case label from the subject. Despite the identity of reference there is a difference in semantic role and therefore a different case label, as in sentence (25).

(25) Harry /shaved /himself.   A,O
  A V   O

7.5.3 Lexicalized roles. Lexicalized roles are case roles that are incorporated into the surface verb form. Since the case is incorporated into the verb, it does not normally appear in surface structure. If it does, it appears as a second copy of a role already expressed in the verb. Modal roles, as well as propositional roles, may be lexicalized into the verb form. The most common form of lexicalization is Object incorporation. When a verb and a noun with the same spelling occur in the lexicon, the verb often incorporates the noun. Lexicalized objects occur with A-O, A-E-O, A-B-O, and A-O-L verbs, as in sentences (26-30).

(26) He /worked /all day.   A,*O /O-lex
  WORK = do work
(27) He /questioned /the suspect.   A,E,*O /O-lex
  QUESTION = ask questions of
(28) He /fed /the fishes.   A,B,*O /O-lex
  FEED = give food to
(29) He /watered /the lawn.   A,*O,L /O-lex
  WATER = put water on
(30) Roger /skinned /the lion.   A,*O,L /O-lex
  SKIN = remove skin from

The locative case is also frequently lexicalized. Verbs of motion frequently incorporate into the verb the adverbial representing the direction of the motion. Verbs which are similar to container nouns often have the locative container noun lexicalized. These lexicalized locatives occur with both process O-L and action A-O-L verbs, as in sentences (31-34).

(31) The balloon /descended.   O,*L /L-lex
     DESCEND = go down
(32) The sun /rose.   O,*L /L-lex
     RISE = come up
(33) Richard /bottled /the beer.   A,O,*L /L-lex
     BOTTLE = put in bottles
(34) The sheriff /jailed /Robin.   A,O,*L /L-lex
     JAIL = put in jail

Modal cases are incorporated into the verb, but this is not a sufficient reason to consider them to be propositional cases. A verb is a complex of features and incorporates many elements expressing manner, means, or medium. These features help to distinguish verbs but do not add anything to the predicate-argument structure. The instrument case is often lexicalized into the verb, as in sentence (35).

(35) He /kicked /the dog.   A,O
     KICK = hit with the foot

If lexicalized roles are expressed on the surface, then the resulting sentence is redundant and considered unacceptable. But if the lexicalized role can be modified in some way, then the modified role may appear as a copy of the lexicalized role, as in sentence (36).

(36) He /bottled /the beer /in green bottles.   A,O,*L /L-lex
     *He bottled the beer in bottles.

7.6 Evaluation of the matrix model. Case grammar theory is a theory of sentence semantics in which the content of a single clause is represented in terms of a verb and the cases required by that verb's semantic valence. The case grammar matrix model is a particular model within that theory, an alternative model based upon the best insights of other models within that theory. The case grammar matrix model remains within the case grammar tradition in the selection of logical structure, the system of cases, the case frames used, the system of derivation adopted, and the use of covert roles.

The logical structure of the model consists of an S dominating a Verb and one, two, or three cases. The case system consists of five cases: Agent, Experiencer, Benefactive, Object, Locative. The Object case is obligatory to every case frame; Experiencer, Benefactive, and Locative cases are mutually exclusive. Case frames are arranged in the form of a 3 x 4 matrix of case frames with state, process, and action verbs in one dimension and basic, experiential, benefactive, and locative in the other. Verbs which are morphologically related constitute a set with one form as intrinsic and other forms derived from it by means of the four derivational units: inchoative, resultative, causative, and decausative. A theory of covert case roles, including deletable roles, coreferential roles, and lexicalized roles, is used to explain the absence of certain case roles in surface structure.

7.6.1 **Logical structure.** The logical structure is made up of logical elements arranged in a particular order. The concept of case grammar as a semantic valence theory is taken from Fillmore (1977). Case grammar is a system which describes the inner semantics of a clause using the verb's semantic valence as a base. The elements of a logical structure are the predicate and the arguments required by the predicate. These elements are taken from traditional logic. Case grammar uses a predicate-argument structure and only differs from traditional logic in naming the arguments as cases. The order of elements in a case grammar description is a subject choice hierarchy order. Cases are listed in left-to-right order according to their availability as a subject choice.

The matrix model uses this logical structure, substantially the structure suggested by Fillmore (1971), with the elements ordered left to right according to the subject choice hierarchy proposed by Fillmore (1971). This logical structure was chosen as the one most independent of surface syntax and most in conformity with logical principles. Consequently, it is the most versatile, the easiest to use, and is easily adaptable to any system of syntactic representation. This structure is recognizable as the representation that most accurately represents the case frame. It has the added advantage of being adaptable to later insertion of the modality elements according to the methods of generative semantics.

7.6.2 **Case system.** The case system is the list of cases used in the model. Available case systems are localist and nonlocalist. The localist systems tend to resolve into five cases: Agent, Object, Location, Source, and Goal. But if one establishes a nonlocalist system, then the choice of cases is much wider. The list of cases used in the matrix model is basically formed from those cases which are common to nonlocalist systems. It is closest to Chafe (1970) except for ambient verbs, Instrument, and Complement. Instrument is excluded because it has no feature in the verb and therefore does not spring from the verb's valence. Complement is excluded because it never occurs in subject position and seems to be a variant of the Object case. Locatives are unified under a single case label (Fillmore 1968).

7.6.3 **Case frames.** Case frames in the matrix model are arranged in a 3 x 4 matrix with state, process, and action verbs in one dimension and basic, experiential, benefactive, and locative domains in the other. The notion of the matrix comes from Chafe (1970), in which the basic verb types: state, process, action, and action-process are first developed and then tested in the various domains represented by the experiencer, benefactive, and locative cases. The action verb type was discarded because of the adoption of an obligatory Object.

The case frame matrix depends upon the tactics used to arrange cases into case frames. These tactics include the following principles: (1) there is an obligatory theme or Object case in every frame, (2) Experiencer, Benefactive, and Locative cases are mutually exclusive, and (3) no case may be repeated in a case frame except the O case. The obligatory O hypothesis is held by Anderson (1971), by Gruber (1965), and Jackendoff (1972). Most models can not use the obligatory O case because they split the Object case into such variants as factitive, complement, and effected objects. The use of Experiencer, Benefactive, and Locative cases as domain markers which are mutually exclusive is taken from Chafe (1970). The use of double O frames despite the one-instance-per-clause principle is based upon Anderson (1971) and clearly repeated in Anderson (1976).

Within the obligatory O hypothesis there is no Action verb which is not at the same time an action-process; therefore any action is assumed to be action-process. Likewise, there can be no zero-place predicates or ambient verbs in Chafe's sense, if the Object case is always present. The resulting model then allows one-, two-, or three-place predicates but no zero-place predicates.

Within the unified Locative hypothesis there is no separate expression for Location, Source, Path, and Goal. Stative locatives and directional locatives are in complementary distribution, as in Fillmore (1968). State locative verbs require stative locatives, motion verbs require directional locatives. The unified locative case means that only one locative will be required by the verb's semantic valence.

The verb remains indifferent to the particular expression of the locative. While the verb's valence requires only a single locative, it permits multiple expressions of the locative. With state locative there is a single place in which the object is located; with motion verbs there is a single motion trajectory which may be described in terms of Source, Path, Goal, or any combination of these.

Although the one-instance-per clause principle of Fillmore is retained for most cases, an exception must be made for predicate nominals with *be* and *become* and for those action verbs which take both an object and an object complement such as *call*, *elect*. In other models either the predicate nominal problem has been overlooked or less satisfactory solutions have been advanced to explain those two-place predicates which involve two similar noun phrases.

7.6.4 Derivation. The case grammar matrix model adopts the bidirectional derivational system proposed by Chafe (1970) as the best way to relate verbs which are derived from the same morphological root. Given that the system is language specific, it helps to organize the lexicon by providing lexical redundancy rules which apply to the particular language under investigation. The bidirectional derivation system tends to name the derivational units rather than explain them. Therefore it is useful to view the basic derivational units in terms of the abstract inchoative and causative predicates in representing these forms in logical structure. The backwards derivations described by Chafe, such as the decausative and resultative, are useful in that they describe derivational relationships that might be overlooked in a uni-directional system. The decausative is used to represent those pseudointransitive forms that are derived from basic action verbs. The resultative is used to describe those resultative adjectives which are derived from an intrinsic process and must be distinguished from the passive forms with which they are ambiguous.

The derivational system is used in Chafe (1970) to reduce the size of the lexicon. Rather than list every entry in the lexicon, Chafe would list only the intrinsic form of the verb in the lexicon and introduce the derived forms by adding the particular derivational unit in the course of sentence generation. In a full entry system of the type advocated by Jackendoff (1976), each form would be listed in the lexicon but these would be related by lexical redundancy rules which specify how the various lexical items are related. The establishment of the derivational system not only organizes the lexicon in an exact way but also helps the analyst in text analysis when he realizes that verbs may occur in state, process, and action forms in the text and that these must be distinguished from each other. The occurrence of English homophonous transitive /intransitive pairs makes this particularly necessary when doing an analysis of English text.

7.6.5 Covert case roles. The theory of covert case roles becomes crucial in a model that adopts the obligatory O hypothesis since the presence of the Object case in each frame is not always obvious. The theory is basically taken from Fillmore (1971) and occurs to some degree in all case grammar models.

(1) Deletable roles were first introduced by Fillmore (1968) and are used by most case grammarians. Deletion is an obvious product of text analysis where the verb occurs sometimes with and sometimes without a given case. Only Chafe seems to neglect the principle of deletable roles by analyzing verbs without objects as actions and analyzing the same verbs as Action-completable when they occur with an object. The theory of deletable roles allows a single analysis for a verb with its full complement of case roles, whether or not all roles actually occur in a particular sentence.

(2) Coreferential roles were neglected in Fillmore (1968), causing Jackendoff to prefer Gruber's thematic relations, in which coreference was explicitly used as a tool. But Fillmore adopts coreferential roles in 1971 and future models. All other case grammarians make use of coreferential roles except Chafe. Anderson (1971) clearly adds two labels to a single noun phrase whenever the semantics of the verb requires it.

(3) Lexicalized roles were neglected in Fillmore (1968) but introduced in Fillmore (1971) with regard to the Instrument case in such verbs as *slap*, *kick*, *kiss*. They do not occur in Chafe but occur in Anderson (1971) under the title of 'reduced clauses' as in *help* = 'give help to'. None of the case grammarians seems to indicate the wide range of lexicalized cases in English. Some indication of this range is shown by comparing all lexical entries where a verb and a noun have exactly the same form. In most of these instances, the verb form will incorporate the noun form into its meaning.

7.7 Conclusion. Case grammar models are effective to the extent that they can be put into practice. The advantages and disadvantages of the model are soon discovered when the model is applied to a language text. The matrix model was tested using the complete text of Ernest Hemingway's *The Old Man and the Sea.*

(1) Text analysis. To begin the analysis, the complete text of the novel was rewritten one clause to a line, with the clauses numbered in order for ready reference. Each clause was assigned a case frame, with particular attention to deletable, coreferential, and lexicalized roles. In this analysis, the dependent clauses within the text, including infinitives and participles, were assigned the same case frame as would be assigned to a comparable simple declarative sentence.

The verbs and their case frames were then collected into an alphabetical lexicon. Multiple occurrences of the same verb were tested to see if the meaning of the verb was the same or different. Decisions were based upon the meaning of the verb in context, what the author intended to convey. Since semantics affects syntax, strong correlations were often found between the meaning of a verb and its syntactic use. The verbs and their case frames were then collected into a case grammar lexicon, where the verbs were listed according to their case frame classification.

(2) Statistical results. When all of the occurrences in the text had been gathered into an alphabetical lexicon, a count was made of the occurrences of each verb in running text. There were 4858 clauses in the text. Along the verb type dimension of the matrix, the number of occurrences was: 40% state verbs, 12% process verbs, and 48% action verbs. Along the domain dimension of the matrix, the number of occurrences was: 38% basic verbs, 28% experiential verbs, 6% benefactive verbs, and 28% locative verbs. The number of process verbs (12%) suggests that the state /action dichotomy is not sufficient for verb classification. The relatively large number of experiential verbs (38%) suggests that these verbs of sensation, emotion, cognition, and communication have a significant role in narrative text.

A count was also made of the verb entries in the lexicon, once the duplicates were eliminated. There were 2351 different verb entries in the lexicon. Along the verb type dimension, the number of verbs was: 41% state verbs, 15% process verbs, and 44 % action verbs. Along the domain dimension, the number of verbs was: 46% basic verbs, 18% experiential verbs, 6% benefactive verbs, and 30% locative verbs. The relatively small number of experiential verb entries (10%), compared with the number of occurrences of these verbs (38%), suggests experiential verbs had a high frequency of occurrence.

(3) Foreign languages. The model was then applied to a wide range of European languages, including Spanish, French, German, Dutch, Portuguese, and Norwegian. It was also applied to non-European languages, such as Chinese, Japanese, Thai, Korean,

Vietnamese, Persian, and Arabic. In all of these languages, the case frames of the matrix proved to be necessary and sufficient for the classification of the verb system, although the syntactic correlates of these frames and the syntactic tests for establishing them varied from language to language.

(4) Computational linguistics. Case grammar theory is useful for natural language processing. In language analysis there is a need for a more comprehensive classification of verbs. Case grammar provides a semantic valence for the verb, a valence which predetermines the number and kind of noun phrases expected with the verb in context. It is no wonder then that computational linguists have turned to some form of case grammar theory in the development of natural language parsers, a movement that continues to expand in both academic and professional circles.

With the need to assign thematic relations to logical form, the need for semantic classification in natural language processing, with the applications of case grammar to language description, translation, and English as a foreign language, it is likely that case grammar theory, in some form or another, will be around for many years to come.

Appendix I. Alphabetical lexicon. The alphabetical lexicon is a list of the 320 predicates used in Chapters 1 through 6 with all duplicates removed and with the case frames adjusted in accordance with the case grammar matrix model. The lexical items are listed in alphabetical order.

abound in	Os,L	be on	Os,L
abound with	L,Os	be open	Os
accept	A,B,O	be pleasing to	Os,L
acquire (-agt)	B,O	be pleased with	L,Os
acquire (+agt)	A,B,O	be sad	Os
admit (enter)	A,O,L	be (=feel) sad	E=Os
allow (happen)	A,O	be slack	Os
allow (person)	A,B,O	be strewn on	Os,L
amuse (-agt)	O,E	be strewn with	L,Os
amuse (+agt)	A,O	be tight	Os
arrive (-agt)	O,L	be true	Os
arrive (+agt)	A=O,L	be under	Os,L
awaken,iv	O	be (=feel) warm	E=Os
awaken,tv	A,O	be warm	Os
be + time	Os,T	be wide	Os
be + poss	Os,B	be windy	Os
be + N	Os,Os	be with	O,L
be apparent	Os,E	become + N	O,O
be broken	Os	believe	E,Os
be careful with	A,O	belong to	Os,B
be cautious	A,*O	blame	A,B,O
be cold	Os	borrow	A,B,O
be (=feel) cold	E=Os	break,iv	O
be dead	Os	break,tv	A,O
be deaf	Os	bring	A,O,L
be dry	Os	build	A,O
be due	Os,B	buy	A,B,O
be (=feel) hot	E=Os	cause (-agt)	O,O
be hot (w)	Os	cause (+agt)	A,O
be hot	Os	change,iv	O,O
be in	Os,L	change,tv	A,O
be interesting	O,E	climb	A=O,L
be known to	Os,E	coerce	A,B,O
be late	Os	come (-agt)	O,L

come (+agt)	A=O,L	frighten (-agt)	O,E
construct	A,O	frighten (+agt)	A=O,E
contain (-agt)	L,Os	gallop	A,*O
contain (+agt)	A,O,*L	get	A,B,O
continue (-agt)	O	give	A,B,O
continue (+agt)	A,O	go (=extend)	Os,L
cook,iv	O	go (-agt)	O,L
cook,tv	A,O	go (+agt)	A=O,L
cost	Os,Os	grant	A,B,O
cough	O	grow,iv	O
crawl	A=O,L	grow,tv	A,O
cross (-agt)	O,L	hand	A,B,O
cross (+agt)	A=O,L	happen	O
cure,tv	A,O	have	B,Os
cut,iv	O	have in	L,Os
cut,tv	A,O	have on	L,Os
dance	A,O	have with	L,Os
deafen,tv	A,O	hear	E,Os
deprive	A,B,O	heat,iv	O
develop into	O,O	heat,tv	A,O
die	O	help	A,B,O
do	A,O	hit	A,O
drink	A,O	hit (=move)	A,O,L
drive (=action)	A,*O	hold	A,O,L
drive (=go)	A=O,L	imagine	E,O
drop (-agt)	O,L	insert	A,O,L
drop (+agt)	A,O,L	keep,iv	O
dry,iv	O	keep,tv	A,O
dry,tv	A,O	kick	A,O
eat	A,O	kill	A,O
elect	A,O,O	kiss	A,O
empty,iv	L,O	knit	A,O
empty,tv	A,O,L	know	E,Os
enter	A=O,L	last (time)	O,T
expect	E,O	laugh	A,O
fall	O,L	lead	A,O,L
fear	E,Os	lead (=extend)	Os,L
feel	E,O	lean,iv	Os,L
fight	A,O	lean,tv	A=O,L
find	B,O	learn (-agt)	E,O
fix (=fasten to)	A,O,L	learn (+agt)	A=E,O
fix (=repair)	A,O	leave behind	A,O,L
float,iv	O	leave (=depart)	A=O,L
float,iv (=go)	O,L	lend	A,B,O
fly (=action)	A,*O	let (happen)	A,O
fly (=go)	A=O,L	let (=allow)	A,B,O
follow	Os,L	lie (-agt)	Os,L
force	A,B,O	lie (+agt)	A=O,L
free	A,B,O	lift	A,O

like	E,Os	regard	E,O
listen to	A=E,O	release	A,B,O
live,iv	Os,L	remain (-agt)	O
look + adj	Os,E	remain (+agt)	A,O
look at	A=E,O	remember	E,O
lose	B,O	remind (+agt)	A,E,O
love	E,Os	remind (-agt)	E,Os,Os
make	A,O	remove	A,O,L
march,iv	A=O,L	require	B,Os
mean	Os,Os	resemble	Os,Os
measure	Os,Os	restrain	A,B,O
meet	A,O,L	retain	A,O,L
melt,iv	O	ride (=action)	A,*O
melt,tv	A,O	ride (=go)	A=O,L
move,iv (-agt)	O,L	rise	O,*L
move,iv (+agt)	A=O,L	rob	A,B,O
move,tv	A,O,L	roll,iv (-agt)	O,L
murder	A,O	roll,iv (+agt)	A=O,L
need	B,Os	roll,tv	A,O,L
obtain	A,B,O	run (=action)	A,*O
occupy (-agt)	Os,L	run (=go)	A=O,L
occupy (+agt)	A=O,L	run (=operate)	A,O
occur	O	save	A=B,O
offer	A,B,O	say	A,E,O
open,iv	O	scream	A,*O
open,tv	A,O	see	E,Os
owe	B,Os	seem	Os,E
own	B,Os	sell	A,B,O
paint	A,*O,L	send	A,O,L
permit	A,B,O	shove	A,O,L
persuade	A,E,O	show	A,E,O
pierce	O,L	sing	A,O
place	A,O,L	sink,iv	O,*L
plant	A,O,L	sit (-agt)	Os,L
play	A,O	sit (+agt)	A=O,L
please	O,E	skin,tv	A,*O,L
possess	B,Os	slacken,iv	O
pounce	A=O,L	slacken,tv	A,O
pour	A,O,L	slap	A,O
precede	Os,L	slip	O,L
predict	A,O	smear	A,O,L
prohibit	A,B,O	smell + adj	Os,E
push	A,O,L	smell (-agt)	E,Os
put	A,O,L	smell (+agt)	A=E,O
rain (w)	O	sneeze	O
raise	A,O,*L	snow (w)	O
read	A,O	sound + adj	Os,E
receive (-agt)	B,O	speak	A,E,O
receive (+agt)	A=B,O	spend (time)	A=O,T

spray	A,O,L	tell	A,E,O
stab	A,O	terrorize	A,O
stack	A,O,L	think (-agt)	E,Os
stand (-agt)	Os,L	think (+agt)	A=E,O
stand (+agt)	A=O,L	throw	A,O,L
stay,iv	O	tighten,iv	O
stay,tv	A,O	tighten,tv	A,O
steal	A,B,O	transport	A,O,L
stretch	Os,L	try	A,O
strew	A,O,L	turn into	O,O
strike (=hit)	A,O	turn out	O
strike (impress)	E,Os,Os	undergo	A,O
stuff	A,O,L	understand	E,Os
surround	Os,L	use	A,O
suspect	E,Os	wake up,iv	O
swallow	A,O	wake up,tv	A,O
swarm in	O,L	walk (=action)	A,*O
swarm with	L,O	walk (=go)	A=O,L
sweep	A,O	want	E,Os
swim (=action)	A,*O	watch	A=E,O
swim (=go)	A=O,L	water	A,*O,L
take (=move)	A,O,L	weigh	Os,Os
take (=steal)	A,B,O	widen,iv	O
talk	A,E,O	widen,tv	A,O
taste + adj	Os,E	win (-agt)	B,O
taste (-agt)	E,Os	win (+agt)	A=B,O
taste (+agt)	A=E,O	work	A,*O
teach	A,E,O	write	A,O

Appendix II. Case grammar lexicon. The case grammar lexicon is a list of the 320 predicates used in Chapters 1 through 6 with all duplicates removed and the case frames adjusted according to the case grammar matrix model. The lexical items are listed according to their case frames. Within each frame, the list is in alphabetical order.

A. Basic verbs (121)

1. State verbs (22)

With single Os
+ [___Os] (16)

be broken
be cold
be dead
be deaf
be dry
be hot
be hot (w)
be late
be open
be sad
be slack
be tight
be true
be warm
be wide
be windy

With double Os
+ [___Os,Os] (6)

be + N
cost
mean
measure
resemble
weigh

2. Process verbs (31)

With single O
+ [___O] (26)

awaken,iv
break,iv
continue (-agt)
cook,iv
cough
cut,iv
die
dry,iv
float,iv
grow,iv
happen
heat,iv
keep,iv
melt,iv
occur
open,iv
rain (w)
remain (-agt)
slacken,iv
sneeze
snow (w)
stay,iv
tighten,iv
turn out
wake up,iv
widen,iv

With double O
+ [___O,O] (5)

become + N
cause (-agt)
change,iv
develop into
turn into

3. Action verbs (68)

With O lexicalized
+ [___A,*O] /O-lex (10)

be cautious
drive (=action)
fly (=action)
gallop
ride (=action)
run (=action)
scream
swim (=action)
walk (=action)
work

With both roles overt
+ [A,O] (57)

allow (happen)
amuse (+agt)
awaken,tv
be careful with
break,tv
build
cause (+agt)
change,tv
construct
continue (+agt)
cook,tv
cure,tv
cut,tv
dance
deafen,tv
do
drink
dry,tv
eat
fight
fix (=repair)
grow,tv
heat,tv
hit

keep,tv
kick
kill
kiss
knit
laugh
let (happen)
lift
make
melt,tv
murder
open,tv
play
predict
read
remain (+agt)
run (=operate)
sing
slacken,tv
slap
stab
stay,tv
strike (=hit)
swallow
sweep
terrorize
tighten,tv
try
undergo
use
wake up,tv
widen,tv
write

With double O
+ [___A,O,O] (1)

elect

B. Experiential verbs (52)

1. State experiential (26)

With E=Os coreference
+ [___E,*Os] /E=Os (4)

be (=feel) cold
be (=feel) hot
be (=feel) sad

be (=feel) warm

With E subject
+ [___E,Os] (12)

believe
fear
hear
know
like
love
see
smell (-agt)
suspect
taste (-agt)
think (-agt)
understand
want

With O subject
+ [___Os,E] (8)

be apparent
be known to
look + adj
seem
smell + adj
sound + adj
taste + adj

With double O
+ [___E,Os,Os] (2)

remind (-agt)
strike (impress)

2. Process experiential (10)

With E subject
+ [___E,O] (6)

expect
feel
imagine
learn (-agt)
regard
remember

With O subject

+ [___O,E] (4)

amuse (-agt)
be interesting
frighten (-agt)
please

3. Action experiential (16)

With A=E coreference
+ [___A,*E,O] /A=E (7)

learn (+agt)
listen to
look at
smell (+agt)
taste (+agt)
think (+agt)
watch

With A=O coreference
+ [___A,E,*O] /A=O (1)

frighten (+agt)

With all roles overt
+ [___A,E,O] (8)

persuade
remind (+agt)
say
show
speak
talk
teach
tell

C. Benefactive verbs (44)

1. State benefactive (9)

With B subject
+ [___B,Os] (6)

have
need
owe
own
possess

require

With Os subject
+ [___Os,B] (3)

be + poss
be due
belong to

2. Process benefactive (5)

With B subject
+ [___B,O]

acquire (-agt)
find
lose
receive (-agt)
win (-agt)

3. Action benefactive (30)

With A=B coreference
+ [___A,*B,O] /A=B (3)

receive (+agt)
save
win (+agt)

With all roles overt
+ [___A,B,O] (27)

accept
acquire (+agt)
allow (person)
blame
borrow
buy
coerce
deprive
force
free
get
give
grant
hand
help
lend
let (=allow)

obtain
offer
permit
prohibit
release
restrain
rob
sell
steal
take (=steal)

D. Locative verbs (100)

1. State locative (25)

With Os subject
+ [___Os,L] (18)

abound in
be in
be on
be pleasing to
be strewn on
be under
follow
go (=extend)
lead (=extend)
lean,iv
lie (-agt)
live,iv
occupy (-agt)
precede
sit (-agt)
stand (-agt)
stretch
surround

With L subject
+ [___L,Os] (7)

abound with
be pleased with
be strewn with
contain (-agt)
have in
have on
have with

2. Process locative (17)

With O lexicalized
+ [___O,*L] /O-lex (2)

rise
sink,iv

With O subject
+ [___O,L] (13)

arrive (-agt)
be with
come (-agt)
cross (-agt)
drop (-agt)
fall
float,iv (=go)
go (-agt)
move,iv (-agt)
pierce
roll,iv (-agt)
slip
swarm in

With L subject
+ [___L,O] (2)

empty,iv
swarm with

3. Action locative (58)

With A=O coreference
+ [___A,*O,L] /A=O (23)

arrive (+agt)
climb
come (+agt)
crawl
cross (+agt)
drive (=go)
enter
fly (=go)
go (+agt)
lean,tv
leave (=depart)
lie (+agt)
march,iv
move,iv (+agt)
occupy (+agt)

pounce
ride (=go)
roll,iv (+agt)
run (=go)
sit (+agt)
stand (+agt)
swim (=go)
walk (=go)

With O lexicalized
+ [___A,*O,L] /O-lex (3)

paint
skin
water

With L lexicalized
+ [___A,O,*L] /L-lex (2)

contain (+agt)
raise

With all roles overt
+ [___A,O,L] (30)

admit (enter)
bring
drop (+agt)
empty,tv
fix (=fasten to)
hit (=move)
hold
insert
lead
leave
meet
move,tv
place
plant
pour
push
put
remove
retain
roll,tv
send
shove
smear
spray

stack
strew
stuff
take (=move)
throw
transport

E. Temporal verbs (3)

1. State temporal

With Os subject
+ [___Os,T] (1)

be + time

2. Process temporal

With O subject
+ [___O,T] (1)

last (time)

3. Action temporal

With A=O coreference
+ [___A,*O,T] /A=O (1)

spend (time)

References

Abraham, Werner. 1978. *Valence, Semantic Case, and Grammatical Relations.* Amsterdam: John Benjamins.

Aid, Frances M. 1973. *Semantic Structures in Spanish.* Washington, D.C.: Georgetown University Press.

Allwood, Jens, Lars-Gunnar Andersson, and Osten Dahl. 1977. *Logic in Linguistics.* Cambridge: Cambridge University Press.

Anderson, John M. 1971. *The Grammar of Case: Towards a Localistic Theory.* Cambridge: Cambridge University Press.

_____. 1976. *On Case Grammar.* London: Croom Helm.

Bach, Emmon, and R. Harms, eds. 1968. *Universals in Linguistic Theory.* New York: Holt, Rinehart, and Winston.

Becker, Alton. 1967. Conjoining in a tagmemic grammar of English. *Georgetown University Round Table on Languages and Linguistics 1967.* Washington, D.C.: Georgetown University Press. 109-121.

Binnick, Robert. 1968. On the nature of the lexical item. *Chicago Linguistic Society* 4.1-11.

Bolinger, Dwight. 1975. *Aspects of Language.* 2nd edition. New York: Harcourt, Brace, Jovanovich.

Brend, Ruth M. 1974. *Advances in Tagmemics.* Amsterdam: North Holland.

Chafe, Wallace L. 1970. *Meaning and the Structure of Language.* Chicago: Chicago University Press.

Chomsky, Noam. 1981. *Lectures on Government and Binding.* Dordrecht, Holland: Foris Publications.

Comrie, Bernard. 1977. *Aspect.* Cambridge: Cambridge University Press.

Cook, Walter A., S.J. 1979. *Case Grammar: Development of the Matrix Model (1970-1978).* Washington, D.C.: Georgetown University Press.

_____. 1985. Case grammar applied to the teaching of English. *Scientific and Humanistic Dimensions of Language.* Festschrift for Robert Lado. Kurt Jankowsky, ed. Amsterdam: John Benjamins.

Dowty, David R. 1972. *Studies in the Logic of Verb Aspect and Time Reference in English.* Austin: University of Texas.

Fillmore, Charles J. 1966. A proposal concerning English prepositions. *Georgetown University Round Table on Languages and Linguistics 1966.* Washington, D.C.: Georgetown University Press. 19-34.

_____. 1968. The case for case. *Universals in Linguistic Theory.* Emmon Bach and Robert Harms, eds. New York: Holt, Rinehart, and Winston. 1-88.

_____. 1969. Towards a modern theory of case. *Modern Studies in English.* David Reibel and Sanford Shane, eds. Englewood Cliffs, N.J.: Prentice-Hall. 361-375.

_____. 1970. Lexical entries for verbs. *Foundations of Language* 4.373-393.

_____. 1971. Types of Lexical information. *Semantics: An Interdisciplinary Reader.* Danny Steinberg and Leon Jakobovits, eds. Cambridge: Cambridge University Press. 370-92.

_____. 1971. Some problems for case grammar. *Georgetown University Round Table on Languages and Linguistics 1971.* Washington, D.C.: Georgetown University Press. 35-56.

_____. 1975. *Principles of Case Grammar: The Structure of Language and Meaning.* Trans. H. Tanaka and M. Funaki. Tokyo: Sanseido Publishing Co.

_____. 1977. The case for case reopened. *Syntax and Semantics.* Peter Cole and Jerrold Sadock, eds. New York: Academic Press 8.59-81.

Fodor, J.D. 1977. *Semantics: Theories of Meaning in Generative Grammar.* New York: Thomas Y. Crowell.

Green, Georgia M. 1969. On the notion 'related lexical entry'. *Chicago Linguistics Society* 5.76-87.

_____. 1972. Some observations on the syntax and semantics of instrumental verbs. *Chicago Linguistic Society* 8.83-92.

Gruber, Jeffrey S. 1976. *Lexical Structures in Syntax and Semantics.* Amsterdam: North Holland.

Hale, Austin. 1974. On the systematization of box 4. *Advances in Tagmemics.* Ruth Brend, ed. Amsterdam: North Holland. 55-74.

Harris, Mary Dee. 1985. *Introduction to Natural Language Processing.* Reston, Va.: Reston Publishing Co.

Helbig, Gerhard. 1971. *Beitrage zur Valenztheorie.* The Hague: Mouton.

Ikegami, Yoshihiko. 1969. *The Semological Structure of English Verbs of Motion.* New Haven, Conn.: Yale University Press.

Inoue, K. 1974. Experiencer. *Studies in Descriptive and Applied Linguistics.* Tokyo: International Christian University. 139-162.

Jackendoff, Ray S. 1972. *Semantic Interpretation in Generative Grammar.* Cambridge, Mass.: MIT Press.

_____. 1976. Toward an explanatory semantic representation. *Linguistic Inquiry* 7.1.89-150.

_____. 1983. *Semantics and Cognition.* Cambridge, Mass.: MIT Press.

_____. 1987. The status of thematic relations in linguistic theory. *Linguistic Inquiry* 18.3.369-411.

Jankowsky, Kurt. 1985. *Scientific and Humanistic Dimensions of Language.* Amsterdam: John Benjamins.

Lakoff, George. 1966. Stative adjectives and verbs in English. *Mathematical Linguistics and Automatic Translation.* A.G. Ottinger, ed. Cambridge, Mass.: Harvard University Press.

_____. 1970. *Irregularity in Syntax.* New York: Holt, Rinehart, and Winston.

_____. 1972. Linguistics and natural logic. *Semantics of Natural Language.* Donald Davidson and Gilbert Harmon, eds. Dordrecht, Holland: D. Reidel. 545-665.

_____. 1976. Toward generative semantics. *Syntax and Semantics.* James D. McCawley, ed. New York: Academic Press. 7.43-61.

Lambert, Dorothy Mack. 1969. *The Semantic Syntax of Metaphor: A Case Grammar Analysis.* Unpublished Ph.D. dissertation. University of Michigan.

Leech, Geoffrey N. 1969. *Towards a Semantic Description of English.* Bloomington: Indiana University Press.

_____. 1971. *Meaning and the English Verb.* London: Longmans.

_____. 1974. *Semantics.* Baltimore, Md.: Penguin Books.

Longacre, Robert E. 1964. *Grammar Discovery Procedures.* The Hague. Mouton.

_____. 1976. *An Anatomy of Speech Notions.* Lisse: The Peter DeRitter Press.

Lyons, John. 1968. *Introduction to Theoretical Linguistics.* Cambridge: Cambridge University Press.

_____. 1977. *Semantics.* Cambridge: Cambridge University Press.

McCawley, James D. 1971. Prelexical syntax. *Georgetown University Round Table on Languages and Linguistics 1971.* Washington, D.C.: Georgetown University Press. 19-34.

_____. 1976. *Grammar and Meaning.* New York: Academic Press.

McCoy, Ana Maria. 1969. *A Case Grammar Classification of Spanish Verbs.* Unpublished Ph.D. dissertation. University of Michigan.

Mellema, Paul. 1974. A brief against case grammar. *Foundations of Language* 11.39-76.

Morgan, Jerry L. 1969. On arguing about semantics. *Papers in Linguistics* 1.49-70.

Moskey, Stephen. 1979. *Semantic Structures and Relations in Dutch: An Introduction to Case Grammar.* Washington, D.C.: Georgetown University Press.

Newmeyer, Frederick J. 1980. *Linguistic Theory in America.* New York: Academic Press.

Nilsen, Don Lee Fred. 1972. *Toward a Semantic Specification of Deep Case.* The Hague: Mouton.

_____. 1973. *The Instrumental Case in English.* The Hague: Mouton.

Pepinsky, Harold B. 1974. A metalanguage for systematic research on human communication via natural language. *Journal of the American Society for Information Science* 25.1.59-69.

Perlmutter, David M. 1970. The two verbs 'begin'. *Readings in English Transformational Grammar.* Roderick A. Jacobs and Peter S. Rosenbaum, eds. Washington, D.C.: Georgetown

University Press. 107-19.

Pike, Kenneth L. 1967. *Language in Relation to a Unified Theory of the Structure of Human Behavior*. The Hague: Mouton.

_____. 1971. Crucial issues in the development of tagmemics. *Georgetown University Round Table on Languages and Linguistics 1971*. Washington, D.C.: Georgetown University Press. 79-98.

_____, and Evelyn Pike. 1977. *Grammatical Analysis*. Arlington, Texas: Summer Institute of Linguistics Press.

Platt, John T. 1971. *Grammatical Form and Grammatical Meaning: A Tagmemic View of Fillmore's Deep Structure Case Concepts*. Amsterdam: North Holland.

Postal, Paul M. 1971. *Crossover Phenomena*. New York: Holt, Rinehart, and Winston.

_____. 1971. On the surface verb 'remind'. *Studies in Linguistic Semantics*. Charles Fillmore and Terence Langendoen, eds. New York: Holt, Rinehart, and Winston. 181-270.

_____. 1974. *On Raising*. Cambridge, Mass.: The MIT Press.

Quirk, Randolph, Sidney Greenbaum, Geoffrey Leech, and Jan Svartvik. 1985. *A Comprehensive Grammar of the English Language*. New York: Longmans.

Rogers, Andy. 1971. Three kinds of physical perception verbs. *Chicago Linguistic Society* 7.206-22.

Ross, John R. 1972. Act. *Semantics of Natural Language*. Donald Davidson and Gilbert Harmon, eds. New York: Humanities Press. 70-126.

Shank, Roger, and Kenneth Colby. 1973. *Computer Models of Thought and Language*. San Francisco: W.H. Freeman.

Somers, H.L. 1982. The use of verb features in arriving at a 'meaning representation'. *Linguistics* 20:237-265.

Starosta, Stanley. 1971. Lexical derivatation in case grammar. *University of Hawaii Working Papers in Linguistics* 3:83-101.

_____. 1973. The faces of case. *Language Sciences* 25:1-14.

_____. 1978. The one per sent solution. *Valence, Semantic Case, and Grammatical Relations*. Werner Abraham, ed. Amsterdam: John Benjamins. 459-571.

Stockwell, Schacter, and Partee. 1973. *The Major Syntactic Structures of English*. New York: Holt, Rinehart, and Winston.

Tesnière, Lucian. 1958. *Eléments de Syntaxe Structurale*. Paris: Klincksieck.

Von Wright, Georg Henrik. 1963. *Norm and Action*. New York: Humanities Press.

_____. 1971. *Explanation and Understanding*. Ithaca, N.Y.: Cornell University Press.

Winograd, Terry. 1983. *Language as a Cognitive Process*. Reading, Mass: Addison-Wesley.

Milton Keynes UK
Ingram Content Group UK Ltd.
UKHW040025030224
437022UK00001B/17